THE
TEACHER'S OUTLINE & STUDY BIBLE™
I TIMOTHY

Copyright © 1996 by Alpha-Omega Ministries, Inc.
All rights reserved throughout the world. No part of
The Teacher's Outline & Study Bible™ may be
reproduced in any manner without written permission.

The Teacher's Outline & Study Bible™ is written for God's people to use both in their personal lives and in their teaching. Leadership Ministries Worldwide wants God's people to use *The Teacher's Outline & Study Bible*™. The purpose of the copyright is to prevent the reproduction, misuse, and abuse of the material.

May our Lord bless us all as we live, preach, teach, and write for Him, fulfilling His great commission to live righteous and godly lives and to make disciples of all nations.

Please address all requests for information or permission to:
 Leadership Ministries Worldwide
 1928 Central Avenue
 Chattanooga, TN 37408
 Ph.# (423) 855-2181   FAX (423) 855-8616
 E-Mail info@lmw.org   http://www.lmw.org

Library of Congress Catalog Card Number: 94-073070

International Standard Book Number: 978-1-57407-298-3

PRINTED IN THE U.S.A.

PUBLISHED BY LEADERSHIP MINISTRIES WORLDWIDE

1   2   3   4   5   03   04   05   06

THE
TEACHER'S OUTLINE & STUDY BIBLE™
I TIMOTHY

KING JAMES VERSION

LEADERSHIP MINISTRIES WORLDWIDE
CHATTANOOGA, TN

LEADERSHIP MINISTRIES WORLDWIDE

DEDICATED

To all the men and women of the world who preach and teach the Gospel of our Lord Jesus Christ and to the Mercy and Grace of God

- Demonstrated to us in Christ Jesus our Lord.

  "In whom we have redemption through His blood, the forgiveness of sins, according to the riches of His grace." (Ep.1:7)

- Out of the mercy and grace of God His Word has flowed. Let every person know that God will have mercy upon him, forgiving and using him to fulfill His glorious plan of salvation.

  "For God so loved the world, that he gave His only begotten Son, that whosoever believeth in Him should not perish, but have everlasting life. For God sent not his son into the world to condemn the world, but that the world through him might be saved." (Jn.3:16-17)

  "For this is good and acceptable in the sight of God our Saviour; who will have all men to be saved, and to come unto the knowledge of the truth." (1 Ti.2:3-4)

The Teacher's Outline & Study Bible™

is written for God's servants to use in their study, teaching, and preaching of God's Holy Word...

- To share the Word of God with the world.

- To help the believer, both minister and layman alike, in his understanding, preaching, and teaching of God's Word.

- To do everything we possibly can to lead men, women, boys and girls to give their hearts and lives to Jesus Christ and to secure the eternal life which He offers.

- To do all we can to minister to the needy of the world.

- To give Jesus Christ His proper place, the place the Word gives Him. Therefore, no work of Leadership Ministries Worldwide will ever be personalized.

ACKNOWLEDGMENTS

Every child of God is precious to the Lord and deeply loved. And every child as a servant of the Lord touches the lives of those who come in contact with him or his ministry. The writing ministries of the following servants have touched this work, and we are grateful that God brought their writings our way. We hereby acknowledge their ministry to us, being fully aware that there are so many others down through the years whose writings have touched our lives and who deserve mention, but the weaknesses of our minds have caused them to fade from memory. May our wonderful Lord continue to bless the ministry of these dear servants, and the ministries of us all as we diligently labor to reach the world for Christ and to meet the desperate needs of those who suffer so much.

THE GREEK SOURCES

1. *Expositor's Greek Testament*, Edited by W. Robertson Nicoll. Grand Rapids, MI: Eerdmans Publishing Co., 1970.

2. Robertson, A.T. *Word Pictures in the New Testament*. Nashville, TN: Broadman Press, 1930.

3. Thayer, Joseph Henry. *Greek-English Lexicon of the New Testament*. New York: American Book Co.

4. Vincent, Marvin R. *Word Studies in the New Testament*. Grand Rapids, MI: Eerdmans Publishing Co., 1969.

5. Vine, W.E. *Expository Dictionary of New Testament Words*. Old Tappan, NJ: Fleming H. Revell Co.

6. Wuest, Kenneth S. *Word Studies in the Greek New Testament*. Grand Rapids, MI: Eerdmans Publishing Co., 1953.

THE REFERENCE WORKS

7. *Cruden's Complete Concordance of the Old & New Testament*. Philadelphia, PA: The John C. Winston Co., 1930.

8. Josephus' *Complete Works*. Grand Rapids, MI: Kregel Publications, 1981.

9. Lockyer, Herbert, Series of Books, including his Books on *All the Men, Women, Miracles, and Parables of the Bible*. Grand Rapids, MI: Zondervan Publishing House.

10. *Nave's Topical Bible*. Nashville, TN: The Southwestern Co.

11. *The Amplified New Testament*. (Scripture Quotations are from the Amplified New Testament, Copyright 1954, 1958, 1987 by the Lockman Foundation. Used by permission.)

12. *The Four Translation New Testament* (Including King James, New American Standard, Williams - New Testament In the Language of the People, Beck - New Testament In the Language of Today.) Minneapolis, MN: World Wide Publications.

13. *The New Compact Bible Dictionary*, Edited by T. Alton Bryant. Grand Rapids, MI: Zondervan Publishing House, 1967.

14. *The New Thompson Chain Reference Bible*. Indianapolis, IN: B.B. Kirkbride Bible Co., 1964,

THE COMMENTARIES

15. Barclay, William. *Daily Study Bible Series*. Philadelphia, PA: Westminster Press.

16. Bruce, F.F. *The Epistle to the Colossians*. Westwood, NJ: Fleming H. Revell Co., 1968.

17. ———. *Epistle to the Hebrews*. Grand Rapids, MI: Erdmanns Publishing Co., 1964.

18. ———. *The Epistles of John*. Old Tappan, NJ: Fleming H. Revell Co., 1970.

19. Criswell, W.A. *Expository Sermons on Revelation*. Grand Rapids, MI: Zondervan Publishing House, 1962-66.

20. Greene Oliver. *The Epistles of John*. Greenville, SC: The Gospel Hour, Inc., 1966.

21. ———. *The Epistles of Paul the Apostle to the Hebrews*. Greenville, SC: The Gospel Hour, Inc., 1965.

22. ———. *The Epistles of Paul the Apostle to Timothy & Titus*. Greenville, SC: The Gospel Hour, Inc., 1964.

23. ———. *The Revelation Verse by Verse Study*. Greenville, SC: The Gospel Hour, Inc., 1963.

24. Henry, Matthew. *Commentary on the Whole Bible*. Old Tappan, NJ: Fleming H. Revell Co.

25. Hodge, Charles. *Exposition on Romans & on Corinthians*. Grand Rapids, MI: Eerdmans Publishing Co., 1972-1973.

26. Ladd, George Eldon. *A Commentary On the Revelation of John*. Grand Rapids, MI: Eerdmans Publishing Co., 1972-1973.

27. Leupold, H.C. *Exposition of Daniel*. Grand Rapids, MI: Baker Book House, 1969.

28. Newell, William R. *Hebrews, Verse by Verse.* Chicago, IL: Moody Press.

29. Strauss, Lehman. *Devotional Studies in Philippians.* Neptune, NJ: Loizeaux Brothers.

30. ———. *Colossians & 1 Timothy.* Neptune, NJ: Loizeaux Brothers.

31. ———. *The Book of the Revelation.* Neptune, NJ: Loizeaux Brothers.

32. *The New Testament & Wycliffe Bible Commentary*, Edited by Charles F. Pfeiffer & Everett F. Harrison. New York: The Iverson Associates, 1971. Produced for Moody Monthly. Chicago Moody Press, 1962.

33. *The Pulpit Commentary*, Edited by H.D.M. Spence & Joseph S. Exell. Grand Rapids, MI: Eerdmans Publishing Co., 1950.

34. Thomas, W.H. Griffith. *Hebrews, A Devotional Commentary.* Grand Rapids, MI: Eerdmans Publishing Co., 1970.

35. ———. Griffith. *Studies in Colossians & Philemon.* Grand Rapids, MI: Baker Book House, 1973.

36. *Tyndale New Testament Commentaries.* Grand Rapids, MI: Eerdmans Publishing Co., Began in 1958.

37. Walker, Thomas. *Ac.of the Apostles.* Chicago, IL: Moody Press, 1965.

38. Walvoord, John. *The Thessalonian Epistles.* Grand Rapids, MI: Zondervan Publishing House, 1973.

OTHER SOURCES

39. Barnhouse, Donald Grey. *Let Me Illustrate.* Grand Rapids, MI: Fleming H. Revell Co., A Division of Baker Book House, 1967.

40. Foster, Elon, Editor. *6000 Classic Sermon Illustrations.* Grand Rapids, MI: Baker House, 1993.

41. *Gods and Generals.* Warner Bros., 2003.

42. Green, Michael P. *1500 Illustrations for Biblical Preaching.* Grand Rapids, MI: Baker Books, 2000, #1460.

43. Knight, Walter B. *Knight's Treasury of 2000 Illustrations.* Grand Rapids, MI: Eerdmans Publishing Company, 1963.

44. ———. *Three Thousand Illustrations for Christian Service*. Grand Rapids, MI: Eerdmans Publishing Company, 1947.

45. Larson, Craig B., Editor. *Choice Contemporary Stories & Illustrations*. Grand Rapids, MI: Baker Books, 1998.

46. ———. *Illustrations for Preaching and Teaching*. Grand Rapids, MI: Baker Books, 1993.

47. Martin, Walter R. *The Kingdom of the Cults*. Minneapolis, MN: Bethany House Publishers, 1982.

48. Morris, Leon. *The Epistles of Paul to the Thessalonians*. "Tyndale New Testament Commentaries." Grand Rapids, MI: Eerdmans Publishing Company, Began in 1958.

49. Tan, Paul Lee. *Encyclopedia of 7,700 Illustrations: Signs of the Times*. Rockville, MD: Assurance Publishers, 1985.

50. Tozer, A.W. *Man: The Dwelling Place of God*. Carol Stream, IL: Christianity Today, Vol. 41, No.5.

MISCELLANEOUS ABBREVIATIONS

&	=	And
Bckgrd.	=	Background
Bc.	=	Because
Circ.	=	Circumstance
Concl.	=	Conclusion
Cp.	=	Compare
Ct.	=	Contrast
Dif.	=	Different
e.g.	=	For example
Et.	=	Eternal
f.	=	Following
Govt.	=	Government
Id.	=	Identity or Identification
Illust.	=	Illustration
K.	=	Kingdom
No.	=	Number
N.T.	=	New Testament
O.T.	=	Old Testament
Pt.	=	Point
Quest.	=	Question
Rel.	=	Religion
Resp.	=	Responsibility
Rev.	=	Revelation
Rgt.	=	Righteousness
Thru	=	Through
V.	=	Verse
Vs.	=	Verses

HOW TO USE

THE TEACHER'S OUTLINE AND STUDY BIBLE™
(TOSB)

To gain maximum benefit, here is all you do. Follow these easy steps, using the sample outline below.

1 STUDY TITLE

2 MAJOR POINTS

3 SUBPOINTS

4 COMMENTARY, QUESTIONS, APPLICATION, ILLUSTRATIONS
(Follows Scripture)

1. First: Read the **Study Title** two or three times so that the subject sinks in.
2. Then: Read the **Study Title** and the **Major Points** (Pts.1,2,3) together quickly. Do this several times and you will quickly grasp the overall subject.

B. The Steps to Peace (Part II): Prayer & Positive Thinking, 4:6-9	
1. Peace comes through prayer 　a. The charge: Do not worry or be anxious 　b. The remedy: Prayer 　　1) About everything 　　2) With requests 　　3) With thanksgiving 　c. The promise: Peace 　　1) Peace that passes all understanding 　　2) Peace that keeps our hearts & minds 2. Peace comes through positive thinking 　a. The charge: Think & practice things that are... 　　1) True 　　2) Honest 　　3) Just 　　4) Pure	6 Be careful for nothing; but in every thing by prayer and supplication with thanksgiving let your requests be made known unto God. 7 And the peace of God, which passeth all understanding, shall keep your hearts and minds through Christ Jesus. 8 Finally, brethren, whatsoever things are true, whatsoever things are honest, whatsoever things are just, whatsoever things are pure, whatsoever things are lovely, whatsoever

3. Now: Read both the **Major Points** and **Subpoints**. Do this slower than Step 2. Note how the points are beside the applicable verse and simply state what the Scripture is saying—in Outline form.
4. Read the **Commentary**. As you read and re-read, pray that the Holy Spirit will bring to your attention exactly what you should study and teach. It's all there, outlined and fully developed, just waiting for you to study and teach.

TEACHERS, PLEASE NOTE:

⇒ Cover the **Scripture** and the **Major Points** with your students. Drive the **Scripture** and **Major Points** into their hearts and minds.

(Please continue on next page)

⇒ Cover *only some of the commentary* with your students, not all (unless of course you have plenty of time). Cover only as much commentary as is needed to get the major points across.

Do NOT feel that you must...
- cover all the commentary under each point
- share every illustration
- ask all the questions

An abundance of commentary is given so you can find just what you need for...
- your own style of teaching
- your own emphasis
- your own class needs

PLEASE NOTE: It is of utmost importance that you (and your study group) grasp the Scripture, the Study Title, and Major Points. It is this that the Holy Spirit will make alive to your heart and that you will more likely remember and use day by day.

MAJOR POINTS include:

APPLICATIONS:
Use these to show how the Scripture applies to everyday life.

ILLUSTRATIONS:
Simply a window that allows enough light in the lesson so a point can be more clearly seen. A suggestion: Do not just "read" through an illustration if the illustration is a story, but learn it and make it your own. Then give the illustration life by communicating it with *excitement & energy*.

QUESTIONS:
These are designed to stimulate thought and discussion.

A CLOSER LOOK:
In some of the studies, you will see a portion boxed in and entitled: "A Closer Look." This discussion will be a closer study on a particular point. It is generally too detailed for a Sunday School class session, but more adaptable for personal study or an in depth Bible Study class.

PERSONAL JOURNAL:
At the close of every lesson there is space for you to record brief thoughts regarding the impact of the lesson on your life. As you study through the Bible, you will find these comments invaluable as you look back upon them.

Now, may our wonderful Lord bless you mightily as you study and teach His Holy Word. And may our Lord grant you much fruit: many who will become greater servants and witnesses for Him.

REMEMBER!

THE TEACHER'S OUTLINE & STUDY BIBLE™ is the only study material that actually outlines the Bible verse by verse for you right beside the Scripture. As you accumulate the various books of *THE TEACHER'S OUTLINE & STUDY BIBLE*™ for your study and teaching, you will have the Bible outlined book by book, passage by passage, and verse by verse.

The outlines alone makes saving every book a must! (Also encourage your students, if you are teaching, to keep their student edition. They also have the unique verse by verse outline of Scripture in their version.)

Just think for a moment. Over the course of your life, you will have your very own personalized commentary of the Bible. No other book besides the Bible will mean as much to you because it will contain your insights, your struggles, your victories, and your recorded moments with the Lord.

> **"Study to show thyself approved unto God, a workman that needeth not to be ashamed, rightly dividing the word of truth" (2 Ti.2:15).**

> **"All scripture is given by inspiration of God, and is profitable for doctrine, for reproof, for correction, for instruction in righteousness: that the man of God may be perfect, throughly furnished unto all good works" (2 Ti.3:16-17).**

A Special Note for the Bible Study Leader

Dear Teacher,

⇒   The teaching material you hold in your hands gives your church the *maximum flexibility* in scheduling for the church year or for any Bible study program. *The Teacher's Outline and Study Bible*™ (TOSB) has been designed to help you in your teaching ministry. The wealth of material makes the TOSB the most unique Bible study material anywhere. The name says it all:

⇒   The *Teacher's* has been designed just for you, God's dear servant, the teacher of God's Holy word.

⇒   *Outline* makes the material unique as every verse has been outlined—point by point—subject by subject—just for you.

⇒   *Study* allows you, the teacher, to study commentary that has been developed and has drawn upon over forty different sources. At your disposal are well-thought-out points that explain in simple language what the Scripture means. Suggestions for opening and closing each lesson assure that your students will be caught up from the beginning to the end. Practical points of application help you to bring the truth to whatever level of student you are teaching. Gripping illustrations have been interspersed through each lesson, illustrations guaranteed to hold the attention of your students as you drive home the point.. finally, questions that are thought-provoking and discussion-oriented are a part of *every* point in the lesson. Imagine—all the benefits of the time spent collecting this study material are right in *your* hands, waiting for you to glean what *you need* for your next lesson.

⇒   *Bible* is the foundation of *The Teacher's Outline and Study Bible*™. God's Holy Word, outlined for you—verse by verse, point by point, subject by subject—gives you, the teacher, the great advantage of having God's Word outlined, explained, made practical, and illustrated.

"Go ye therefore, and teach all nations"

(Mt.28:19)

Outline of 1 Timothy

***The Teacher's Outline & Sermon Bible*™** is *unique*. It differs from all other Study Bibles & Sermon Resource Materials in that every Passage and Subject is outlined right beside the Scripture. When you choose any *Subject* below and turn to the reference, you have not only the Scripture, but you discover the Scripture and Subject already outlined for you—*verse by verse*.

For a quick example, choose one of the subjects below and turn over to the Scripture, and you will find this marvelous help for faster, easier, and more accurate use.

A suggestion: For the quickest overview of 1 Timothy, first read *all the major titles* (I, II, III, etc.), then come back and read the subtitles.

Outline of 1 Timothy

		Page
Introduction to 1 Timothy		1
Introduction: The Minister and His Young Disciple, 1:1-2		3
I.	**False and True Teachers in the Church, 1:3-20**	
	A. The Danger of False Teachers, 1:3-11	10
	B. The Testimony of a True Minister, 1:12-17	18
	C. The Young Minister (Charge 1): To be a Warrior, 1:18-20	26
II.	**Duties and Order in the Church, 2:1–3:13**	
	A. The First Duty of the Church—Pray, 2:1-8	36
	B. The Women of the Church, 2:9-15	46
	C. The Overseers of the Church, 3:1-7	55
	D. The Deacons of the Church, 3:8-13	65
III.	**Behavior and Relationships in the Church, 3:14–6:21**	
	A. The Description of the Church, 3:14-16	72
	B. The Warning About False Teachers and Their Apostasy, 4:1-5	81
	C. The Young Minister (Charge 2): To Be a Good Minister, 4:6-16	88
	D. The Spirit of Relationships, 5:1-2	100
	E. The Christian Widows, 5:3-16	105
	F. The Elders or Officials, 5:17-20	113
	G. The Young Minister (Charge 3): To Be an Impartial Minister, 5:21-25	118
	H. The Believing Slaves or Employees, 6:1-2	126
	I. The False Teachers, 6:3-5	131
	J. The Secret of Contentment, 6:6-10	139
	K. The Young Minister (Charge 4): To Be a Man of God, 6:11-16	145
	L. The Rich Man and the Minister: The Final Charge, 6:17-21	153
Subject Index		161
Illustration Index		169

THE FIRST EPISTLE OF PAUL THE APOSTLE TO

TIMOTHY

INTRODUCTION

AUTHOR: Paul, the Apostle.

DATE: Uncertain. Probably A.D. 61-64.

The books of 1 Timothy and Titus seem to have been written while Paul was traveling and ministering between two Roman imprisonments. The date depends upon the answer to this question: Did Paul suffer one or two Roman imprisonments? The book of Acts mentions only one imprisonment and closes with Paul in prison in Rome. It says nothing about his death. As one discusses this question, one major thing needs to be kept in mind. Paul prayed fervently that God would release him from prison. And he asked others to pray fervently for his release (Ph.1:25-26; Phm.22). Did God answer his prayer as requested? No one knows for sure. However, several factors point rather decisively to his being released and later suffering a second imprisonment.

1. The Life and Movements of Paul. Paul says in Tit.1:5 that he had been to Crete on a mission tour. And in Tit.3:12 he says that he was spending the winter in Nicopolis. These events do not fit in with any of the accounts in Acts. The evidence seems to be that God answered his prayer and had him released from prison.

2. The Life and Movements of Paul's Companions. Note the following two examples, and there are others. In 1 Ti.1:3 Paul says that he told Timothy to stay in Ephesus. But there is no record of this event in Scripture. Paul had made only two visits to Ephesus. One was a very short visit with little if any ministry. There is no mention whatsoever about Timothy (Ac.18:19-22). The second was his three year ministry in which Timothy had a part. But when it came time for Paul to move on, he sent Timothy and Erastus to Macedonia. He did not ask Timothy to stay in Ephesus. When then did Paul tell Timothy to stay in Ephesus? There just is no record of such a visit in Scripture. Thus all indications point to a third visit by Paul and Timothy—a visit after his first imprisonment and before an unrecorded second imprisonment.

Again, in 2 Ti.4:20 Paul writes, "Trophimus have I left at Miletum sick." Paul was in Miletum before his first Roman imprisonment, but he did not leave Trophimus there sick (Ac.20:17). Trophimus went on to Rome with Paul (Ac.21:29). When then was Trophimus left at Miletum sick? The only clear answer seems to be that Paul made another visit to Miletum—after his first imprisonment and right before a second unrecorded imprisonment.

3. The Time Sequence Between the Writing of the Prison Epistles and the Pastoral Epistles. The Prison Epistles (Ephesians, Philippians, Colossians, and Philemon) were written while Paul was in prison in Rome. He says so in each epistle. Note the following example: Philemon 24 says that Demas is a follower of Christ, but 2 Ti.4:10 says that he had deserted. The letter to Timothy was definitely written after the prison letter to Philemon. When? The evidence points toward a time after his first imprisonment and before a second unrecorded imprisonment. This seems to be the only clear explanation.

As stated above, 1 Timothy and Titus seem to have been written right after Paul had been released from his first imprisonment in Rome and was traveling about ministering. At some point in those few years he was rearrested and imprisoned in Rome for a second time. During this second imprisonment he wrote 2 Timothy before he was executed. His execution was probably between A.D. 65-68.

TO WHOM WRITTEN: "To Timothy, my own son in the faith" (1 Ti.1:2). Timothy's father was a Greek and an unbeliever, but his mother was a Jew and a believer. Her name was Eunice and his grandmother's name was Lois (2 Ti.1:5). Timothy was not circumcised; hence it would seem that he was educated in Greek ways and customs (Ac.16:3). When Paul met Timothy, Timothy was already a Christian believer with a strong testimony, so strong in fact that Paul arranged for him to become his missionary partner (Ac.16:1f). Timothy's maturity and importance are seen in Acts 16 when the word "he" of verse one is changed very rapidly to "they" of verse four. Timothy became a son to Paul (1 Co.4:17). He was esteemed so highly and loved so deeply by Paul that Paul said he was the one man whose mind was at one with his own (Ph.2:19). He was probably chosen by Paul to become Paul's successor (see note—Ph.1:1). From this point on, he was seen either ministering with Paul or else being sent out by Paul to minister to certain churches. He was with Paul in Paul's first imprisonment (Co.1:1; Phm.1). Apparently, Paul was released from prison and Timothy began to travel with him again (see 1 Timothy, Introduction, Date). On this journey Paul left him in Ephesus to correct some errors that had arisen, while Paul himself traveled on into Macedonia to visit the churches there. Soon thereafter Paul was arrested and imprisoned in Rome a second time. As soon as possible Timothy joined him (2 Ti.4:11, 21), but this time Timothy was imprisoned also. However, Timothy was later released (He.13:23), while Paul was either beheaded or released and began a mission tour into Spain. (See note, Timothy—Ph.2:19-24 for more discussion.)

PURPOSE: Paul had three purposes for writing Timothy.
  1. To encourage Timothy in his Christian life and walk.
  2. To warn against false teaching and doctrinal error.
  3. To teach the qualifications and order of officials in the church. Believers needed to know how to behave in the church: "That thou mayest know how thou oughtest to behave thyself in the house of God" (1 Ti.3:15).

SPECIAL FEATURES:
  1. 1 Timothy is "A Pastoral Epistle." There are two other Pastoral Epistles: 2 Timothy and Titus. They are called Pastoral Epistles because they deal primarily with the pastoral care, oversight, and organization of the church. They tell believers how they ought to behave in the house of God (1 Ti.3:15). Interestingly, the term *pastoral* has a long history. It was first used by Thomas Aquinas in A.D. 1274. He called 1 Timothy "an epistle of pastoral rule" and 2 Timothy "an epistle of pastoral care." The term "Pastoral Epistles," however, began to be widely used only after D.N. Berdot (A.D. 1703) and Paul Anton (A.D. 1726) so described them (Donald Guthrie. *The Pastoral Epistles*. "The Tyndale New Testament Commentaries." Grand Rapids, MI: Eerdmans, 1972, p.11).
  2. 1 Timothy is "A Personal Epistle." It was written to a young disciple who was loved as a son. The epistle is filled with warm and affectionate feelings and filled with instructions that were to govern Timothy's personal behavior.
  3. 1 Timothy is "An Ecclesiastical Epistle." It was written to answer questions about church organization, doctrinal purity, and personal behavior. Two things were happening. First, the number and sizes of churches were growing rapidly, and second, the apostles were aging. In both cases the apostles were just unable to personally reach and instruct all the churches; therefore, they had to write if the churches were to be rooted and grounded in the Lord.
  4. 1 Timothy is "An Apologetic Epistle." It is a defense of the faith. The first rumblings and early development of false teaching had just begun to appear (Gnosticism. See Colossians, Introductory Notes, Purpose.) Therefore, Paul warns the believers and defends the truth against heretical and false teaching.

THE FIRST EPISTLE OF PAUL THE APOSTLE TO TIMOTHY

CHAPTER 1

INTRODUCTION: THE MINISTER & HIS YOUNG DISCIPLE, 1:1-2

Outline	Text

1. The minister's call & credentials: An apostle
  a. By the command of God
  b. By Christ our hope
2. The disciple's privilege & need
  a. His privilege: A true son in the faith
  b. His need: Grace, mercy, & peace
	Paul, an apostle of Jesus Christ by the commandment of God our Saviour, and Lord Jesus Christ, which is our hope;
	2 Unto Timothy, my own son in the faith: Grace, mercy, and peace, from God our Father and Jesus Christ our Lord.

Introduction
THE MINISTER AND HIS YOUNG DISCIPLE
1 Timothy 1:1-2

Study 1: THE MINISTER AND HIS YOUNG DISCIPLE

Text: 1 Timothy 1:1-2

Aim: To go and make disciples: To grow young Christian believers in the faith.

Memory Verse:
> "Go therefore and make disciples of all the nations, baptizing them in the name of the Father and the Son and the Holy Spirit" (Matthew 28:19, NASB).

INTRODUCTION:
What have you done in the past five years that will have lasting value? Sometimes we can get so caught up in *doing* that we forget *what* we are supposed to do. If you were employed by a store that sold power-tools to craftsmen, you would want to sell tools that would benefit your customers, something that would help them produce their finest work. You would be wasting your time and theirs if you tried to sell them something inferior or something they would not use.

Strange as it may seem, many Christians are busy doing everything except what they are called to do, that is, make disciples. The challenge from Scripture is to stop getting sidetracked and get busy doing the Lord's work. Start producing disciples for Christ. A disciple made in Jesus' name will produce lasting results. Like the excellent craftsman, the believer needs to have the correct tools in order to produce a quality disciple. Nothing else will do.

One thing that is desperately needed in the church is the vital ministry of making disciples, of nourishing and nurturing men and women as sons and daughters of the

1 TIMOTHY 1:1-2

faith. In seeing the relationship that existed between the Apostle Paul and Timothy, we should be challenged more and more to make disciples—to get to the task of growing leaders within God's church.

OUTLINE:
1. The minister's call and credentials: an apostle (v.1).
2. The disciple's privilege and need (v.2).

1. THE MINISTER'S CALL AND CREDENTIALS: AN APOSTLE (v.1).

Paul calls himself an apostle of Jesus Christ. The word *apostle* means a person who is sent out or sent forth. An apostle is a representative, an ambassador, an envoy, a person who is sent out into one country to represent another country. Three things are true of the apostle:
⇒ he belongs to the king or country who sends him out.
⇒ he is commissioned to be sent out.
⇒ he possesses all the authority and power of the person who sends him out.

Paul makes three forceful points.
1. *He was an apostle by the command of God.* The word command means to be under orders, to be placed under obligation. It is the instructions given by some high official that must be carried out, for example, the word of a king. The word command has the sense of compulsion, force, and necessity.

Paul—the minister of God—was a man sent forth by the command and order of the King of kings, God Himself. The compulsion, force, and necessity of God's command drove him to be a minister of Jesus Christ.

APPLICATION:
The stress of Paul upon his apostleship seems to indicate that Timothy was to share the letter of First Timothy with the church as a whole. What Paul was writing to Timothy was coming from an apostle of Christ; therefore, the whole church was to heed the exhortations.

2. *He was an apostle because of God our Savior.* This is one of the great titles of God. God is the first source of our salvation. We are saved because God loves us.

> "For God so loved the world, that he gave his only begotten Son, that whosoever believeth in him should not perish, but have everlasting life" (Jn.3:16).

If God did not love us, we would not be saved. We would be wiped off the face of the earth, utterly destroyed, condemned, and punished throughout all of eternity without any hope of ever being saved. But God does love us; therefore, He has provided the way for us to be saved. God is our Savior.
⇒ The point is this: since God is our Savior, man never has to die; he can be delivered from sin, death, and judgment to come. This is another reason Paul was driven to serve Christ. People all around him were...
• enslaved by sin
• gripped by death
• doomed to face the judgment of God

Therefore, Paul was driven to represent Jesus Christ in this world of sin and death. He was forced by the inner compulsion of God our Savior to carry the glorious message of salvation to the whole world: the message that God is interested in the whole world. God is our Savior.

> "And my spirit hath rejoiced in God my Saviour" (Lu.1:47).
> "To the only wise God our Saviour, be glory and majesty, dominion and power...now and ever" (Jude 25).

3. *He was an apostle because of Jesus Christ who is our hope.* Men long and hope for all kinds of things...
- recognition, acceptance, esteem, friends
- security and victory over the trials of life
- deliverance from death and eternal life

The reason man longs for these things is because he lacks them. Even if he possesses some sense of them, he still senses a great deal of lack: a great deal of emptiness, incompleteness, unfulfillment, and insecurity within his soul. Why? Because the human soul can never be at rest until it has the absolute assurance that it is acceptable to God and is going to live forever. The human soul was made for God and for the hope of God. Therefore, there is only one way a person can ever have this absolute assurance: Jesus Christ must live within his heart. Jesus Christ is a person's hope of glory (Co.1:27). When a person receives Jesus Christ into his heart and life, the divine nature of Christ...
- makes the person acceptable to God
- gives the person the recognition, acceptance, and friendship of God and of all other believers (the church)
- gives the person security and gives him supernatural power to conquer the trials of life
- delivers the person from death and gives him the inheritance of eternal life

On top of all this, the most wonderful thing happens: Christ gives the person the absolute assurance and hope of all these. The person becomes perfectly complete and satisfied in Jesus Christ our hope (Co.2:10).

The point is this: since Christ is our hope, Paul was driven to serve Christ. He was forced by the inner compulsion to offer the hope of Christ to a world that was gripped by the hopelessness of despair, trouble, and death.

> "Christ in you, the hope of glory" (Co.1:27).
> "Why art thou cast down, O my soul? and why art thou disquieted within me? hope in God: for I shall yet praise him, who is the health of my countenance, and my God" (Ps.43:5).

ILLUSTRATION:
Do you fully understand the power of hope? It is hope in Christ that will carry you through the most desperate trials and temptations of life. Listen to this believer's story.

> *I wanted to quit several times. For me, life was losing its meaning and I wanted out. God had given me a test that seemed impossible to pass. In the span of two years I had lost my means of employment, teetered on the edge of divorce, and sank to the depths of despair.*
>
> *It seemed there was no end to the misery. But in the depths of my heart, a flicker of hope remained as I prayed in faith. I simply refused to believe that Christ would allow me to fall by the wayside. Like a wounded soldier pressing on in the line of fire, my only hope was in Christ. As I prayed and trusted in His ability to redeem my situation, the picture became brighter and brighter.*

1 TIMOTHY 1:1-2

> *At first, the circumstances looked worse. Many people around me reminded me of the "friends of Job." But eventually the sovereign mercy and power of God began to take effect: the waters of destruction began to part. In the midst of chaos, God began to put all the pieces of the puzzle together. The job of my greatest desire became available. My marriage was saved and is stronger than ever. Like a prisoner who has been set free from the fetters of bondage, life is now being experienced and enjoyed instead of just being endured.*

Hope will carry you a long way if it is placed in Christ alone.

QUESTIONS:
1. What things in verse one qualified Paul to be an apostle? How do these qualifications apply to your ministry?
2. Where are you to focus your hope? What are some *wrong* people and things that you can focus your hope upon?
3. How alive is hope in your life? What can you do to cultivate hope?

2. THE DISCIPLE'S PRIVILEGE AND NEED (v.2).

Timothy was greatly privileged, for he was treated as a son by a minister of God, by Paul himself. (See Author—Introduction.) Note that Paul calls Timothy "my own son in the faith." When Paul first met Timothy, Timothy was only ten to twelve years old. But even at that young age, his love for the Lord was apparently strong and noticed by Paul. When Paul returned to Lystra on his next missionary journey, Paul was so stricken with Timothy's spiritual maturity that he invited him to become a disciple. Later, Paul was to say that Timothy was the one person whose mind was as one with his own (Ph.2:19). Paul took him under his wing and began to disciple him in the Lord—to teach him all he knew. What a wonderful privilege: to be discipled by Paul the apostle.

Note the greeting by Paul. He names three qualities that a disciple must possess.
1. There is the grace of God and of Christ.
2. There is the mercy of God and of Christ (see **A CLOSER LOOK: Mercy—1 Ti.1:2** for discussion).
3. There is the peace of God and of Christ (see **A CLOSER LOOK: Peace—1 Ti.1:2** for discussion).

QUESTIONS:
1. Has God ever entrusted someone into your care or you into someone else's care for spiritual discipleship? What special memories come to mind?
2. What three qualities must a disciple possess? Do you lack any of these? What can you do in order to deepen your experience with each of these qualities?
3. Did you have an opportunity to share the gospel of peace this past week? By word? By example? By your lifestyle? How would you evaluate your experience? What would you do differently the next time?

A CLOSER LOOK:

(1:2) **Timothy:** Timothy was just a child when Paul visited Lystra on his first mission (about five or six years before). He was probably somewhere around ten to twelve years old. He was still a young man when Paul wrote his first letter to Timothy (1 Ti.4:12). All this means Timothy was somewhere around eighteen years old when Paul met him on his second mission to Lystra.

It is also possible that Paul led Timothy to the Lord on his first mission tour, but it is more probable that Timothy's mother and grandmother led him to the Lord.

1 TIMOTHY 1:1-2

Acts seems to read as though Paul did not know or remember Timothy from his first mission (Ac.16:1-3). In either case, his spiritual maturity at this point was strong enough for Paul to challenge him to join his mission corps. The facts of his life seem to be as follows:

Timothy's father was a Greek and an unbeliever, but his mother was a Jew and a believer. Her name was Eunice and his grandmother's name was Lois (2 Ti.1:5). Timothy was not circumcised; hence it would seem that he was educated in Greek ways and customs (Ac.16:3). When Paul met Timothy, Timothy was already a Christian believer with a strong testimony, so strong in fact that Paul arranged for him to become his missionary partner (Ac.16:1f). Timothy's maturity and importance are seen in Acts 16 when the word "he" of verse one is changed very rapidly to "they" of verse four. Timothy became a son to Paul (1 Co.4:17). He was esteemed so highly and loved so deeply by Paul that Paul said he was the one man whose mind was one with his own (Ph.2:19). He was probably chosen by Paul to become Paul's successor (see Ph.1:1). From this point on, he was seen either ministering with Paul or else being sent out by Paul to minister to certain churches. He was with Paul in Paul's first imprisonment (Co.1:1; Phm.1). Apparently, Paul was released from prison and Timothy began to travel with him again (see 1 Timothy, Introduction, Date). On this journey Paul left him in Ephesus to correct some errors that had arisen, while Paul himself traveled on into Macedonia to visit the churches there. Soon thereafter Paul was arrested and imprisoned in Rome a second time. As soon as possible Timothy joined him (2 Ti.4:11, 21), but this time Timothy was imprisoned also. However, Timothy was later released (He.13:23), while Paul was either beheaded or released and began a mission tour into Spain.

QUESTIONS:
1. How intimate was the relationship between Paul and Timothy? Do you have any relationships that would compare to theirs? What can you do to develop this kind of relationship with a Christian believer?
2. Why is it important to have a Timothy or a Paul in your life?

A CLOSER LOOK:

(1:2) **Mercy:** feelings of pity, compassion, affection, kindness. It is a desire to succor; to tenderly draw unto oneself and to care for. Two things are essential in order to have mercy: seeing a need and being able to meet that need. God sees our need and feels for us (Ep.2:1-3). Therefore, He acts; He has mercy upon us...
- God withholds His judgment
- God provides a way for us to be saved

Mercy arises from a heart of love: God has mercy upon us because He loves us. His mercy has been demonstrated in two great ways:
⇒ God has withheld His judgment from us—withheld it even when we deserved it.
⇒ God has provided a way for us to be saved through the Lord Jesus Christ.

When Jesus Christ died, He died for our sins. He took our sins upon Himself and bore the judgment of sin for us. Therefore, if we trust Christ as our Savior, God does not count sin against us. Instead, He counts the righteousness of Christ for us. We become acceptable to God through the righteousness of Christ. The great mercy of God is this...
- He allowed Christ, His very own Son, to die for us. He actually allowed His own Son to bear the punishment of our sins for us
- He loves us so much that He will forgive our sins if we will only trust Christ

1 Timothy 1:1-2

> The point is this: it is absolutely necessary for both the minister and the disciple to know and possess the mercy of God and of Christ. A person who has not experienced the mercy of God does not know God. Of all people, the minister and disciple of Christ must know the mercy of God.

ILLUSTRATION:

Is mercy a part of your life? Is it something you practice daily? The following story is a striking example of someone changed by mercy.

> *Like many young married couples, Dan and Tracy went into their marriage without understanding money management. It did not take them long to go from debt-free to debt-ridden. A combination of bad advice, unplanned hospital bills, and bad circumstances left them trapped, never having enough money. Month after month they fell further and further into debt.*
>
> *As the pressure increased, Dan prayed one of those "I'll pray, but it will do no good" kind of prayers. He said, "Lord, I know we do not deserve a second chance, but we've learned so much about good stewardship and what not to do, I'd love to start all over again." In a whispered hush, he said "Amen."*
>
> *Sometime later, Dan and Tracy shared with their pastor their desire to get their finances in order. The pastor sensed their sincerity and wanted to help them overcome their crushing debt. But how?*
>
> *Expecting harsh condemnation for being such poor stewards, Dan and Tracy were shocked at the mercy extended to them by the pastor. Two weeks later, another group of Christians got involved in Dan and Tracy's life. These unnamed Christian businessmen had started a ministry to help couples just like them. The burden of the businessmen was to supply funds at no interest to Christians who were in need—as long as the couples would...*
> - *agree to live by a budget*
> - *repay the loan so others could benefit from their ministry*
> - *no longer use credit cards*
>
> *As Dan signed the needed paperwork, his earlier prayer came back to mind. "Lord, You are so merciful. I deserved condemnation, but You provided mercy."*

How can you provide mercy to someone in need today?

QUESTIONS:
1. What strikes you the most about the mercy of God?
2. When is it the easiest for you to provide mercy to others?
3. When is it the most difficult for you to offer mercy to others?

A CLOSER LOOK:

(1:2) **Peace:** means to be bound, joined, and weaved together with God and with everyone else. It means to be assured, confident, and secure in the love and care of God. It means to have a sense, a consciousness, a knowledge that God will...

- provide
- guide
- strengthen
- sustain
- deliver
- encourage
- save
- give life, real life, both now and forever

1 TIMOTHY 1:1-2

A person can experience true peace only as he comes to know Jesus Christ. Only Christ can bring peace to the human heart, the kind of peace that brings deliverance and assurance to the human soul.

> "Peace I leave with you, my peace I give unto you: not as the world giveth give I unto you. Let not your heart be troubled, neither let it be afraid" (Jn.14:27).

QUESTIONS:
1. How is true *peace* described?
2. Why would Paul want Timothy to have *peace* in his life? Why should *peace* be a part of your life?
3. What is the key to keeping *God's peace* in your life?

SUMMARY:

Do you desire to do those things which will last? You can if you are willing to make disciples, to nourish and nurture young Christian believers in the faith. You have a wonderful example in the life of Paul and Timothy:

1. The minister's call and credentials: an apostle.
   a. By God's command
   b. By God our Savior
   c. By Christ our hope
2. The disciple's privilege and need.
   a. A true son in the faith
   b. His need: Grace, mercy, and peace

Who are *you* investing in for the future?

PERSONAL JOURNAL NOTES:
(Reflection and Response)

1. The most important thing that I learned from this lesson was:

2. The area that I need to work on the most is:

3. I can apply this lesson to my life by:

4. Closing Statement of Commitment:

1 Timothy 1:3-11

Outline	Scripture	Notes
	I. FALSE & TRUE TEACHERS IN THE CHURCH 1:3-20	teachers of the law; understanding neither what they say, nor whereof they affirm.
	A. The Danger of False Teachers, 1:3-11	7 But we know that the law is good, if a man use it lawfully; 8 Knowing this, that
1. False teachers teach a different doctrine	3 As I besought thee to abide still at Ephesus, when I went into Macedonia, that thou mightest charge some that they teach no other doctrine.	the law is not made for a righteous man, but for the lawless and disobedient, for the ungodly and for sinners, for unholy and profane, for murderers of fathers
2. False teachers give heed to endless speculations & controversies rather than to God's work	4 Neither give heed to fables and endless genealogies, which minister questions, rather than godly edifying which is in faith: so do.	and murderers of mothers, for manslayers, 9 For whoremongers, for them that defile themselves with mankind, for men-
3. False teachers put empty discussion above love a. Above a pure heart b. Above a good conscience c. Above a sincere faith	5 Now the end of the commandment is charity out of a pure heart, and of a good conscience, and of faith unfeigned: 6 From which some having swerved have turned aside unto vain jangling; 7 Desiring to be	stealers, for liars, for perjured persons, and if there be any other thing that is contrary to sound doctrine; 10 According to the glorious gospel of the blessed God, which was committed to my trust.
		4. False teachers put ambition & personal ideas above the truth

		5. False teachers put self-righteousness above God's gospel
		a. False teachers do not understand the law & its purposes
		  1) Law is not given to righteous people, but to unrighteous people: To everyone who is guilty of any sin or evil
		  2) Law is given to restrain people, to keep them from committing wickedness
		b. False teachers do not understand the real measuring rod used by God: The gospel

Section I
FALSE AND TRUE TEACHERS IN THE CHURCH
1 Timothy 1:3-20

Study 1: THE DANGER OF FALSE TEACHERS

Text: 1 Timothy 1:3-11

Aim: To fearlessly defend the faith.

Memory Verse:
> "Neither give heed to fables and endless genealogies, which minister questions, rather than godly edifying which is in faith: so do" (1 Timothy 1:4).

1 Timothy 1:3-11

INTRODUCTION:
There are few things that can turn the stomach of a nation more than that of a traitor. Remember Benedict Arnold? Arnold, as you may recall, was an American who spied on his own countrymen during the Revolutionary War. He was found guilty of treason and executed.
But note: as bad as Arnold's betrayal was, a false teacher who operates in the church is even more repulsive. While Arnold's betrayal of America was a temporary thing, a false teacher's damage to the Kingdom of God is eternal because he leads souls away from God into everlasting damnation.

This is the first charge to Timothy and to all believers: be a defender of the faith. We must guard against and correct false teachers.

OUTLINE:
1. False teachers teach a different doctrine (v.3).
2. False teachers give heed to endless speculations and controversies rather than to God's work (v.4).
3. False teachers put empty discussion above love (vv.5-6).
4. False teachers put ambition and personal ideas above the truth (v.7).
5. False teachers put self-righteousness above God's gospel (vv.8-11).

1. FALSE TEACHERS TEACH A DIFFERENT DOCTRINE (v.3).

Timothy was in Ephesus and Paul was in Macedonia, a great distance apart. Ephesus was in Asia and Macedonia was in Europe, north of Greece. Note that Paul had to urge Timothy to stay at Ephesus. The church was in trouble because false teaching had seeped in, and the church needed Timothy. Apparently, Timothy felt incapable and wanted to join Paul until Paul could return to Ephesus and handle the situation himself. However, false teaching is so serious a matter that it has to be handled immediately when it raises its ugly head. Therefore, Timothy had to remain in Ephesus so that he could charge the church to stop the false teaching. The word *charge* is a strong word. It is a military word that means to pass commands down through the ranks. Timothy was to give orders and charge the false teachers to stop teaching false doctrine, and if this did not work, he was to order and charge the church to handle the false teachers. This says several things about the church at Ephesus.

1. The leaders had not heeded the word of Paul when he had met with them earlier (Ac.20:17-38). He had warned them about false teachers.

> "Take heed therefore unto yourselves, and to all the flock, over the which the Holy Ghost hath made you overseers, to feed the church of God, which he hath purchased with his own blood. For I know this, that after my departing shall grievous wolves enter in among you, not sparing the flock. Also of your own selves shall men arise, speaking perverse things, to draw away disciples after them. Therefore watch, and remember, that by the space of three years I ceased not to warn every one night and day with tears" (Ac.20:28-31).

2. The leaders had not insisted upon the purity of the gospel as Paul had done and taught. They had allowed the Word of God to become corrupted.

> "For we are not as many, which corrupt the word of God: but as of sincerity, but as of God, in the sight of God speak we in Christ" (2 Co.2:17).

3. Timothy was to charge the ministers, teachers, and leaders to preach no other doctrine than the doctrine of God's Word.

1 TIMOTHY 1:3-11

⇒ They were not to add to the doctrine of God's Word.
⇒ They were not to take away from the doctrine of God's Word.
⇒ They were not to formulate new doctrines for the church.

They were not to make what they thought were improvements nor to correct what they thought were defects in the Word of God. They were not to change or alter the Word of God to any degree whatsoever. In the clear words of this verse: "charge some that they teach no other doctrine."

> "I marvel that ye are so soon removed from him that called you into the grace of Christ unto another gospel: which is not another; but there be some that trouble you, and would pervert the gospel of Christ. But though we, or an angel from heaven, preach any other gospel unto you than that which we have preached unto you, let him be accursed. As we said before, so say I now again, If any man preach any other gospel unto you than that ye have received, let him be accursed" (Ga.1:6-9).

QUESTIONS:
1. Why did Paul give such strong orders to Timothy? How does this charge apply to your life?
2. What did the church at Ephesus fail to do in defense of the gospel? How do these failures effect churches in your community?
3. Why do some people add their own doctrines to God's Word? What can you do to ensure that you will not follow your own *ideas* and *doctrines* (instead of God's)?

2. FALSE TEACHERS GIVE HEED TO ENDLESS SPECULATIONS AND CONTROVERSIES RATHER THAN TO GOD'S WORK (v.4).

No better description of false teaching could be given than what this verse gives:
⇒ "[False teaching] is fables and endless genealogies, which give rise to questions, rather than godly edifying."

1. The word *fables* refers to all forms of false and fictional teaching or doctrine. It means the false ideas and speculations of men about God and Christ and the teachings of God's Word. The doctrines of men are only speculations, fables, narratives, stories, fictions, and falsehoods.[1]

> "But refuse profane and old wives' fables, and exercise thyself rather unto godliness" (1 Ti.4:7).
> "And they shall turn away their ears from the truth, and shall be turned unto fables" (2 Ti.4:4).

2. The word *genealogies* refers to those who take comfort in a godly heritage. The Jews were guilty of this. They took great pride in their godly forefathers, so much so that they felt that the godliness of their forefathers rubbed off on them. The more godly forefathers they had in their roots, the more prestigious and acceptable they felt before God and men. They felt that the stronger their roots, the more man and God would accept and esteem them. Note the reference to "endless genealogies." There were apparently those who were spending enormous amounts of time in structuring and discussing

---
[1] A.T. Robertson. *Word Pictures in the New Testament*, Vol.4. (Nashville, TN: Broadman Press, 1931), p.561.

1 TIMOTHY 1:3-11

the godly heritage of the past. Apparently, the practice had seeped into the church. There were those...
- who were stressing heritage over Christ
- who were depending upon a godly heritage for salvation instead of trusting Christ
- who were spending more time in genealogies than in edifying and building up the godliness of the church
- who were concentrating upon questions and theories rather than upon building godly behavior among believers

APPLICATION:
Some persons take great comfort in their godly heritage. They actually feel that God would never reject them...
- because of their godly wives, husbands, children, parents
- because they have a godly pastor or friend with whom they are close

> "Who can bring a clean thing out of an unclean? Not one" (Jb.14:4).
> "There is a generation that are pure in their own eyes, and yet is not washed from their filthiness" (Pr.30:12).

ILLUSTRATION:
It was Billy Graham who once stated bluntly, "Being born in America does not make you a Christian any more than being born in a garage makes you a car." In the same sense, being born in a godly family or being born in a Christian hospital does not make you a Christian.

> Charles was a young man who was full of life. Raised by Jewish parents, he discovered Christ during his adult years and gave his life to Christ. Charles became quite an evangelist to both the Jew and the Gentile. As he shared his testimony, his words were sharp: "Without Jesus in my life, I would have died and gone to hell."
>
> Interestingly enough, Charles' friend Gary did not have the same belief. Gary had a special love for the Jews. He believed that because the Jews were God's chosen people throughout Old Testament history, they did not need to make a decision for Christ. In essence, they earned a place in heaven because of their "godly heritage," because of their family ties to Abraham and other godly fathers of Israel.
>
> But when another believer asked Gary what would have happened to Charles if he had died before making a decision to accept Christ, Gary's answer was haunting: "I'm not sure where he would have gone."

While people speculate about eternity, heaven is passing them by. Be sure you understand that your entrance into heaven is only through Jesus Christ, not through a godly heritage.

QUESTIONS:
1. What is your guarantee of entering heaven? Where do some people place their trust?
2. How would you respond to Gary's belief about the Jews?
3. Do you know someone who is trusting in his godly heritage instead of in Christ? Trusting that God will accept him because of his mother's, father's, wife's, or husband's faith? How can you witness to him?

1 TIMOTHY 1:3-11

3. FALSE TEACHERS PUT EMPTY DISCUSSION ABOVE LOVE (vv.5-6).

The end of God's commandment to men is love (agape, God's kind of love). Therefore, ministers and teachers are to focus upon growing in love and in teaching love. The great call of believers is...
- to know the love of God and to love God
- to love each other as brothers in the Lord
- to love the lost of the world so much that we are driven to take the gospel to them

But note where this kind of love comes from. Its source is not found in men; it does not just arise out of the heart of man. The love which we are to know and possess comes from three sources.

⇒ *Love comes from a pure heart*: a heart forgiven by God and cleansed from all impurities; a heart that is not weighed down by selfishness, worldliness, envy, covetousness, and immorality.

⇒ *Love comes from a good conscience*: a conscience that knows there is nothing between it and God, between it and men; a conscience that knows it has been true to God's Word and has taught no error.

⇒ *Love comes from unfeigned or sincere faith*: a faith that is set upon God and His Word, that holds to God's Word and trusts and teaches God's Word and God's Word only.

The end of God's commandment—of all that God has ever said to man—is love. Therefore, a true believer commits his life to learn more and more about the love of God and to teach the love of God more and more. But to do this he must be totally committed...
- to having a pure heart before God
- to having a good (clear) conscience before God
- to following the faith, that is, the teachings and doctrine of God's Word

However, this is not true with some—not true with false teachers. Note exactly what Scripture says: some have swerved and turned aside to empty discussions. The term "vain jangling" sounds just like what false teaching amounts to: vain, empty clamor and noise. The term means empty arguments, discussions, and speculations—the speculative ideas of men about God, Christ, and the Word of God. Note that false teachers swerve and turn aside from the doctrines of God's Word to these vain janglings.

> "Now the Spirit speaketh expressly, that in the latter times some shall depart from the faith, giving heed to seducing spirits, and doctrines of devils; speaking lies in hypocrisy; having their conscience seared with a hot iron" (1 Ti.4:1-2).

QUESTIONS:
1. According to verse 5, what is the great call of a Christian believer? Which one of these needs your immediate attention? Why?
2. What is the source of the love that is described here? List some of the wrong places to find the source of love?
3. What did Paul mean by "vain jangling"? Give some practical examples of how this is done.

1 TIMOTHY 1:3-11

4. FALSE TEACHERS PUT AMBITION AND PERSONAL IDEAS ABOVE THE TRUTH (v.7).

The picture is that of a person who is ambitious...
- to be recognized as an original teacher or preacher
- to be recognized as a creative person
- to be recognized as the creator of a novel idea or doctrine
- to be recognized as the author of a new concept or doctrine
- to be recognized as the founder of a new movement

The picture is that of a person who so desires to fit in with the latest fashion of teaching that he neglects or ignores the truth. He disregards the truth in order to fit in with his peers. The false teacher's ambition is allowed to cloud his understanding of the truth.

William Barclay points out that the false teacher who is ambitious often...
- demonstrates arrogance instead of humility
- focuses upon teaching rather than learning
- looks down upon simple-minded people
- regards those who do not agree with his conclusions as ignorant fools[2]

> "But in vain they do worship me, teaching for doctrines the commandments of men" (Mt.15:9).

ILLUSTRATION:
We must never forget that the Bible is our only reliable guide for truth. No person can be the authority on truth, no matter how much education or experience he has. As A.W. Tozer said:

The devil is a better theologian than any of us and is a devil still.[3]

QUESTIONS:
1. Do you know any teachers who lord their education or experience over others? Whose focus is upon themselves instead of upon God and His Word? What should you do when facing this kind of attitude? What is your responsibility as a true believer?
2. What safeguards have you built to protect yourself from this type of false teacher? Or to keep yourself from *being* this type of teacher?

5. FALSE TEACHERS PUT SELF-RIGHTEOUSNESS ABOVE GOD'S GOSPEL (vv.8-11).

These verses show that the false teachers who had infiltrated the church were Jewish legalists. These said that a person became acceptable to God...
- by Christ and the law
- by receiving Christ plus keeping the law
- by becoming righteous in Christ and by doing the righteousness of the law

They rejected the teaching that a person was saved by grace through faith alone. To them a person could not be saved unless he...

---

2 William Barclay. *The Letters to Timothy, Titus, and Philemon.* "The Daily Study Bible." (Philadelphia, PA: The Westminster Press, 1959), p.37.
3 A.W. Tozer. *Man: The Dwelling Place of God.* (Carol Stream, Il: Christianity Today), Vol. 41, No.5.

1 TIMOTHY 1:3-11

- became good enough to please God
- did enough good to make himself acceptable to God

What is wrong with this? There is nothing wrong with doing good, but there is a great deal wrong with thinking and teaching that a person can do enough good to make himself acceptable to God. God is perfect; therefore, a person would have to become perfect to be acceptable to God.

⇒ Man is already short of perfection; he is already imperfect; therefore, he can never be acceptable to God—not by any merit or work of his own.

⇒ Man already comes so short and is so sinful, he can never stop coming short and sinning. Every man comes short, sins, fails, trespasses, and transgresses—no matter who he is. He is depraved and lives a depraved life, a life short of God's glory (Ro.3:23).

This is the reason God gave man the law: not to show man that he is righteous (lawful), but to show him just how far short he really is of God's glory—how unrighteous he is and how much he needs the love and grace of God. God gave the law to show man how much he needs a Savior, the Lord Jesus Christ, the Son of God Himself. This is what man fails to see. This is what the false teachers fail to see.

1. False teachers do not understand the law and its purposes. God gave the law to man to show him how short he comes (unrighteousness) and to restrain evil. Note this:

⇒ The law was given to man—to all men.
⇒ The law was not made for the righteous but for the unrighteous.
⇒ Therefore, all men must be unrighteous because the law was given to all men.

Scripture gives a list of the people to whom God gave the law. Note how the list covers all of society. Every person is guilty of having broken the law of God.

a. The law is given to the lawless and disobedient (rebellious): all who fail to live as God wills and commands. If a person could fail just once (he cannot, but if he could), he would still need the law to let him know that he is short of the standard, has to pay the penalty, and must not violate the standard any more.

b. The law is given to the ungodly and sinners: all who act contrary to God's nature and come short of perfection.

c. The law is given to the unholy and profane: all who refuse to set their lives apart to God and dedicate themselves to God; all who deny and question God and spiritual things, who exalt themselves and this world above God and the spiritual world.

d. The law is given to "those who strike and beat and [even] murder fathers and strike and beat and [even] murder mothers" and for other murderers (Amplified New Testament).

e. The law is given to whoremongers and to those who defile themselves with mankind, that is, all impure and immoral persons and all homosexuals.

f. The law is given to men-stealers or kidnappers.

g. The law is given to liars and to those who commit perjury.

h. The law is given to anything else that is contrary to the sound doctrine (teaching) of God's Word.

Note how no person is left out of the list: every human being who has ever lived or ever will live needs the law, for every person is short of God's glory; that is, every man is unrighteous. Therefore, no person can ever be acceptable to God. Righteousness is not by the law—not by being good and doing good. False teachers fail to see this.

2. False teachers do not understand the real measuring rod of God: the gospel—the glorious gospel of the blessed God. The blessed God has made a way for man to be-

1 TIMOTHY 1:3-11

come acceptable to Him. It is not the way of law and works but the way of the gospel. When a person accepts the gospel of God, God accepts that person. What is the gospel?

> "That Christ Jesus came into the world to save sinners" (1 Ti.1:15).
>
> "For God so loved the world, that he gave his only begotten Son, that whosoever believeth in him should not perish, but have everlasting life. For God sent not his Son into the world to condemn the world; but that the world through him might be saved. He that believeth on him is not condemned: but he that believeth not is condemned already, because he hath not believed in the name of the only begotten Son of God" (Jn.3:16-18).

QUESTIONS:
1. What traits does a legalist display? Are any of these traits a temptation for you? Why or why not?
2. Why did God give man the law?
3. How does the legalist pervert the law of God?
4. Using very simple terms, what is the gospel?

SUMMARY:

The warning that Paul gave Timothy is very clear: false teachers are armed and dangerous, and they are to be taken seriously. Why? Because...

1. False teachers teach a different doctrine.
2. False teachers give heed to endless speculations and controversies rather than to God's work.
3. False teachers put empty discussion above love.
4. False teachers put ambition and personal ideas above the truth.
5. False teachers put self-righteousness above God's gospel.

PERSONAL JOURNAL NOTES:
(Reflection & Response)

1. The most important thing that I learned from this lesson was:

2. The area that I need to work on the most is:

3. I can apply this lesson to my life by:

4. Closing Statement of Commitment:

1 TIMOTHY 1:12-17

	B. The Testimony of a True Minister, 1:12-17	15 This is a faithful saying, and worthy of all acceptation, that Christ Jesus came into the world to save sinners; of whom I am chief.	2. Christ saved Paul
			  a. Christ came to save sinners
			  b. Christ has now saved the "worst" sinner

1. Christ Jesus appointed Paul to serve
  a. Christ strengthened him
  b. Christ considered him trustworthy
  c. Christ forgave his terrible sins
	12 And I thank Christ Jesus our Lord, who hath enabled me, for that he counted me faithful, putting me into the ministry; 13 Who was before a blasphemer, and a persecutor, and injurious: but I obtained mercy, because I did it ignorantly in unbelief.	16 Howbeit for this cause I obtained mercy, that in me first Jesus Christ might show forth all longsuffering, for a pattern to them which should hereafter believe on him to life everlasting.	c. Christ saved him as an example of His great mercy

d. Christ poured out His grace upon Paul	14 And the grace of our Lord was exceeding abundant with faith and love which is in Christ Jesus.	17 Now unto the King eternal, immortal, invisible, the only wise God, be honour and glory for ever and ever. Amen.	3. Christ is to be praised

Section I
FALSE AND TRUE TEACHERS IN THE CHURCH
1 Timothy 1:3-20

Study 2: THE TESTIMONY OF A TRUE MINISTER

Text: 1 Timothy 1:12-17

Aim: To share a convincing gospel, a gospel that changes lives.

Memory Verse:
"And I thank Christ Jesus our Lord, who hath enabled me, for that he counted me faithful, putting me into the ministry" (1 Timothy 1:12).

INTRODUCTION:
We live in perilous times, days of gross immorality, lawlessness, and violence. Yet God has placed each believer in a strategic place, a place where the glorious power of the gospel must be proclaimed.

God's solution for the havoc produced by the false teachers of the world is to raise up true believers who are faithful to the gospel. Instead of responding to the tug of the false teacher's lies, the true believer is pulled by the irresistible draw of the Word of God—a pull that keeps him walking in the truth.

It was Edmund Burke who once commented, "The only thing necessary for the triumph of evil is for good men to do nothing."

Be determined to stand up for the truth. Tell of the marvelous truth of God's Word whenever, wherever, and to whomever He gives you the opportunity.

This passage is a contrast with the former passage (1 Ti.1:3-11), presenting a strong contrast between the true minister and false teachers. These verses cover the testimony of Paul, who was a true minister. It is a passage that every minister and believer of the church should heed.

1 TIMOTHY 1:12-17

OUTLINE:
1. Christ Jesus appointed Paul to serve (vv.12-14).
2. Christ saved Paul (vv.15-16).
3. Christ is to be praised (v.17).

1. CHRIST JESUS APPOINTED PAUL TO SERVE (vv.12-14).

This is a critical fact. Paul says that he did not make himself a minister nor did other persons choose him to be a minister. He did not choose the ministry because he thought it would be a good profession nor because people thought he would make a good minister. He was in the ministry for one reason only: Christ Jesus had chosen him and put him into the ministry. Note four facts.

1. Christ Jesus enabled Paul. The word *enabled* means to strengthen and give power to. The power of Paul's ministry came from Christ. Christ gave him the strength to minister. Paul's strength and power to minister did not come from his...
- trying to stir up power within himself
- talking about the results and power in his ministry
- trying to program strength and power into his ministry
- trying to shout power into his preaching

Christ Himself put Paul into the ministry; therefore Christ Himself strengthened and empowered Paul for the ministry. No person has the power to do spiritual warfare; no person can penetrate the spirits of other people. If a person is to minister to people, he must be empowered by Christ, for only Christ can penetrate the spirits of people. Therefore, the minister must possess the power of Christ.

APPLICATION:
This is a critical fact. It means that a person cannot make himself a minister nor can other persons choose him to be a minister—not a true minister, not a minister who pleases Christ and can be blessed by Christ. Why? Because no person can carry on a successful ministry in his own strength, not a ministry that truly reaches people for Christ and delivers them from sin, death, and the judgment to come. Only Christ can do this. This is the reason the believer must be enabled by Christ; he must minister in the strength and power of Christ.

A person who is in the ministry because he has chosen the ministry as a profession or because people thought he would make a good minister is only serving a humanistic religion. Of course, a humanistic minister—a minister who ministers only in his human strength—does some good through social and emotional development. But he does much harm in that he leads people into a false security. How? He is not able to spiritually save a person—not a single person—from sin, death, and the judgment to come. Only Christ Jesus can do this. Therefore, the only way a minister can be what he should be...
- is to be put in the ministry by Christ Jesus
- is to be enabled (strengthened and empowered) by Christ Jesus

> "Ye have not chosen me, but I have chosen you, and ordained you, that ye should go and bring forth fruit, and that your fruit should remain: that whatsoever ye shall ask of the Father in my name, he may give it you" (Jn.15:16).
>
> "Whereof I was made a minister, according to the gift of the grace of God given unto me by the effectual working of his power" (Ep.3:7).

1 Timothy 1:12-17

2. **Christ Jesus counted him trustworthy.** This is a most wonderful thought, that Christ would count us trustworthy. He trusts us to be faithful, and in the final analysis, He knows that we will be faithful to Him. This is one of the reasons He chooses and puts us in the ministry.

APPLICATION 1:
No matter how far down a ministering believer falls, he should always remember that Christ Jesus has counted him faithful. Christ knows that the believer who truly ministers for Christ will arise and begin to serve with renewed fervor. This is the reason Christ called the believer: because in the final analysis the believer must be faithful. Why do we say this? Because of the forgiveness and power and faithfulness of Christ. Therefore, any believer who has fallen must arise and seek the forgiveness of Christ and begin to walk anew in the strength and power of Christ. He must begin anew to serve and minister—all for Christ.

APPLICATION 2:
William Barclay has an excellent message for us as we deal with our dear brothers and sisters who have fallen.

> It was to Paul an amazing thing, that he, the arch-persecutor, had been chosen as the missionary and the pioneer of Christ. It was not only that Jesus Christ had forgiven him; it was that Christ had trusted him. Sometimes in human affairs we forgive a man who has committed some mistake or who has been guilty of some sin, but we make it very clear that his past makes it impossible for us to trust him again with any responsibility. But Christ had not only forgiven Paul, He had entrusted him with His work to do. The man who had been the persecutor of Christ had been made the ambassador of Christ.[1]

"Moreover it is required in stewards, that a man be found faithful" (1 Co.4:2).

We must be as faithful and forgiving to others as Christ is to us!

3. **Christ Jesus forgave his terrible sins.** Paul mentions three terrible sins of which he had been guilty.
   ⇒ Blasphemy: he had insulted, reviled, cursed, and railed the name of Christ.
   ⇒ Persecutor: he had been so angry at Christ that he had set out to wipe the Lord's name off the face of the earth. Therefore, he had been set against all believers—set upon destroying them all.
   ⇒ Injurious: insolent; to treat and use others despitefully; to be brutal and violent and to enjoy it; to be in a fiery rage and to inflict it upon others. William Barclay says that the word...

> Indicates a kind of arrogant sadism; it describes the man who is out to inflict pain and injury for the sheer joy of inflicting it....that is what Paul was once like in regard to the Christian Church. Not content with words of insult, he went to the limit of legal persecution. Not content with legal persecution, he went to the limit of sadistic brutality in his attempt to stamp out the Christian faith."[2]

However despite all this evil, God had mercy upon Paul. Paul had not known that Christ was really the true Messiah. He thought that he knew God and that his religion

---

[1] William Barclay. *The Letters to Timothy, Titus, and Philemon*, p.48.
[2] ibid., p.52.

was the true religion. He felt that any religion that stood against his religion was to be stamped out. Therefore, when Paul attacked Christ and His followers, he did it ignorantly in unbelief. He just did not believe that Jesus Christ could possibly be the Messiah.

The point is this: God had mercy upon Paul. He took pity upon Paul despite his terrible sins.

> "Who is a God like unto thee, that pardoneth iniquity, and passeth by the transgression of the remnant of his heritage? he retaineth not his anger for ever, because he delighteth in mercy" (Mi.7:18).

4. Christ Jesus poured out His grace upon Paul. Remember: grace means the undeserved favor and blessings of God.
⇒ Christ favored Paul even when he did not deserve it.
⇒ Christ blessed Paul even when he did not deserve it.

And note: Christ favored and blessed him exceedingly and abundantly, that is, superabundantly and beyond measure. Christ did two things for Paul.
⇒ Christ stirred faith in Paul: the faith to believe, trust, and serve and to keep on serving no matter the trial, problem, or fatigue.
⇒ Christ stirred love in Paul: the love to still reach out and do all he could for people even when they rejected, ridiculed, abused, and persecuted him.

> "Or despisest thou the riches of his goodness and forbearance and longsuffering; not knowing that the goodness of God leadeth thee to repentance?" (Ro.2:4).

QUESTIONS:
1. What was the source of Paul's power for the ministry? How can this source be applied to your ministry or as a lay servant of the Lord?
2. Some people enter the ministry for all of the wrong reasons. What are some of those reasons? Why are these temptations for some?
3. How and why does God trust you?
4. What one sin has God *not* forgiven you? Think for a moment. What is the most evil thing that you have done? Can you trust Christ to forgive you for that sin? Why or why not?
5. What impact did the grace of God have on Paul? What impact does God's grace have on you? What impact should it have on you?

2. CHRIST SAVED PAUL (vv.15-16).

Three significant points are made in these two verses.

1. Christ Jesus came into the world to save sinners. This is a faithful saying or statement. It is a true message that can be trusted, and the glorious message is worthy of everyone accepting it. Not a single person should reject or ignore the message.

"**Christ Jesus came into the world to save sinners.**" Christ actually left the spiritual world or dimension to come into the physical world in order to save the human race. He saves us from sin, death, and the judgment to come. No matter how sinful a person is—no matter how great a sin or sins he has committed—Christ Jesus came to save him. And the person can be saved.
⇒ The point is this: every true minister has been saved by Christ or else he is not a true minister. It is just as necessary for a minister to be saved as it is for anyone else. Every person needs to be saved, and once he has been saved—no matter how terrible his sin—Christ can put him into the ministry.

1 TIMOTHY 1:12-17

"For the Son of man is come to seek and to save that which was lost" (Lu.19:10).

"Wherefore he is able also to save them to the uttermost that come unto God by him, seeing he ever liveth to make intercession for them" (He.7:25).

2. Christ Jesus has now saved the chief sinner. The worst sins in the world are the sins of...
- blasphemy: being filled with anger and malice against Christ; cursing and blaspheming His name with a bitter hostility
- persecuting believers and trying to annihilate them off the face of the earth
- injuring believers; being brutal and violent against believers and enjoying it

This had been Paul, but note the wonderful truth: **"Christ Jesus came into the world to save sinners."** And Paul was the chief sinner; therefore, Christ Jesus had come to save him.

APPLICATION:
Christ will save anyone who confesses that he is a sinner and that he needs to be saved—any sinner who truly confesses and repents of his sin. No matter how terrible the sin, if the person will confess and turn from his sin, Christ will save him. Why? Because Christ Jesus came to save sinners. This was His very purpose for coming into the world.

The point is this: every true minister is to know how terrible a sinner he is. He is as much a sinner as Paul was. The minister is to be as conscious of being a sinner as much as anyone else. He is to be aware that he is "the chief" of sinners or else he lacks a true sense of God's holiness and of man's depravity.

"But when Jesus heard that, he said unto them, They that be whole need not a physician, but they that are sick. But go ye and learn what that meaneth, I will have mercy, and not sacrifice: for I am not come to call the righteous, but sinners to repentance" (Mt.9:12-13).

3. Christ Jesus saved Paul as a pattern of His great mercy. Very simply, Paul is the prime example...
- that any sinner, no matter how terrible his sin, can be saved—if he will only receive Christ and begin to follow Him day by day.
- that any believer can be delivered from sin and from the power of sin, no matter how strong the enslavement is—if he will only receive the power of Christ and follow Him with a renewed commitment.

The point is this: the true minister is a pattern of the Lord's great longsuffering. The Lord has saved the minister from sin, truly saved him; therefore, the true minister stands as a dynamic example of God's eternal mercy and eternal grace.

"The Lord is not slack concerning his promise, as some men count slackness; but is longsuffering to us-ward, not willing that any should perish, but that all should come to repentance" (2 Pe.3:9).

ILLUSTRATION:
Scripture is very clear about who has taken the initiative to save us. Unquestionably, it is Jesus Christ. Unfortunately, sometimes we keep running from the only One who can save us!

1 TIMOTHY 1:12-17

> *In 1981, a Minnesota radio station reported a story about a stolen car in California. Police were staging an intense search for the vehicle and the driver, even to the point of placing announcements on local radio stations to contact the thief.*
>
> *On the front seat of the stolen car sat a box of crackers that, unknown to the thief, were laced with poison. The car owner had intended to use the crackers as rat bait. Now the police and the owner of the VW Bug were more interested in apprehending the thief to save his life than to recover the car.*
>
> *So often when we run from God, we feel it is to escape his punishment. But what we are actually doing is eluding his rescue.*[3]

Are you running from God's punishment or from His rescue?

QUESTIONS:
1. Why did Jesus Christ come into the world?
2. What conditions does Christ put on people who want to be saved? Have you met these conditions? Why or why not?
3. Why did God save a sinner like Paul? Why did God save you?

A CLOSER LOOK:

(1:16) **Paul:** Paul was chosen to be the pattern for all other men. The pattern of what? Of longsuffering—that God's mercy can save anyone. Paul had been the arch-persecutor of the church, storming into the homes and arresting and murdering the followers of Christ. But God, who is longsuffering and not willing that any should perish, reached down and had mercy upon Paul. God forgave Paul and saved him.

Paul declared a marvelous truth: if God could save him, God could save anyone. No matter how great the sinner, the longsuffering and mercy of God are greater. Paul is proof; he is the pattern of God's mercy.

QUESTIONS:
1. Who do you believe is beyond God's ability to save?
2. Why is it important that God is longsuffering?
3. Why was Paul considered to be the pattern of God's mercy?
4. What feelings come to your mind when you think about the mercy of God?

3. CHRIST IS TO BE PRAISED (v.17).

Thinking of the glorious salvation that Christ had given him led Paul to break forth into praise. This is a great doxology:
- ⇒ God is "the King eternal": the word eternal is literally ages. God is the King, the sovereign majesty of the ages, both this age and the age to come.
- ⇒ God is "immortal": that is, incorruptible. He has no seed of corruption, no seed of aging, deterioration, or decay within His being. God cannot die. He alone has immortality (1 Ti.6:16).
- ⇒ God is "invisible": that is, He cannot be seen by people, not with physical eyes in the physical dimension or world.

---

[3] Craig B. Larson, Editor. *Illustrations for Preaching & Teaching.* (Grand Rapids, MI: Baker Books, 1993), p.207.

1 Timothy 1:12-17

⇒ God is "the only wise God": that is, He is the only living and true God, the only God who actually possesses intelligence and wisdom, who can truthfully interact with the world and save men.

> "**But ye are a chosen generation, a royal priesthood, an holy nation, a peculiar people; that ye should show forth the praises of him who hath called you out of darkness into his marvelous light**" (1 Pe.2:9).

ILLUSTRATION:
The only legitimate response from a sinner who is saved by grace is this: unreserved praise for the eternal King of glory. Your praise is to rise from a changed heart.

> *A story is told in which a man went to church with an angel as his guide. Every seat in the church was filled, but there was something strange about it all. The organist moved his fingers over the keys but no music came forth from the pipes. The choir arose to sing, and their lips moved, but not a sound was to be heard. The pastor stepped to the pulpit to read the Scriptures, but not a sound was heard.*
>
> *The congregation joined in repeating the prayer, but not a single sound was heard. The pastor again stepped to the pulpit, and went through all the motions of preaching, but the man with the angel heard nothing. So he turned to the angel and said,*
>
> *"What does this mean? I see that a service is being held, but I hear nothing."*
>
> *The angel replied, "You hear nothing because there is nothing to be heard. You see this service just as God sees it. These are not putting their hearts into it, and so God hears nothing. He hears only that which comes from the heart, and not that which comes from the lips only."*
>
> *As the angel was speaking, back in the last pew they heard a child saying, "Our Father, which art in heaven, hallowed be thy name,' etc. The angel said, 'You are hearing the only part of this service that God hears. He hears this little child's prayer because she means what she says, and put her heart and soul in it."* [4]

Can your praise be heard by God? Or are you talking to yourself?

QUESTIONS:
1. When is it easiest for you to offer true praise to God? Why?
2. What can you do to cultivate a deeper worship of God in your life?
3. Meditate on verse 17 again. What items of praise come to mind? Take some time today and praise Him for them!

---

[4] *Selected from The Gospel for Youth.* Walter B. Knight. *Knight's Treasury of 2,000 Illustrations.* (Grand Rapids, MI: Eerdmans Publishing Company, 1992), p.447-448.

1 TIMOTHY 1:12-17

SUMMARY:

There is indeed a flood of gross immorality, lawlessness, and violence sweeping across the land. Remember: God has placed you in a strategic position so that you, along with other believers, can turn the tide by proclaiming the glorious power of the gospel. Do you have the kind of testimony that can change your culture? You can if...

1. Christ Jesus appoints you to serve.
2. Christ saves you.
3. Christ is to be praised by you.

PERSONAL JOURNAL NOTES:
(Reflection & Response)

1. The most important thing that I learned from this lesson was:

2. The area that I need to work on the most is:

3. I can apply this lesson to my life by:

4. Closing Statement of Commitment:

1 Timothy 1:18-20

	C. The Young Minister (Charge 1): To Be a Warrior, 1:18-20	19 Holding faith, and a good conscience; which some having put away concerning faith have made shipwreck:	2. The weapons of war: Faith & a good conscience
1. The charge: To fight the good fight			3. The warning: Conscience can be rejected & faith can be shipwrecked or destroyed
a. Timothy's special call to the ministry	18 This charge I commit unto thee, son Timothy, according to the prophecies which went before on thee, that thou by them mightest war a good warfare;	20 Of whom is Hymenaeus and Alexander; whom I have delivered unto Satan, that they may learn not to blaspheme.	
b. His call was to stir him to fight a good spiritual war for the Lord			a. Two specific examples
			b. The discipline
			1) Delivered to Satan
			2) Corrective discipline

Section I
FALSE AND TRUE TEACHERS IN THE CHURCH
1 Timothy 1:3-20

Study 3: THE YOUNG MINISTER (CHARGE 1): TO BE A WARRIOR

Text: 1 Timothy 1:18-20

Aim: To actively work at becoming spiritually fit.

Memory Verse:
"This charge I commit unto thee, son Timothy, according to the prophecies which went before on thee, that thou by them mightest war a good warfare" (1 Timothy 1:18).

INTRODUCTION:
Years ago in the United States, a popular poster featured Uncle Sam with his finger pointing to the reader saying, "Uncle Sam Needs You!" With that invitation, Americans left behind homes and careers to become a part of the greatest military force on the face of the earth.

Much preparation went into honing these soldiers and sailors into a fighting machine. The basic training that the raw recruits experienced turned them from private citizens into powerful commandos, which were then turned loosed on the enemy.

All believers are called to be warriors in this world—warriors for God. But the minister of God is called to do even more: he is called to take charge and to lead in being a warrior. Have you responded to the call to join God's army? Are you in "battle shape"? Are you fighting the enemy?

This is a great study for the young minister or for any person who is sensing the call to serve God.

OUTLINE:
1. The charge: to fight the good fight (v.18).
2. The weapons of war: faith and a good conscience (v.19).
3. The warning: conscience can be rejected and faith can be shipwrecked or destroyed (vv.19-20).

1 TIMOTHY 1:18-20

1. THE CHARGE: TO FIGHT THE GOOD FIGHT (v.18).

Paul is giving a "charge" to Timothy. The word means a command, an urgent command, a military command. It is a command that lays upon a person the most urgent and critical obligation. *"The ministry is not a matter to be trifled with, but an order from the commander-in-chief."*[1] The *charge* is always a command from a superior that is to be transmitted to others; that is, this charge—the charge to fight a good warfare—is to be given to the young minister and he, in turn, is to pass the charge on to others.[2]

> **"And the things that thou hast heard of me among many witnesses,**
> **the same commit thou to faithful men, who shall be able to teach others also" (2 Ti.2:2).**

Note two points in this verse.

1. Timothy had a special call to the ministry. Remember: Timothy had a strong testimony for Christ before the church and his community (Ac.16:2).

   APPLICATION:
   Note two significant points:
   1) A person must be called to the ministry by the Spirit of God. The ministry is not just another profession where a person serves society and makes a living. The Christian ministry is the call of God—the call that puts a person right in the midst of spiritual war that fights for the souls and minds of people.
   2) When a person is called by the Spirit of God, he must not reject the call. He must do exactly what Paul says: jump right into the midst of the battle and fight a good warfare!

2. Timothy's call was to stir him to fight a good warfare. He was never to forget his call—never to forget the predictions of his home church, the predictions that he would fight a good warfare in the ministry for Christ—all for Christ. He was to keep these expectations of his home church before his mind and use them to stir him to fight for Christ.
   ⇒ Note: Paul is recommitting this charge to Timothy. Apparently Timothy needed to be recharged. He was facing the critical issue of false teaching in the church at Ephesus, and he was shrinking from it. But God's call was clear: he was to fight a good warfare—to struggle even to the point of death if need be.

Believers, ministers and laymen alike, must never forget: the ministry is a sacred trust, a sacred commitment. God has taken the most precious and sacred thing to Him—the very gospel of His dear Son—and placed that message into the hands of men. Therefore, the minister must not fail. He must arise and charge right to the forefront of the warfare, the spiritual warfare that is being fought for the souls and minds of people.

   APPLICATION:
   A spiritual warfare is being fought for the minds and souls of people. The minister of God is to be right in the middle of the conflict. He is God's instrument to teach men—to teach them the way to God and righteousness. If God's ministers do not fight and struggle to lead men to God, then literally millions of souls will

---

[1] Donald Guthrie. *The Pastoral Epistles.* "Tyndale New Testament Commentaries." (Grand Rapids, MI: Eerdmans Publishing Company, Began in 1958), p.67.
[2] *Expository Dictionary of New Testament Words.* (Old Tappan, NJ: Fleming H. Revell, 1966).

1 TIMOTHY 1:18-20

perish without ever knowing the way to God—without ever knowing that a person can actually live forever in the presence of God. This is the reason ministers must arise and lead the charge into the battle for the minds and souls of men. So much depends upon the minister of God—so many souls, the hope and lives of so many—that he must be faithful and fight a good warfare.

QUESTIONS:
1. What distractions prevent you from being able to fight a good warfare? What needs your immediate attention now?
2. Where is the battleground of spiritual warfare in your life? What can you do to strengthen yourself to fight a good warfare?
3. Do you ever want to quit the battle? What can you do to recharge your spiritual batteries?

2. THE WEAPONS OF WAR: FAITH AND A GOOD CONSCIENCE (v.19).

Note that the young minister is to "hold"—that is, keep—the faith and a good conscience.

1. "The faith" means the truth of Christianity and of Christ and of the Word of God. It is the faith that the minister holds in Christ, in the very teachings of Christ and of the Word of God. The faith of the minister is the very basis, foundation, and structure of his life. The faith of the Lord Jesus Christ and of the Word of God is his life. As the minister fights the spiritual battles of this life, he is to cling to the commands, instructions, and words of his commander-in-chief. He is not to turn away from the commands and words of the Lord Jesus Christ—not even for a minute.

2. The minister is to hold "a good conscience" (see **A CLOSER LOOK: Conscience—1 Ti.1:19** for discussion).

QUESTIONS:
1. How does "the faith" keep the believer in fighting shape?
2. What leeway does God give you in fully obeying His commands and instructions?
3. How trustworthy is your conscience? What is the key to holding a good conscience?

A CLOSER LOOK:

(1:19) **Conscience:** very simply stated, conscience is the inner sense of right and wrong. Contrary to what some teach, conscience does not come from training, education, society, or environment. Scripture says that conscience is innate; that is, a man is born with a consciousness of right and wrong.

> "For when the Gentiles, which have not the law, do by nature the things contained in the law, these, having not the law, are a law unto themselves: which show the work of the law written in their hearts, their conscience also bearing witness, and their thoughts the mean while accusing or else excusing one another" (Ro.2:14-15).

However, the conscience has to be developed and matured through education and environment. It is just like a small baby: it is there, existing, but it is undeveloped and immature until it is fed and taught what to do. In fact the conscience, just like a small child, is either developed or defiled—one or the other—through environment and

1 TIMOTHY 1:18-20

education. Every person is born with a conscience, but its value and health are determined by how well it is fed and trained with righteousness and godliness. The better it is fed and taught, the more effective and valuable it will become.

The point is this: a good and healthy conscience comes from living a righteous and godly life before God. A bad and defiled conscience comes from living an unrighteous and ungodly life in this world. If a person violates his conscience (does wrong), his conscience pricks and nags him. He feels remorse, regret, and guilt. If he corrects his behavior and asks God for forgiveness, God removes the guilt—completely and totally. If he continues to violate his conscience, three things happen.

⇒ The conscience becomes hardened. It no longer directs the person. The pricking and nagging and pull to do right is dulled. The person becomes callused and hardened to righteousness. He no longer has the direction of conscience and the consciousness of what is right. He is left alone in the world to walk in unrighteousness and ungodliness just as he wills.

⇒ Some persons refuse to listen and they react against conscience, they strike out in hostility and rebellion, living more and more unrighteously and ungodly.

⇒ Other persons refuse to listen to conscience, sensing more and more failure. This can and often does lead to withdrawal, depression, and all kinds of emotional and mental problems.

Scripture says the following about the conscience.
1. The work of conscience.
   a. The conscience convicts of sin.

> "And they which heard it, being convicted by their own conscience, went out one by one, beginning at the eldest, even unto the last: and Jesus was left alone, and the woman standing in the midst" (Jn.8:9).

ILLUSTRATION:
Most of us can relate to being caught with our hand in the cookie jar and the guilt that comes along with it.

> *A little ten-year old boy learned this valuable lesson early in life. It seems the "cool" thing to do was to go to the school store and slip pencils and pens into your pocket without getting caught. So after successfully pocketing several items, the boy thought to himself, "This is too easy. Today the pencils—tomorrow...who knows?"*
>
> *Soon, word came through the grapevine that any student caught stealing would be harshly punished. In this little boy's mind, the punishment was translated into the horrible thought that Mom and Dad would find out.*
>
> *Panic-stricken, the little boy felt both scared and sorry. Under his breath, he prayed this simple prayer: "God, if I get out of this, I'll never steal anything ever again." Later, as the "cool" kids headed off to the store after class, he went the opposite direction to rid himself of the stolen supplies.*

This little boy grew up to become a solid citizen, but he still regretted one thing: he did not return the stolen items. He just threw them away.

Thankfully, when your conscience convicts you of sin, God does not throw you away. Instead, He redeems all those who ask for forgiveness.

1 TIMOTHY 1:18-20

b. The conscience (at least at first) bears witness to what is right even if a person does not have the law of God.

> "**For when the Gentiles, which have not the law, do by nature the things contained in the law, these, having not the law, are a law unto themselves: which show the work of the law written in their hearts, their conscience also bearing witness, and their thoughts the mean while accusing or else excusing one another**" (Ro.2:14-15).

c. The conscience confirms the feelings and actions of a person.

> "**I say the truth in Christ, I lie not, my conscience also bearing me witness in the Holy Ghost**" (Ro.9:1).

d. The conscience is to stir a person to live in simplicity and godly sincerity.

> "**For our rejoicing is this, the testimony of our conscience, that in simplicity and godly sincerity, not with fleshly wisdom, but by the grace of God, we have had our conversation in the world, and more abundantly to you-ward**" (2 Co.1:12).

e. The conscience is to stir a person to be a testimony to others, to be a testimony before every man's conscience…
- by renouncing dishonesty.
- by not handling the Word of God deceitfully.

> "**But have renounced the hidden things of dishonesty, not walking in craftiness, nor handling the word of God deceitfully; but by manifestation of the truth commending ourselves to every man's conscience in the sight of God**" (2 Co.4:2).

QUESTIONS:
1. What is your conscience supposed to do?
2. How do you to cultivate a healthy conscience? Are you doing the best that you can do? What can you do to improve the quality of your conscience?

2. The source of a good, clear, pure, and healthy conscience.
   a. A good and healthy conscience comes from obeying the laws of the state.

   > "**Wherefore ye must needs be subject, not only for wrath, but also for conscience sake**" (Ro.13:5).

   b. A good and healthy conscience comes from love which flows from a pure heart and a sincere faith.

   > "**Now the end of the commandment is charity out of a pure heart, and of a good conscience, and of faith unfeigned**" (1 Ti.1:5).

   c. A good and healthy conscience comes from holding fast to one's faith and to a good conscience.

   > "**Holding faith, and a good conscience; which some having put away concerning faith have made shipwreck**" (1 Ti.1:19).

   d. A good and healthy conscience comes from serving God.

1 TIMOTHY 1:18-20

"I thank God, whom I serve from my forefathers with pure conscience, that without ceasing I have remembrance of thee in my prayers night and day" (2 Ti.1:3).

    e. A good and healthy conscience comes from being cleansed by the blood of Christ.

> "How much more shall the blood of Christ, who through the eternal Spirit offered himself without spot to God, purge your conscience from dead works to serve the living God?" (He.9:14).

    f. A good and healthy conscience comes from the will to live honestly in all things.

> "Pray for us: for we trust we have a good conscience, in all things willing to live honestly" (He.13:18).

    g. A good and healthy conscience comes from suffering wrong for the sake of God.

> "For this is thankworthy, if a man for conscience toward God endure grief, suffering wrongfully" (1 Pt.2:19).

    h. A good and healthy conscience comes from good behavior in Christ.

> "Having a good conscience [behavior]; that, whereas they speak evil of you, as of evildoers, they may be ashamed that falsely accuse your good conversation in Christ" (1 Pt.3:16).

QUESTIONS:
1. What keeps your conscience healthy and pure?
2. Why is it so important that you keep a clear conscience?

3. Some facts about conscience.
    a. A person is to live in all good conscience.

> "And Paul, earnestly beholding the council, said, Men and brethren, I have lived in all good conscience before God until this day" (Ac.23:1).

    b. A person is to have a conscience void of offense before God and men.

> "And herein do I exercise myself, to have always a conscience void of offense toward God, and toward men" (Ac.24:16).

    c. The conscience can be weak.

> "But when ye sin so against the brethren, and wound their weak conscience, ye sin against Christ" (1 Co.8:12; cp. 1 Co.8:7, 10).

    d. A person is not to do anything that would violate the conscience of another person.

> "But if any man say unto you, This is offered in sacrifice unto idols, eat not for his sake that showed it, and for conscience sake: for the earth is the Lord's, and the fulness thereof: conscience, I say, not thine own, but of the other" (1 Co.10:28-29).

1 TIMOTHY 1:18-20

e. Conscience can be put away and faith can be shipwrecked.

"Holding faith, and a good conscience; which [conscience] some having put away concerning faith have made shipwreck" (1 Ti.1:19).

f. The conscience can be seared (branded either as following God or devils).

"Speaking lies in hypocrisy; having their conscience seared with a hot iron" (1 Ti.4:2).

g. The conscience and mind are both defiled (made impure, unclean) through defilement and unbelief.

"Unto the pure all things are pure: but unto them that are defiled and unbelieving is nothing pure; but even their mind and conscience is defiled" (Tit.1:15).

h. Keeping the law and being religious cannot make the conscience perfect.

"[The tabernacle] which was a figure for the time then present, in which were offered both gifts and sacrifices, that could not make him that did the service perfect, as pertaining to the conscience" (He.9:9).

i. Seeking for a good conscience toward God saves us by the resurrection of Jesus Christ.

"The like figure whereunto even baptism doth also now save us (not the putting away of the filth of the flesh, but the answer of a good conscience toward God,) by the resurrection of Jesus Christ" (1 Pe.3:21).

4. Scripture mentions at least seven kinds of conscience.[3]
   a. There is the good (clear, pure, healthy) conscience.

   "And Paul, earnestly beholding the council, said, Men and brethren, I have lived in all good conscience before God until this day" (Ac.23:1).

   b. There is a conscience void of offense.

   "And herein do I exercise myself, to have always a conscience void of offense toward God, and toward men" (Ac.24:16).

   c. There is a weak conscience.

   "Howbeit there is not in every man that knowledge: for some with conscience of the idol unto this hour eat it as a thing offered unto an idol; and their conscience being weak is defiled....For if any man see thee which hast knowledge sit at meat in the idol's temple, shall not the conscience of him which is weak be emboldened to eat those things which are offered to idols....But when ye sin so against the brethren, and wound their weak conscience, ye sin against Christ" (1 Co.8:7, 10, 12).

---

[3] This idea comes from Thomas Walker. *The Acts of the Apostles*. (Chicago, IL: Moody Press, 1965), p.487.

> d. There is a pure conscience.
>
> "Holding the mystery of the faith in a pure conscience" (1 Ti.3:9).
>
> e. There is a seared conscience.
>
> "Speaking lies in hypocrisy; having their conscience seared with a hot iron" (1 Ti.4:2).
>
> f. There is a defiled conscience.
>
> "Unto the pure all things are pure: but unto them that are defiled and unbelieving is nothing pure; but even their mind and conscience is defiled" (Tit.1:15).
>
> g. There is an evil conscience.
>
> "Let us draw near with a true heart in full assurance of faith, having our hearts sprinkled from an evil conscience, and our bodies washed with pure water" (He.10:22).
>
> **QUESTIONS:**
> 1. How would you define the term "conscience"?
> 2. What does your conscience do for you?
> 3. What are the sources of a good conscience?
> 4. In what circumstances would you be tempted to ignore your conscience? Why? What can you do to protect your conscience?

3. THE WARNING: CONSCIENCE CAN BE REJECTED AND FAITH CAN BE SHIPWRECKED OR DESTROYED (vv.19-20).

The warning is frightening. Conscience can be put away and faith can be shipwrecked. "Put away" means to push away with force. It is a willful and deliberate pushing away of conscience. Conscience says that something is wrong and should not be done, but conscience is ignored and subdued, turned away from and denied.

When a person continues to push his conscience away, something terrible happens: his faith is shipwrecked. His faith is broken to pieces and destroyed. A person must live as Scripture dictates: righteously and godly. If he does not live righteously and godly, then he weakens his faith and soon dashes it upon the storms of evil, worldliness, and false doctrine. His faith is shipwrecked because he pushed his conscience aside, refusing to listen to its call to live righteously and godly. Note two points.

1. Paul gives two specific examples of men who pushed their conscience away and shipwrecked their faith.
   ⇒ Hymenaeus was the man who taught false doctrine, that the resurrection of believers had already taken place (2 Ti.2:17).
   ⇒ Alexander was probably the coppersmith who opposed Paul and did much evil against him (2 Ti.4:14).

2. Paul mentions the discipline which he exercised against the two men. But remember why he disciplined them: they had continued to reject the guidance of their conscience and to turn away from the faith. Therefore, Paul had delivered them to Satan. What does this mean? There are two possible explanations.

1 TIMOTHY 1:18-20

a. The discipline means that the men must be excommunicated from the church. The idea is that outside the church—outside in the world—is the domain of Satan, whereas in the church is the domain of God (Jn.12:31; 16:11; Ac.26:18; Ep.2:12; Co.1:13; 1 Jn.5:19). The men were to be sent back to Satan's world to which they belonged. Perhaps such discipline would humiliate them and bring them to their senses. It was a discipline not only to punish them but to awaken them to righteousness. It was a judgment that took away their Christian privileges with the hope that the discipline would stir them to repent.
b. The discipline means more than excommunication. It is the miraculous subjection of the person to the power of Satan, to be terrified or tormented by him that they might repent and return to Christ.
⇒ The idea is that Paul and the church prayed for some circumstance or difficulty to arise in their lives that would stir them to repent.

People are chastised for sin and spiritual failure. In fact, it is impossible to sin and escape chastisement. Men reap what they sow. There is a spiritual power that inflicts punishment upon sin. However, this should not be surprising in our day, for modern medicine and psychology tell us that misbehavior causes physical, emotional, and mental punishment.

Note that the discipline is remedial; that is, the two men were disciplined in order to try to lead them back to Christ. The men were delivered to Satan so that they might learn not to blaspheme.

> "For this cause [continuing in sin] many are weak and sickly among you, and many sleep. For if we would judge ourselves, we should not be judged. But when we are judged, we are chastened of the Lord, that we should not be condemned with the world" (1 Co.11:30-32).
>
> "Blessed is the man whom thou chastenest, O LORD, and teachest him out of thy law" (Ps.94:12).

ILLUSTRATION:
What happens to a person who puts away his conscience? According to Scripture, his faith can be shipwrecked. Ignoring his conscience will cause him to drift farther and farther off course. Destruction awaits. A person must pay attention to the instruction God provides in His Word. In *Returning to Your First Love*, Pastor Tony Evans writes:

> I'll never forget the time my younger brother rebelled against my father. He didn't like my father's rules....Now, little brother was the...wrestling champion....At 250 pounds, he was big and strong....
>
> My father told my brother to do something...but my brother didn't think he should have to do it. So he frowned, shook his head, and said, "No!"
> Dad said, "Oh yes!"
> Little brother said, "No!"
> My father...took him upstairs, and helped him pack his suitcase. My brother jumped [at the opportunity] and said, "Yeah, I'm leaving! I don't' have to take this!"
> And he walked out of the house. But he forgot a few things. He forgot he didn't have a job. He forgot it was snowing outside. He forgot he didn't have a car. He jumped [at the opportunity], but he forgot that when you don't have anything, you don't jump.

1 TIMOTHY 1:18-20

So twenty minutes later...knock, knock! Brother was at the door wanting to come home. My father delivered him to the elements that he might be taught respect....

When he was put out, my brother was no longer under the protective custody of our home. He had to fend for himself. [4]

Ignoring your conscience leaves you out in the cold, fending for yourself instead of being under the protection of God and in the safe haven of a family of believers.

QUESTIONS:
1. What risks are you taking if you ignore your conscience?
2. Men reap what they sow. Can any good come from 'putting away' your conscience?
3. Do you think Paul's judgment was unloving towards Hymenaeus and Alexander? Explain your answer.

SUMMARY:

How about you? Would you respond to the call and enlist in the army of God? As you become spiritually fit, you will learn...

1. The charge: to fight the good fight.
2. The weapons of war: faith and a good conscience.
3. The warning: conscience can be rejected and faith can be shipwrecked or destroyed.

PERSONAL JOURNAL NOTES:
(Reflection & Response)

1. The most important thing that I learned from this lesson was:

2. The area that I need to work on the most is:

3. I can apply this lesson to my life by:

4. Closing Statement of Commitment:

---

[4] Craig B. Larson. *Choice Contemporary Stories & Illustrations*. (Grand Rapids, MI: Baker Books, 1998), #58.

1 TIMOTHY 2:1-8

CHAPTER 2

II. DUTIES & ORDER IN THE CHURCH, 2:1–3:13

A. The First Duty of the Church—Pray, 2:1-8

1. **Pray for everyone**
   a. By requests & special prayers
   c. By intercession
   d. By thanksgiving
2. **Pray for civil authorities**
   a. That we may lead quiet & peaceable lives
   b. That we may lead godly & holy lives
3. **Pray for everyone to be saved**

I exhort therefore, that, first of all, supplications, prayers, intercessions, and giving of thanks, be made for all men; 2 For kings, and for all that are in authority; that we may lead a quiet and peaceable life in all godliness and honesty. 3 For this is good and acceptable in the sight of God our Saviour; 4 Who will have all men to be saved, and to come unto the knowledge of the truth. 5 For there is one God, and one mediator between God and men, the man Christ Jesus; 6 Who gave himself a ransom for all, to be testified in due time. 7 Whereunto I am ordained a preacher, and an apostle, (I speak the truth in Christ, and lie not;) a teacher of the Gentiles in faith and verity. 8 I will therefore that men pray every where, lifting up holy hands, without wrath and doubting.

a. Because God is our Savior & He wills for all men to be saved
b. Because there is only one God, not the many gods of men
c. Because there is only one Mediator who can save us
d. Because Christ is the ransom, the Redeemer for all
e. Because ministers are ordained or appointed to proclaim the salvation of God

4. **Pray everywhere & pray in the right spirit**

Section II
DUTIES AND ORDER IN THE CHURCH
1 Timothy 2:1–3:13

Study 1: THE FIRST DUTY OF THE CHURCH—PRAY

Text: 1 Timothy 2:1-8

Aim: To make a strong commitment: To live a life marked by prayer.

Memory Verse:
> "I will therefore that men pray every where, lifting up holy hands, without wrath and doubting" (1 Timothy 2:8).

INTRODUCTION:

Would you pray any differently if you could actually see into the spiritual world, into the spiritual dimension of being? If that kind of sight could be granted for a moment, you would see the intense conflict being waged for your soul. You would quickly realize that Satan's fight for your soul is no game. Satan means business.

But know this: the Christian believer has been given a strategic part to play in waging war against Satan's onslaught against humanity. The prayers of intercession that are offered up to God are like destructive missiles to the enemy's plans. Are you doing your part?

This begins a significant section in the teaching of 1 Timothy, a section that covers the duties and order of the church. The first duty of the church is basic: it is the duty of prayer.

1 TIMOTHY 2:1-8

OUTLINE:
1. Pray for everyone (v.1).
2. Pray for civil authorities (v.2).
3. Pray for everyone to be saved (vv.3-7).
4. Pray everywhere and pray in the right spirit (v.8).

1. PRAY FOR EVERYONE (v.1).

Not a single person is to be omitted or left out of our prayers. We are to pray for all persons:
- ⇒ the high and the low
- ⇒ the educated and the uneducated
- ⇒ the important and the unimportant
- ⇒ the rich and the poor
- ⇒ the leader and the follower
- ⇒ the old and the young
- ⇒ the friend and the enemy

Pray for all men. Do not neglect, ignore, or bypass any person. Every person needs prayer; every person needs God: His salvation, care, direction, approval, and acceptance. Therefore, pray for all men.

Note: this is an exhortation to pray, which means that it is both an encouragement and a charge. The believer is given the encouragement and charge to pray just as a soldier is encouraged and charged to fight.

"First of all" stresses just how important prayer is. "First of all"—above all else, of supreme importance—put prayer first. "First of all"—before all else—pray for all men.

Note that four kinds of prayer are mentioned. This also stresses the importance of praying for all men.

1. There is *supplication*. This refers to the prayers that focus upon special needs—deep and intense needs. When we see special needs in the lives of people—all people—we are to supplicate for them. That is, we are to be carrying the need before God with a great sense of urgency, pleading and begging for the person or persons. The idea is that of intense and deep brokenness before God in behalf of others—that God would help and save the person.

APPLICATION:
Just think what a different world this would be, what a different community we would have if we really took the names and needs of people before God and pleaded for them in an intense brokenness and in tears. Just think...
- how many more loved ones would be saved and helped
- how many more within our community, state, country, and world would be saved and helped
- how fewer problems would exist within society

Scripture emphatically declares:

"Ye have not, because ye ask not" (Ja.4:2).

2. There are *prayers*. This refers to the special times of prayer that we set aside for devotion and worship. We are to have set times for prayer, times that we set aside to worship God and when we pray for all men.

3. There are *intercessions*. This refers to bold praying, to standing before God in behalf of another person. Christ is our Intercessor, the One who stands between God and us in our behalf. But we are to intercede for men, to carry their names and lives

1 TIMOTHY 2:1-8

before God and to boldly pray for them, expecting God to hear and answer—all in the name of Christ. We are to intercede for all men—to stand in the gap between them and God, boldly praying and asking God to be merciful and gracious in salvation and in deliverance.

4. There is *thanksgiving*. This means that we thank God for hearing and answering—thank Him for what He has done and is going to do for all men.

> "But I say unto you, Love your enemies, bless them that curse you, do good to them that hate you, and pray for them which despitefully use you, and persecute you" (Mt.5:44).

ILLUSTRATION:
One of the greatest challenges issued to believers is to pray. But do you pray like your prayers make a difference? For many years, Patrick thought prayer was a good idea; he even bought books on prayer. But prayer was not a *priority* to him. Ironically, Patrick had just been appointed chairman of his church's missions committee, which to him meant running the organization like a business...until he met Tim.

Tim was a missionary from China who was home on furlough after an emotionally and spiritually draining time on the mission field. Tim came to Patrick's first missions committee meeting in order to report on his ministry. Tim opened his report with these remarks:

> *Without the faithful prayers of this committee and its chairman, I would not be here today. Many times, my wife and I were on the verge of quitting, leaving China behind in the ruin of our failed attempts to share the gospel with those precious people. But just when we started to pack, we remembered all the folks back home who promised to pray for us. Patrick, I'd like to thank you and your committee for your faithfulness in prayer.*
>
> *Patrick sunk in his seat as he mumbled, "You're welcome Tim." Later, Patrick had this conversation with God: "Lord, I'm sorry for being so slack. If I had taken the time to pray for Tim and his wife, they would have been spared a lot of grief. I commit myself to a renewed prayer-life, with Your help.*

On a sign in front of Patrick's church was this message: "Seven Days Without Prayer Makes One Weak." Your lack of prayer not only weakens your life, it affects others as well. Who needs your help today? Pray!

QUESTIONS:
1. Who do you need to add to your prayer list?
2. How often do you pray without any directions from the Lord? In what ways can you mature in your personal prayer life?
3. What prevents you from praying for all men? What can you do to overcome this?
4. Why is it important for you to be familiar with each kind of prayer mentioned in this verse?

2. PRAY FOR CIVIL AUTHORITIES (v.2).

Pray for civil authorities, for kings and for all who are in authority.
- ⇒ No matter how good or how bad they are, pray for them.
- ⇒ No matter how moral or immoral they are, pray for them.
- ⇒ No matter how just or unjust they are, pray for them.

1 TIMOTHY 2:1-8

The thought of praying for evil rulers is shocking to some people. Just think of the evil rulers in the world even today. But remember: Nero was on the throne in Rome when Paul charged believers to pray for the king or emperor. And Nero had already burned Rome and had blamed it on Christian believers. In fact, he was presently launching a violent persecution against the believers.

Donald Guthrie says, *"This Christian attitude towards the State is of utmost importance. Whether the civil authorities are perverted or not they must be made subjects for prayer, for Christian citizens may in this way influence the course of national affairs, a fact often forgotten except in times of special crisis."*[1]

There are two reasons why we are to pray for rulers.

1. We pray for rulers so that we can lead quiet and peaceable lives. The only way the citizens of a nation can live quiet and peaceable lives is for the ruler to be filled...
- with wisdom and knowledge
- with morality and justice
- with courage and boldness
- with compassion and understanding

Therefore, believers must pray for the rulers to be filled to the brim so that the rulers can bring about peace and security throughout the land. Then and only then can the citizens of a land live quiet and peaceable lives.

2. We must pray for rulers so that we can live godly and sincere lives. Believers want freedom of worship for all citizens.
⇒ They want freedom of worship, the right to worship and live for God without being opposed and persecuted.
⇒ They want freedom of life and choice, the right to live sincere or purposeful lives, the right to pursue their own lives and wills without being opposed by a ruler.

APPLICATION:
People desire and even crave freedom: freedom of life and choice, freedom of worship. This is the reason we must pray for rulers...
- for wise and knowledgeable rulers
- for moral and just rulers
- for courageous and bold rulers
- for compassionate and understanding rulers

> **"By the blessing of the upright the city is exalted: but it is overthrown by the mouth of the wicked" (Pr.11:11).**

ILLUSTRATION:
As true believers we are not told to put our *trust* in rulers; we are told to *pray* for them. Our trust is to be in the Lord. Politicians are not the answer to our problems. Jesus is the answer.

Men who feared God established the United States. They knew that any drift from trusting in Him would lead to ruin. The people came in droves from all parts of the world in order to worship God as they saw fit. Listen in on the conversation of one of the early unnamed pilgrims as he prayed to God:

> *Almighty God, You know how hard this new land is for us. At any moment the King of England could cut off his support and leave us to starve. Lord, work in his heart and move him to grant us favor. The freedom to worship You in this new land has been so rich. Touch the king's heart in a way that will*

---

1 Donald Guthrie. *The Pastoral Epistles.* "Tyndale New Testament Commentaries," p.70.

forever secure our ability to worship You in openness. The memories of spiritual slavery to the Church of England and the persecution for resisting their wishes is still very fresh in my mind. Forever burn the memories on my heart so that I will never take for granted my freedoms. May You grace our governor with Your wisdom. Grant him courage to lead us down the right path and may Your compassion fill his heart.

Prayers like these proved to be the source of God's blessing of America. Prayer and peace go hand in hand. Are your prayers making an impact on your leaders, your nation?

QUESTIONS:
1. What does this verse teach you about your civic responsibilities? What can you do to improve in this area?
2. What are the reasons you are to pray for rulers?
3. How do you feel about praying for leaders who are evil? Do you need to change your attitude towards them?

3. PRAY FOR EVERYONE TO BE SAVED (vv.3-7).

There are five reasons given why we are to pray for the salvation of all men, including all rulers.

1. First, God is our Savior and He wills all men to be saved and to come to the knowledge of the truth. As pointed out earlier (1 Ti.1:1), God our Savior is one of the great titles for God. God is our Savior, the source of our salvation. God is the first Person who has cared for and loved man. God loves us and He is not willing that any should perish; therefore, He has taken the initiative and provided the way for us to be saved.

Note: God wills all men to be saved, but not in the sense of a decree. God has not decreed that all men be saved. This is evident by the ungodly and unrighteous lives lived by so many. God wills all men to be saved in the sense that He loves and longs for them to be saved. If any man perishes, it is his own fault. God has done all He can. He has provided the way for man to be saved. If a man is now lost, it is his own choosing.

Note the words "the knowledge of the truth." What truth is it that God wants man to know? The truth that is covered in the points that follow: that there is only one God, and there is only one Mediator who gave Himself a ransom for all—the truth that all can be saved from sin and death and judgment to come through the death of the Lord Jesus Christ. God loves man so much that He has provided the way for man to be saved. That way is the truth, and that truth is the truth that God wants man to know.

> **"Jesus saith unto him, I am the way, the truth, and the life: no man cometh unto the Father, but by me" (Jn.14:6).**

This is the reason we should pray for all men, both rulers and citizens, high and low, educated and uneducated, moral and immoral, just and unjust, civilized and savage, saved and lost. God wants all men to be saved regardless of who they are and no matter how evil they may be.

> **"The Lord is not slack concerning his promise, as some men count slackness; but is longsuffering to us-ward, not willing that any should perish, but that all should come to repentance" (2 Pe.3:9).**

1 TIMOTHY 2:1-8

2. Second, there is only one God not the many gods of men. If there were many gods, then there would be many ways to reach the heavens of the gods. But there are not many gods. Logically, there could not be many gods. When we speak of God, we mean the Infinite and Supreme Majesty of the Universe. There can be only one Supreme Being, only one Infinite Being. If there should be many gods, then they would not be infinite or supreme; therefore, they would not be God.

⇒ The point is this: since there is only one God, there can be only one way to reach Him—only one way to be saved. Why? This is the discussion of the next point.

"Wherefore thou are great, O LORD God: for there is none like thee, neither is there any God besides thee, according to all that we have heard with our ears" (2 S.7:22).

3. There is only one mediator between God and men. Man must have a mediator if he is to be saved, if he is to approach God and be acceptable to God. As asked above, why? Because there is only one perfect Person: God Himself. No man can stand before God, not in his own name or righteousness. Man is imperfect, and God is perfect. Man cannot make himself acceptable to God no matter what he does. If perfection accepted imperfection, it would no longer be perfection. Perfection has to be just and righteous, which means that it has to reject imperfection. God cannot accept imperfect man. God has to be just and righteous and reject man in all the imperfection of his thoughts and behavior.

How, then, can man become acceptable to God? God has to make man acceptable. God Himself has to handle the sin, condemnation, and death of men. But how? There was only one way: God, the Perfect Person, had to become Man. God had to come to earth in such a way that man could understand Him and understand what He was doing. This He did by partaking of flesh and blood and coming to earth in the person of His Son, the Man Christ Jesus.

⇒ God Himself had to conquer sin. He had to live a perfect and sinless life as a man in order to handle sin. By living a perfect and sinless life, He became the Ideal and Perfect Man, the Ideal and Perfect Righteousness that could cover and stand for all men (He.2:14-15).

This is part of what is meant by Jesus Christ being our Mediator. He stands before God as the Perfect Man, and He also stands between God and men as the Perfect Man. He is the Ideal Pattern of all men, of just what a man should be. Therefore, when a man really believes in Jesus Christ...

- God takes that man's belief and counts it as the righteousness of Jesus Christ
- God accepts the man's faith and honor in His Son as righteousness
- God lets the righteousness of His Son, Jesus Christ, cover the man
- God accepts the man's faith as the righteousness of Jesus Christ

Very simply stated, the man is not righteous, but God takes the man's faith in His Son and credits his faith as righteousness. Jesus Christ stands as the Mediator between God and men; He stands as the Mediator of perfection and righteousness for man. The point is this: since there is only one Mediator, we must pray for men to come to know Him. And we must rush to proclaim Him to all men so that they can know about Him and have the opportunity to follow Him.

"And the Word was made flesh, and dwelt among us, (and we beheld his glory, the glory as of the only begotten of the Father,) full of grace and truth" (Jn.1:14).

1 TIMOTHY 2:1-8

QUESTIONS:
1. What reasons are given for us to pray for the salvation of all men?
2. Why is there only one way to become acceptable to God? What is that way? Why is this an essential element for the Christian believer to embrace?

4. The man Christ Jesus gave Himself a ransom for all. The word "ransom" means to exchange something for something else. The man Christ Jesus exchanged His life for the life of man; He gave up His life for the life of man. How? By the cross. Jesus Christ took the sin and condemnation of men upon Himself and bore their judgment for them. Christ died for man; He bore the judgment of God against sin for man.

As the Ideal and Perfect Man, Christ could do this for man. Since He was the Ideal Man, His death was the ideal death. Therefore, His death can stand for and cover the death of all men. If a man really believes and trusts that the death of Jesus Christ is for him...
- God counts the death of Christ for the man
- God actually counts the man as having already died in Christ
- God accepts the man as free from the guilt and condemnation of sin because Christ has already paid the ransom price for sin and death

This is the glorious gospel of God: man can now live forever in the presence of God. Jesus Christ gave Himself as a ransom for sin and death. When man receives Christ Jesus into his heart and begins to follow Christ...
- God gives him life now and forever, abundant life and eternal life. When the man finishes his task upon earth, God will transfer him right into His presence—quicker than a flash of lightning. The man never has to taste death.

The words "testified in due time" mean that God sent His Son in the fulness of time. When it was time for Christ to come to earth, He came.

Now note: we must pray for men to believe that Christ died for them—pray that they might be saved. And we must rush to proclaim the glorious news that Christ Jesus has paid the ransom price for us: we can now be set free from sin, death, and condemnation. We can now live with God eternally.

> **"For the life of the flesh is in the blood: and I have given it to you upon the altar to make an atonement for your souls: for it is the blood that maketh an atonement for the soul" (Le.17:11).**
>
> **"For there is one God, and one mediator between God and men, the man Christ Jesus; who gave himself a ransom for all, to be testified in due time" (1 Ti.2:5-6).**

5. Ministers are ordained or appointed to proclaim the salvation of God. Note: Paul said three things about himself.
   a. God had appointed Paul to be a preacher: a herald, an ambassador who was appointed by a king to go forth and proclaim the message of the king. The minister is a preacher who is sent forth by God to preach the truth about Jesus Christ...
      - that He is the Mediator between God and men
      - that He has given Himself as a ransom for all

   > **"And he said unto them, Go ye into all the world, and preach the gospel to every creature" (Mk.16:15).**

   b. God had appointed Paul to be an apostle: a person who had been sent as a very special witness and on a very special mission. The minister is sent forth on the

1 TIMOTHY 2:1-8

special mission to bear witness that Jesus Christ is the Mediator between God and men. Jesus Christ has paid the ransom price for man.

> "Ye have not chosen me, but I have chosen you, and ordained you, that ye should go and bring forth fruit, and that your fruit should remain: that whatsoever ye shall ask of the Father in my name, he may give it you" (Jn.15:16).

c. God had appointed Paul as a teacher: a person who instructs people into the faith and truth of God's Word. It is the gift to root and ground people in doctrine, reproof, correction, and righteousness.

Note Paul's stress upon his call from God: "I speak the truth in Christ, and lie not." God had called him to proclaim and teach the salvation in Christ Jesus. Apparently, there were some at Ephesus who questioned Paul's call and ministry.

⇒ The point is this: God has called ministers to proclaim the faith and truth of the Mediator and the great ransom price that He paid for man's salvation. Therefore, we must pray for all men—that they will receive the message of the minister and be saved.

> "And Paul dwelt two whole years in his own hired house, and received all that came in unto him, preaching the kingdom of God, and teaching those things which concern the Lord Jesus Christ, with all confidence, no man forbidding" (Ac.28:30-31).

QUESTIONS:
1. Think about your life. How do you feel when you realize that the holy, sinless, perfect Son of God sacrificed His life for you?
2. In light of what Christ did for you, what He saved you from, what should you do for Him? Why is it important for you to proclaim the gospel and pray for others to receive the gospel?

4. PRAY EVERYWHERE AND PRAY IN THE RIGHT SPIRIT (v.8).

A person should never stop praying. He should be praying all day long as he walks throughout the day. He should develop an unbroken communion and fellowship with the Lord, praying for all men—for both the ruler and the citizen, the high and the low, the lost and the saved—all over the world. He should pray for those of his...

- home
- city
- state
- church
- community
- country

He should pray for those in...
- North America
- Central America
- India
- South America
- Africa
- Russia

...and on and on

The believer is to pray and to keep on praying. He is to pray everywhere—no matter where he is. But note: the believer is also told how to pray.

1 Timothy 2:1-8

1. He is to pray "lifting up holy hands"; that is, he is not to come before God having touched or handled "the forbidden things."[2] He is not to come with sin in his life.

> "But your iniquities have separated between you and your God, and your sins have hid his face from you, that he will not hear" (Is.59:2).

2. He is to pray without anger or feelings in his heart against someone else. Very simply...
   - God does not accept us unless we accept others.
   - God does not forgive us unless we forgive others.

> "Therefore if thou bring thy gift to the altar, and there rememberest that thy brother hath ought against thee; leave there thy gift before the altar, and go thy way; first be reconciled to thy brother, and then come and offer thy gift" (Mt.5:23-24).

3. He is to pray without doubting. There is no need to pray if we do not think God is going to hear us. If we ask Him in doubt, we are not trusting His presence and power to meet our need. We are actually denying God's care and power. We are destroying the name of God among men. Therefore, we must believe God when we pray.

> "Therefore I say unto you, What things soever ye desire, when ye pray, believe that ye receive them, and ye shall have them" (Mk.11:24).

ILLUSTRATION:
Does God limit our prayers? Does God listen only to the prayers made within the confines of the church walls? Of course not! Tragically, many in our culture have been bullied into thinking that prayer is for the church only.

> *During the first 170 years of American history, prayer was considered an appropriate thing to do before a ballgame, before school, or during a session of Congress when the need for God's guidance was felt. Previous presidents have often called upon the name of God during times of national crisis.*
>
> *Prayer was never meant to be segregated but to be included in the everyday affairs of believers. On one particular day, a jury had been called together to consider the fate of a person accused of murder. The jury consisted of people from a variety of backgrounds. As it turned out, the foreman of the jury was a woman who loved Jesus Christ. At the urging of another Christian on the jury, she was asked to begin their deliberations in prayer, asking God for His wisdom. Even those who did not know Christ entered in as they had to make some critical decisions in the hours to come.*
>
> *Though prepared for a long and drawn-out deliberation, the jury reached their unanimous decision of guilty in less than an hour. In that secular jury room, God came at their invitation and gave them exactly what they had asked for—His wisdom.*

Are you free enough to pray everywhere?

---

2 William Barclay. *The Letters to Timothy, Titus, and Philemon*, p.74.

1 Timothy 2:1-8

QUESTIONS:
1. Where are the hardest places for you to pray? Why?
2. What can you do in order to expand your prayer life?
3. It is important for us to pray in the right spirit. Why do you think your motives are so important to God?
4. How do you handle any doubts that enter your mind when you pray?

SUMMARY:

Prayer is not an option. It is a commandment. God has given the Church the duty to pray. What are the issues? You must:

1. Pray for everyone.
2. Pray for civil authorities.
3. Pray for everyone to be saved.
4. Pray everywhere and pray in the right spirit.

How are you to do this? It has been said that you must work like everything depends upon you and pray like everything depends upon God. God has done His part...now, will you?

PERSONAL JOURNAL NOTES:
(Reflection & Response)

1. The most important thing that I learned from this lesson was:

2. The area that I need to work on the most is:

3. I can apply this lesson to my life by:

4. Closing Statement of Commitment:

1 Timothy 2:9-15

	B. The Women of the Church, 2:9-15	all subjection. 12 But I suffer not a woman to teach, nor to usurp authority over the man, but to be in silence. 13 For Adam was first formed, then Eve. 14 And Adam was not deceived, but the woman being deceived was in the transgression. 15 Notwithstanding she shall be saved in childbearing, if they continue in faith and charity and holiness with sobriety.	& submissiveness 3. In church, women are not to teach nor to have authority over a man
1. In public, women are to dress modestly	9 In like manner also, that women adorn themselves in modest apparel, with shamefacedness and sobriety; not with broided hair, or gold, or pearls, or costly array;		a. Because God created in an orderly way
a. Dress modestly & sensibly			b. Because God created each with different natures
b. Do not dress to attract attention			c. Because woman was deceived
c. Dress with good deeds	10 But (which becometh women professing godliness) with good works.		4. In the home, mothers will be saved if they continue to live & walk in the Lord
2. In church, women are to learn in silence	11 Let the women learn in silence with		

Section II
DUTIES AND ORDER IN THE CHURCH
1 Timothy 2:1-3:13

Study 2: **THE WOMEN OF THE CHURCH**

Text: 1 Timothy 2:9-15

Aim: To fully appreciate God's role for women within the church.

Memory Verse:
"Favour is deceitful, and beauty is vain: but a woman that feareth the Lord, she shall be praised" (Proverbs 31:30).

INTRODUCTION:
This is a vibrant passage of Scripture, a passage that stirs both men and women to sit up and listen. It even arouses emotions and reactions from some, in particular within societies where women's rights have become a heated issue. The subject is women in the church: the place of women in public, in the church, and in the home or in childbearing.

OUTLINE:
1. In public, women are to dress modestly (vv.9-10).
2. In church, women are to learn in silence and submissiveness (vv.11-14).
3. In church, women are not to teach nor to have authority over a man (vv.12-14).
4. In the home, mothers will be saved if they continue to live and walk in the Lord (v.15).

1. IN PUBLIC, WOMEN ARE TO DRESS MODESTLY (vv.9-10).

The word *adorn* is really a better translation of what Scripture means. The word means the dress, ornaments, and arrangement of clothing upon the body. But the word adorn also refers to behavior and demeanor, that is, the way a woman carries herself, walks, moves, and behaves in public. Remember: this passage is being written to genuine

1 TIMOTHY 2:9-15

Christian women—women who truly believe in the Lord, who wish to honor the Lord and to have a strong testimony for Him. The Christian woman wants to guard her clothing and to dress modestly; she wants to watch the way she dresses, walks, moves, and behaves in public. She wants to bring honor to the Lord and to build a strong testimony—a testimony that she loves the Lord and has committed her life...

- to help people, not to seduce them
- to serve people, not to destroy them
- to point people to Jesus, not to attract them to herself
- to teach people righteous behavior not fleshly and worldly behavior

Scripture covers three things about the adorning or dress of a true Christian woman. All three are revealing. They demonstrate exactly where a woman stands—regardless of what she professes: either with Christ or with the world.

1. The Christian woman is to dress and behave modestly and to keep herself under control at all times.
    ⇒ She is to dress and adorn herself with "shamefacedness"; that is, in public she is to dress and act modestly, somewhat reserved and shy.
    ⇒ She is to dress and adorn herself with "sobriety"; that is, she is to dress and act appropriately, sensibly, controlled, soberly, calmly, quietly, and seriously.

2. The Christian woman is not to dress to attract attention. This is the point of these negative commands. She is not to adorn herself...
    - with braided hair: elaborate hair-styles—hair-styles that are so different that they break away from acceptable customs and attract attention to herself.
    - with gold, or pearls, or expensive clothing: elaborate jewelry and clothing that is extravagant, ostentatious, flamboyant, and that attract attention to herself.

Donald Guthrie says that a woman's mind is mirrored by her dress.[1] How true this is! How a woman dresses shows whether she lives in prayer and devotion to God or has deep feelings and desires for the world and the gaping and lustful attention of men.

3. The Christian woman is to dress and adorn herself with good works. Note exactly what this verse says. Some women profess godliness. Godliness means that they reverence and fear God and are devoted to Him. These are the women who are committed and concerned with good works. As stated earlier, their minds are upon helping, saving, and teaching people, not upon attracting, seducing, and destroying them through lustful and immoral thoughts and sexual behavior.

Now, note a significant fact that is often ignored and sometimes tragically unknown. True beauty is inward not outward. Think for a moment: a woman who is focused upon Christ and good works is at peace with herself. She is filled with assurance and confidence, and she has strong self-image and esteem. She has purpose, meaning, and significance in life and knows that she is perfectly secure and looked after by Christ. Picture such a woman:
    ⇒ her smile—which arises from a joy filling her whole body.
    ⇒ her walk—which has a spring in each step.
    ⇒ her dignity, calmness, serenity, confidence, security, purposefulness.

Picture her beauty. No matter what her facial features are—no matter how modest her clothing is—she is beautiful. Just how true this is can be easily seen in the opposite picture. Picture the woman who lives in and of the world, concerned about her looks and dress and appearance. Picture...

---

[1] Donald Guthrie. *The Pastoral Epistles*, p.74.

- her smile—which arises from an emptiness and reveals a dissatisfaction with life.
- her walk and movements—which reveal an insecurity, loneliness, and fear of not being accepted for what she is within and the need to fit in with her peers.
- her behavior of looseness, restlessness, and her lack of purpose, meaning, and significance.

Picture this woman's behavior. Every man—even if he has known hundreds of women—knows that this woman lacks beauty, no matter how attractive her facial and body features may be. In the eyes of so many in the world, she is good for only one thing: to be used to satisfy the world's greed for money and lust for pleasure.

As stated, beauty is not in looks; beauty is from within. If a woman is beautiful within—if she is really godly and given over to good works—God floods her with a beauty that far surpasses any beauty of the flesh or clothing.

APPLICATION:
Christian women must be focused upon Christ and upon helping the desperate who are in the communities and cities of the world. Christian women must be focused upon godliness—fearing and reverencing God—and upon good works, the good works that are so desperately needed by the lost and poor within our communities and cities.

> **"Whose adorning let it not be that outward adorning of plaiting the hair, and of wearing of gold, or of putting on of apparel; but let it be the hidden man of the heart, in that which is not corruptible, even the ornament of a meek and quiet spirit, which is in the sight of God of great price. For after this manner in the old time the holy women also, who trusted in God, adorned themselves, being in subjection unto their own husbands" (1 Pe.3:3-5).**

QUESTIONS:
1. How does an understanding of these verses help a woman have a good Christian witness?
2. What thoughts come to your mind when you hear the word modesty? Why do you think God wants His people to be modest?
3. In the Christian believer, where is true beauty located? Why does the world put so much stock in the wrong places for beauty?

2. IN CHURCH, WOMEN ARE TO LEARN IN SILENCE AND SUBMISSIVENESS (vv.11-14).

Two striking points are given in these verses. Remember: this passage is being written to genuine Christian women, women who truly love and wish to honor the Lord and to have a strong testimony for Him. The woman who is a true Christian wants to guard her behavior in church as well as in public.

The Christian woman is a follower of Christ, a true believer; therefore, she is to learn all she can about Christ. She is to attend church and read, listen, and study. She is to show and demonstrate her love for the Lord by learning all she can about Him. And note the spirit in which she is to learn. She is to learn...
- in a spirit of *silence* which means quietness
- in a spirit of *subjection* which means submissiveness

1 Timothy 2:9-15

ILLUSTRATION:
It is almost impossible to talk and listen at the same time. If we do most of the talking, we cannot hear God speaking to us. In *When I Relax I Feel Guilty*, author Tim Hansel notes:

> *An American Indian was in downtown New York, walking with his friend who lived in New York City. Suddenly he said, "I hear a cricket."*
> *"Oh, you're crazy," his friend replied.*
> *"No, I hear a cricket. I do! I'm sure of it."*
> *"It's the noon hour. There are people bustling around, cars honking, taxis squealing, noises from the city. I'm sure you can't hear it."*
> *"I'm sure I do." He listened attentively and then walked to the corner, across the street, and looked all around. Finally on the corner he found a shrub in a large cement planter. He dug beneath the leaves and found a cricket. His friend was astounded. But the Cherokee said, "No. My ears are no different from yours. It simply depends on what you are listening to. Here, let me show you." He reached into his pocket and pulled out a handful of change....And he dropped it on the concrete. Every head within a block turned. "You see what I mean?" he said as he began picking up his coins. "It all depends on what you are listening for."* [2]

In a church filled with a variety of sounds, the truth rings clear when we close our mouths and train our ears to listen for God's Word.

APPLICATION:
There is no difference between men and women in learning about Christ. Therefore, this verse could apply to men as well as to women. Everyone is to learn about Christ; therefore, everyone is to approach the Lord and the church in a spirit of quietness and submissiveness. This is true of any student, whether in a public school, university, or church. A student cannot learn if he is always questioning, contradicting, refuting, arguing, and differing with the teacher. A student who sits under a teacher in a spirit of arrogance, pride, and rebellion seldom learns anything. A student can learn only if he comes in a spirit of quietness and submissiveness, a willingness to listen, read, and study under his teacher. In fact, the quieter and more submissive he is to the authority of the professor, the more likely he is to learn.

Therefore, Christian women are to learn of Christ, learn in a spirit of quietness and submissiveness. They are not to be disruptive, arguing, differing, contradicting, grumbling, griping, and complaining in church. They are to learn of Christ in church, and they are to learn in a spirit of quietness and submissiveness.

> **"Study to show thyself approved unto God, a workmen that needeth not to be ashamed, rightly dividing the word of truth" (2 Ti.2:15).**

QUESTIONS:
1. What is the ultimate result and goal of behaving in the proper way at church?
2. Why do you think that God wants you to learn how to be quiet and submissive? What do you need to do to cultivate these traits in your life?

---

[2] Craig B. Larson, Editor. *Illustrations for Preaching & Teaching*, p. 240.

1 TIMOTHY 2:9-15

3. IN CHURCH, WOMEN ARE NOT TO TEACH NOR TO HAVE AUTHORITY OVER A MAN (vv.12-14).

Ears perk up and eyes focus when this statement is read, and in some cases emotions are aroused, especially in societies where the struggle for women's rights are being fought. What does Scripture mean? Scripture is brief and factual. A simple statement is made: **"A woman [is not] to teach, nor to hold authority over a man."** But note: a woman is not forbidden to teach nor forbidden to hold authority. She is only forbidden to teach and to hold authority over a man. Why? Why is she allowed to teach and manage other women and children but not men?

1. Because God created in an organized and orderly fashion; He created everything to have its own order and function. In relation to human beings, God created man first then woman. God created man...

- to be the driving force of creation
- to plow the way
- to take the lead
- to be the initiator
- to oversee the family and its welfare

The woman was created not as a competitor but as a counterpart. She is just as unique a creation as the man and her function is just as important as the man's, but her function upon earth is not the same as man's. In the plan of God's creation, each supports, complements, and works along the side of the other. Therefore, within the church the teaching and administrative leadership of the church is to be headed up by the man.

2. God created man and woman with different natures. Women were created with more of an open and receptive, trusting and intuitive, tender and bearing nature. Because of her receptive and trusting nature, she tends to believe things and to follow along more easily than man. Therefore, she is more easily deceived than man. This is what happened with Adam and Eve when they fell into sin. Eve was deceived and followed along with the temptation, but not Adam. He knew exactly what he was doing. He sinned because he loved the woman and wanted to know the pleasure of sin with her. He knew exactly what he was doing; therefore, he was in the greater wrong.

The point is this: by nature, men are built more to take the lead in teaching and administration; whereas women are built more to receive and follow.

> **"But I would have you know, that the head of every man is Christ; and the head of the woman is the man; and the head of Christ is God" (1 Co.11:3).**

APPLICATION 1:

Note an important question: Does this mean that a woman is never to teach or hold authority over a man?

The New Testament gives example after example of women who held phenomenal positions and ministries in the early days of Christianity.

- ⇒ Mary of Nazareth was chosen by God to bear and rear and teach God's very own Son, the Lord Jesus Christ, while He was on earth (Lu.1:26-38).
- ⇒ Anna, a prophetess, was chosen by God to predict the future of the baby Jesus (Lu.2:36-38).
- ⇒ It was four women who demonstrated raw courage by standing at the foot of Jesus' cross when all the disciples had fled for their lives (Mk.15:40).
- ⇒ Joanna and Susanna supported the work of Christ (Lu.8:3).

1 TIMOTHY 2:9-15

⇒ Martha and Mary opened their home to Jesus time and again (Lu.10:38-39; Jn.11:5).
⇒ Mary Magdalene, because of her great love and devotion for Christ, was chosen by God to be the first to witness the Lord's resurrection (Mt.16:9; Jn.20:11-18).
⇒ Tabitha or Dorcas helped the poor of her city by clothing them (Ac.9:36-43).
⇒ Mary, the mother of John Mark, allowed the early believers to meet in her home (Ac.12:12).
⇒ Lydia courageously stepped forth and became the very first convert to Christ in Europe (Ac.16:13).
⇒ Priscilla, along with her husband Aquila, taught the truth of Christ to the young preacher, Apollos (Ac.18:26).
⇒ Philip the evangelist had four daughters who were prophetesses (Ac.21:9).
⇒ Phebe served the church at Cenchrea, probably as a deaconess (Ro.16:1-2).
⇒ Mary of Rome ministered to Paul and his companions (Ro.16:6).
⇒ Tryphena and Tryphosa were two ladies who labored in the Lord (Ro.16:12).
⇒ The mother of Rufus became a mother to Paul (Ro.16:13).
⇒ Euodia and Syntyche were two women who labored in the gospel (Ph.4:2-3).
⇒ The mother and grandmother of Timothy, Lois and Eunice, taught the Scriptures to Timothy from his earliest childhood (2 Ti.1:5).
⇒ The aged women were to teach the young women (Tit.2.3).

These Scriptures clearly show that women were chosen and gifted by God to hold significant positions and ministries in the early days of Christianity. But it also has to be noted that there is no clear record of a woman serving in the capacity of the head teacher or head authority in the New Testament church (pastor, bishop, or elder). Does this mean that God never raises up a woman to teach all Christians, men and women, or to hold authority on a church-wide or worldwide ministry? In answer to this question, we have to go before the Lord humbly and openly and seek the answer for ourselves. But we must always confess that God is God; therefore, He can do what He wills in order to meet a special need. If He needs to raise up a woman to meet some special teaching or administrative need in the church, He can do it.

APPLICATION 2:
Some commentators say that this passage is to be interpreted only in the context of its day. William Barclay's comment gives an example of this position.

> *The Christian Church did not lay down these regulations as in any sense permanent regulations, but as things which were necessary in the situation in which the early Church found itself....All the things in this chapter are mere temporary regulations laid down to meet a given situation. If we want Paul's real and permanent view on this matter, we get it in Galatians 3:28. "There is neither Jew nor Greek, there is neither bond nor free, there is neither male nor female: for ye are all one in Christ Jesus." In Christ the differences of place and honour and prestige and function within the Church were all wiped out....We must not read this passage as a barrier to all women's work and service within the Church; we must read it in the light of its Jewish background and in the light of the situation in a Greek city. And we must look for Paul's permanent views in the passage which tells us that the differences are*

1 TIMOTHY 2:9-15

wiped out, and that men and women, slaves and freemen, Jews and Gentiles, are all eligible to serve Christ.[3]

But note: this position is most unlikely because of the universal reference to Adam and Eve. Scripture is drawing a universal application from the creation of Adam and Eve. It is because God created in an organized and orderly way and gave specific functions to both man and woman that man is to take the lead in blazing the path through life for his family and the church.

APPLICATION 3:
There is another possible reason why God has forbidden women to stand before men in a position of teaching and authority, a reason that has perhaps been neglected in discussion. By nature men and women are attracted to each other by looking, but man by nature is the more dominant pursuer. Therefore, by nature he is probably more attracted by looking than the woman is. If a man looks at a woman long enough, he will begin to notice any feature of attractiveness about her. This is natural and normal, the way God made man and woman. However, when a woman stands before a man for a long time and the man is forced to continue looking at her, the situation becomes ready-made for temptation to attack his mind with suggestive thoughts. This is not to say that every man who sits under the teaching of a woman and who is forced to look at her is thinking immoral thoughts. It only means that when a man is forced to look and look at a woman, the temptation is more likely to happen.

QUESTIONS:
1. Why is a woman not permitted to teach and to hold authority over a man?
2. Do you think that a woman can be used by God in extraordinary situations?
3. How does trusting God help you to accept these verses and to obey God's instructions?

4. IN THE HOME, MOTHERS WILL BE SAVED IF THEY CONTINUE TO LIVE AND WALK IN THE LORD (v.15).

This is a glorious promise to the true Christian woman. But what does it mean? Women still suffer pain in childbearing and some women, even Christian women, die when giving birth to a child. The verse refers back to Eve and her sin. The judgment upon her sin was that she would suffer pain in childbearing (Ge.3:16). The promise seems to mean one of three things.
 1. When the promise is kept within the context of this passage, it seems to mean this (vv.12-14). The woman does not find her salvation and fulfillment through holding positions of teaching and authority, but through childbearing. The very nature of a woman's being, the primary function of a woman's nature and call upon earth, is to carry on the human race. Therefore, the woman's salvation—that is, her ultimate fulfillment, satisfaction and completeness in life—comes through bearing and rearing children. Her salvation and completeness in life does not come from competing with men to see who blazes the paths and builds the roads through the jungles of this earth. She can do these things, but her salvation—her ultimate fulfillment and satisfaction—does not come by doing these things. Contrariwise, the woman will be saved and totally fulfilled if she...

---

[3] William Barclay. *The Letters to Timothy, Titus, and Philemon*, p.78.

1 Timothy 2:9-15

- will continue in faith: continue believing and trusting
- will continue in love: loving the Lord, her husband, believers, and the lost of the world
- will continue in holiness: living a life totally set apart to Christ and His purpose
- will continue in self-control: disciplining and controlling her life to follow Christ in all things

2. A second possible meaning of the verse is this: the sentence of pain in childbearing (the penalty of her sin) does not prohibit a woman's salvation. She shall be saved if she continues in faith, love, holiness, and self-control.

3. There is one other possible meaning of this passage that needs to be considered. The definite article (the) is in the Greek before the word "childbearing." That is, the verse reads: "She shall be saved in the childbearing." Some commentators feel that "the childbearing" refers to the seed of the woman, that is, to the greatest childbearing that has ever taken place which is the birth of Christ Himself. Therefore, the meaning is this: despite the judgment upon the woman (suffering pain in childbearing), the woman will be saved in the supreme childbearing, that is, in Christ.

Whatever a person's interpretation, note the condition. The promise is based upon the woman...

- already having faith in Christ
- already knowing the love of God
- already living a holy life
- already controlling her life and following Christ

> "Then said they unto him, What shall we do, that we might work the works of God? Jesus answered and said unto them, This is the work of God, that ye believe on him whom he hath sent" (Jn.6:28-29).

ILLUSTRATION:
Christian women should be examples of godliness not worldliness.

> *Corrie Ten Boom was a shining example of a godly woman. Even though she was captured and placed in a Nazi concentration camp during World War II, she would not compromise her testimony. In her book The Hiding Place she described what it was like to try to remain godly in such a terrible place. The guards would offer favors in exchange for sex. Some prisoners would give in out of desperation. For those who would not give in, conditions would worsen. It seemed unbearable, but Corrie held on to her faith in God.*
>
> *Because she was determined to remain godly, the Lord was able to use her later to win many to Christ. She even became a celebrity and wrote her story, which later was made into a movie. Corrie spoke in many places around the world, telling of God's faithfulness in the most trying of times.*
>
> *At one of these speaking engagements, a German man came up to meet her. He was visibly touched by her message of forgiveness. Corrie Ten Boom then had another chance to live what she preached. It was one of the most powerful and liberating moments of her godly life. The man explained that he remembered her from Germany, because he was one of the guards. He offered his hand and begged her forgiveness. Through the enabling of the Spirit, she reached out her hand and forgave the man.*

What can God do through one woman determined to live a godly life? More than anyone could possibly imagine!

1 TIMOTHY 2:9-15

QUESTIONS:
1. What is the secret to contentment?
2. What does this verse tell you about God's promise to save woman?
3. With every one of God's promises to His people there is a condition—something that we must do in response to His action. What is the condition for this promise?

SUMMARY:

God has a special ministry for the Christian woman in public, in the church, and at home. A believing woman can find fulfillment when she applies these timeless principles to her walk with the Lord...

1. In public, women are to dress modestly.
2. In church, women are to learn in silence and submissiveness.
3. In church, women are not to teach nor to have authority over men.
4. In the home, mothers will be saved if they continue to live and walk in the Lord.

PERSONAL JOURNAL NOTES:
(Reflection & Response)

1. The most important thing that I learned from this lesson was:

2. The area that I need to work on the most is:

3. I can apply this lesson to my life by:

4. Closing Statement of Commitment:

1 TIMOTHY 3:1-7

	CHAPTER 3	brawler, not covetous;	
	C. The Overseers or Ministers of the Church, 3:1-7	4 One that ruleth well his own house, having his children in subjection with all gravity;	3. Family qualifications: The minister or overseer must manage his own home
1. The office of overseer or minister a. Is a noble task b. Is to be desired	This is a true saying, If a man desire the office of a bishop, he desireth a good work.	5 (For if a man know not how to rule his own house, how shall he take care of the church of God?)	
2. Personal qualifications	2 A bishop then must be blameless, the husband of one wife, vigilant, sober, of good behavior, given to hospitality, apt to teach; 3 Not given to wine, no striker, not greedy of filthy lucre; but patient, not a	6 Not a novice, lest being lifted up with pride he fall into the condemnation of the devil. 7 Moreover he must have a good report of them which are without; lest he fall into reproach and the snare of the devil.	4. Spiritual qualifications a. Must be spiritually mature b. Reason: A danger of pride 5. Community qualifications

Section II
DUTIES AND ORDER IN THE CHURCH
1 Timothy 2:1–3:13

Study 3:   **THE OVERSEERS OR MINISTERS OF THE CHURCH**

Text: 1 Timothy 3:1-7

Aim: To set your heart upon becoming a leader for God, a leader within the church.

Memory Verse:
> "This is a true saying, If a man desire the office of a bishop, he desireth a good work" (1 Timothy 3:1).

INTRODUCTION:
Do you feel comfortable entrusting your soul to the care of your church leaders? The Bible instructs us to...

> "Obey them that have the rule over you, and submit yourselves: for they watch for your souls, as they that must give account, that they may do it with joy, and not with grief: for that *is* unprofitable for you" (He.13:17).

One of the most important duties of the local church is to ask God for leaders who qualify according to the Scripture. Woe to any body of believers who compromise on this issue. A church that ignores God's criteria for ministers or elders and accepts leaders for the reason of popularity or politics defiles the office of the elder.

The office of bishop is probably the same office as elder or presbyter or minister in the New Testament. All three words refer to the same person, to the minister of the gospel and of the church. What are the qualifications of the minister or elder? Who

1 TIMOTHY 3:1-7

should be preaching the gospel and filling the pulpits of the Lord's church? What kind of person should be considering the ministry and the great privilege of caring for God's people? The importance of this passage cannot be overstressed when it comes to the building and protection of God's church and people.

OUTLINE:
1. The office of overseer or minister (v.1).
2. Personal qualifications (vv.2-3).
3. Family qualifications: the minister or overseer must manage his own home (vv.4-5).
4. Spiritual qualifications (v.6).
5. Community qualifications (v.7).

1. THE OFFICE OF OVERSEER OR MINISTER (v.1).

The office of minister or elder (bishop) is a "good work." The word *good* means honorable, excellent, beneficial, productive. Note that the position of the ministry is not what is stressed, but the work of the ministry. The emphasis is not the esteem and honor of the profession. The emphasis is upon the work of the ministry. It is the work that is honorable, excellent, beneficial, and productive. The work of the ministry is a "good work."

Note another fact: the office of minister or bishop is to be desired. The word *desire* means to seek after with a strong desire, to set one's heart upon. God stirs some hearts to seek the ministry and to dedicate their lives to the work of the ministry.

APPLICATION:
When a person is stirred to commit his life to the ministry, he must say "yes" to the Spirit of God. To say "no" to God's call is to reject God and to miss one's calling and life. It is to miss one's very purpose for being on earth.

> **"But covet earnestly the best gifts: and yet show I unto you a more excellent way" (1 Co.12:31).**

QUESTIONS:
1. What is the relationship between the office of the minister and the work of the ministry? What can happen if an emphasis is placed on the wrong one?
2. Is it wrong to desire this office? Why or why not?
3. Ultimately, who decides whether or not you are a qualified to serve as an elder or minister?

2. PERSONAL QUALIFICATIONS (vv.2-3).

The minister must meet some personal qualifications; he must be a person of great Christian character.
1. The minister or elder must be "blameless": above reproach; not open to attack; not able to be criticized by the enemy at all.[1]
2. The minister or elder must be "the husband of one wife." From the earliest times of church history, this qualification has been interpreted differently. Some have held...

---

[1] *The Pulpit Commentary*, Vol.21. Edited by H.D.M. Spence and Joseph S. Exell. (Grand Rapids, MI: Eerdmans Publishing Co., 1950), p.50.

1 TIMOTHY 3:1-7

- that the elder or minister must have a wife; he must be married to be a minister.
- that the elder or minister must never have more than one wife; he must never marry again, even if his wife died. This position holds that second marriages are completely forbidden.
- that the elder must not have more than one wife at a time. (Remember: polygamy was the common practice of society when the church was first born).
- that an elder must live a life of strict morality; he "must be a loyal husband, preserving marriage in all its purity."2

APPLICATION:
Every minister, believer, and church must go before the Lord and seek the meaning of this qualification for him or herself. But we must be honest and open to hear the Lord and then beg of Him the courage and discipline to do what He says. This is an absolute essential for all who are believers, for nothing is any more traumatic than the loss of a spouse through death or separation and divorce. And if there is ever a time that we must reach out and minister to our brothers and sisters, it is when they lose their spouses.

⇒ The point is this: should a minister or elder be allowed to serve as a minister if he has had more than one wife, either through death or divorce? The Pulpit Commentary has an excellent comment on this point:

> *If we consider the general laxity in regard to marriage, and the facility of divorce, which prevailed among Jews and Romans at this time, it must have been a common thing for a man to have more than one woman living who had been his wife. And this [was] a distinct breach of the primeval law (Ge.ii.24), [and] would properly be a bar to any one being called to the 'office of a bishop'....It is utterly unsupported by any single passage in Scripture that a second marriage should disqualify a man for the sacred ministry. As regards the opinion of the early Church, it was not at all uniform, and amongst those who held that this passage absolutely prohibits second marriages in the case of a [bishop], it was merely a part of the asceticism of the day.*3

A.T. Robertson very simply says, *"Of one wife. One at a time, clearly."*4

William Barclay says, *"In its context here we can be quite certain that this means that the Christian leader must be a loyal husband, preserving marriage in all its purity."*5

Thompson Chain Reference Bible, in listing its subjects, simply says *"Polygamy Forbidden."*

> **"And he answered and said unto them, Have ye not read, that he which made them at the beginning made them male and female, and said, For this cause shall a man leave father and mother, and shall cleave to his wife: and they twain shall be one flesh? Wherefore they are no more twain, but one flesh. What therefore God hath joined together, let not man put asunder" (Mt.19:4-6).**

---

2   William Barclay. *The Letters to Timothy, Titus, and Philemon*, p.87.
3   *The Pulpit Commentary*, Vol.21, p.51.
4   A.T. Robertson. *Word Pictures in the New Testament*, Vol.4, p.572.
5   William Barclay. *The Letters to Timothy, Titus, and Philemon*, p.87.

1 TIMOTHY 3:1-7

3. The minister or elder must be vigilant: temperate, self-controlled, and watchful. He must be vigilant, watch over, and control his own life and the lives of his dear people.

> "Watch and pray, that ye enter not into temptation: the spirit indeed is willing, but the flesh is weak" (Mt.26:41).
>
> "Be sober, be vigilant; because your adversary the devil, as a roaring lion, walketh about, seeking whom he may devour" (1 Pe.5:8).

4. The minister or elder must be "sober": be sober-minded, that is, have a mind that is sound, sensible, controlled, disciplined, and chaste—a mind that has complete control over all sensual desires. Note: if the mind is controlled, a person's whole life—his body and behavior—is controlled. He lives a sober life.

> "Therefore let us not sleep, as do others; but let us watch and be sober. For they that sleep sleep in the night; and they that be drunken are drunken in the night. But let us, who are of the day, be sober, putting on the breastplate of faith and love; and for an helmet, the hope of salvation" (1 Th.5:6-8).

5. The minister or elder must be of "good behavior": well-behaved, orderly, composed, solid, and honest. It is a person who has good conduct, whose character and behavior stands as the ideal and pattern for others.

> "[Love] doth not behave itself unseemly, seeketh not her own, is not easily provoked, thinketh no evil" (1 Co.13:5).

ILLUSTRATION:
We easily disqualify ourselves from having a lasting ministry when our behavior contradicts what we say. This minister's example is one of what not to do.

> *Reggie was the kind of man who used smoke and mirrors to hide his character from the members of his congregation. Inside, he struggled with a personal hell everyday. But on the outside, he presented himself as one who had it all together.*
>
> *He was known for his ability to joke about any topic. One of his favorite jokes was to act effeminate and in a "joking" way give one of his staff members a kiss on the cheek. In a nervous sort of way, everyone would laugh. But in the back of their minds each had serious questions about Reggie's sexual preference. Shocked at even having such notions, the staff would quickly channel their thoughts elsewhere.*
>
> *Word of Reggie's foolish behavior spread through the church and then the community. His church became the talk of the town. As accusations came, he steadfastly denied each one. And when a television reporter came to inquire, Reggie slammed the door in her face.*
>
> *As it turns out, Reggie wasn't joking after all. He was a practicing homosexual who sneaked out of the closet and tried to keep others in the dark by his coarse jesting. In the end, the joke was on Reggie. His services as minister were no longer needed by the congregation. His ruse destroyed lives and brought shame to the name of Christ. After leaving this congregation behind, he went to a new town and started the whole process all over again.*

1 Timothy 3:1-7

Questions:
1. How does trusting Christ help the elder to remain blameless? What special challenges does an elder face with his behavior?
2. Why is it important for an elder to have only one wife? What would be some of the natural consequences if this charge were violated?
3. What is the secret to having a sober life? How victorious are you in this area? What can you do today to get a better handle on this part of your life?

6. The minister or elder must be given to "hospitality": to have an open heart and home; "showing love or being a friend to the believers, especially strangers or foreigners" (Amplified New Testament). The minister helps and entertains as much as he can. He does not open his heart, home, time, or money to the things of the world; but he uses what resources he has to help and minister to people.

> "But a lover of hospitality, a lover of good men, sober, just, holy, temperate" (Tit.1:8).
>
> "Be not forgetful to entertain strangers: for thereby some have entertained angels unawares" (He.13:2).

7. The minister or elder must be "apt to teach": able, capable, skillful, and qualified to teach. William Barclay has such an excellent comment on this point that he must be quoted:

> *It has been said that the duty of the Christian leader is "to preach to the unconverted and to teach the converted." There are two things to be said about this. It is one of the disasters of modern times that the teaching ministry of the Church has not been exercised as it should be. There is any amount of topical preaching; there is any amount of exhortation; but there is little use in exhorting a man to be a Christian when he does not know what being a Christian means. Instruction is a primary duty of the Christian preacher and leader. But the second thing is this. The finest and the most effective teaching is not done by speaking, but by being. Our ultimate duty is not to talk to men about Christ, but to show men Christ. Even the man with no gift of words can teach by living in such a way that in him men see the reflection of the Master. A saint has been defined as someone "in whom Christ lives again."*[6]

> "Teaching them to observe all things whatsoever I have commanded you: and, lo, I am with you alway, even unto the end of the world" (Mt.28:20).

Application:
Note: the minister must be rooted and grounded in the Word of God in order to teach. Short-cuts are not allowed. The sponge that is squeezed will reveal what the sponge has soaked up. The same is true with the minister or elder—what he has been taking in (studying, looking at, living) will surely come out when the pressure is on.

> "O how love I thy law! it *is* my meditation all the day" (Ps.119:97).
>
> "Order my steps in thy word: and let not any iniquity have dominion over me" (Ps.119:133).

---

[6] William Barclay. *The Letters to Timothy, Titus, and Philemon*, p.95.

1 Timothy 3:1-7

8. The minister or elder must not be given to wine: not be a drunkard; not sit around drinking all the time. In order to justify their right to drink, some argue that drinking wine was a common practice in the ancient world even among true Christian believers. However, we must always remember what William Barclay so forcefully points out about the ancient world:
   ⇒ First, the water supply was often inadequate and dangerous.
   ⇒ Second, *"although the ancient world used wine as the commonest of all drinks it used it most abstemiously. When wine was drunk, it was drunk in the proportion of two parts of wine to three parts of water. A man who was drunken would be disgraced in ordinary heathen society, let alone in the Church."*[7]

> **"It is good neither to eat flesh, nor to drink wine, nor any thing whereby thy brother stumbleth, or is offended, or is made weak" (Ro.14:21).**
>
> **"He [the Nazarite] shall separate himself from wine and strong drink, and shall drink no vinegar of wine, or vinegar of strong drink, neither shall he drink any liquor of grapes, nor eat moist grapes, or dried" (Nu.6:3).**

9. The minister or elder must not be a "striker": not combative or violent, not contentious or quarrelsome, not a person who strikes out and contends with another person. The minister must not be a person who strikes other people or who becomes easily upset, irritated, or aggravated with others. He uses neither hand nor tongue against anyone. On the contrary he is kind, gentle, and longsuffering with others.

APPLICATION:
Note: the tongue can be used to strike out at a person as easily as the hand or fist. Many a person has been hurt and damaged by the poisonous venom of a striking tongue.

> **"Let nothing be done through strife or vainglory; but in lowliness of mind let each esteem other better than themselves. Look not every man on his own things, but every man also on the things of others" (Ph.2:3-4).**

10. The minister or elder must not be a lover of worldly gain or possessions. (This is the meaning of filthy lucre.) The minister must be a person who has given all he is and has (money) to minister to people. He must not be a person who has entered the ministry as a profession or as a livelihood. He must be supported and given a livelihood by the church but he is not to be in the ministry in order to get a livelihood. He must not be a person who is out to get, but a person who is committed to giving. He must live of the gospel—God's people must support him so that he can preach the gospel—but he must be dead to the love of money and material possessions. He must give all that he is and has to the cause of Christ—to meet the dire needs of the desperate and dying men, women, and children of this earth. Remember: the following warnings were written to professing Christians.

> **"For the love of money is the root of all evil: which while some coveted after, they have erred from the faith, and pierced themselves through with many sorrows" (1 Ti.6:10).**

---

[7] William Barclay. *The Letters to Timothy, Titus, and Philemon*, p.91.

1 Timothy 3:1-7

11. The minister or elder must be "patient": gracious, kind, gentle, forbearing, reasonable, soft, and tender. The word goes beyond treating someone with justice: it treats a person graciously and tenderly. It reaches beyond justice and touches the person with a gentle hand.

> "But the wisdom that is from above is first pure, then peaceable, gentle, and easy to be entreated, full of mercy and good fruits, without partiality, and without hypocrisy" (Ja.3:17).

12. The minister or elder must not be a brawler: not contentious or a fighter. He must be a man of peace, a mild-mannered person, always under control. Again, this refers to the tongue as well as to the hands. He must be a man who is deeply touched when there is unrest, controversy, or disturbance in the church or among believers. He must be a person who is so touched that he will work and seek for peace.

> "Finally, brethren, farewell. Be perfect, be of good comfort, be of one mind, live in peace; and the God of love and peace shall be with you" (2 Co.13:11).

13. The minister or elder must not be covetous: not a lover of money.

> "And he said unto them, Take heed, and beware of covetousness: for a man's life consisteth not in the abundance of the things which he possesseth" (Lu.12:15).

QUESTIONS:
1. Why is it important for an elder or minister to have great Christian character?
2. How do you feel about the high personal qualifications of an elder? Do you think that they are impossible to meet? What is God's role in equipping a person to be an elder or minister? What is the elder's or minister's role?
3. Are there any of the above areas of your life where you need to improve your witness? If so, what are they? What is the secret to cultivating these traits in your life?

3. FAMILY QUALIFICATIONS: THE MINISTER OR OVERSEER MUST MANAGE HIS OWN HOME (vv.4-5).

The minister or elder must meet one very significant family qualification. The minister or bishop must rule his own household and rule it well. The home is a miniature of the church; the home is the proving ground for leadership in the church. The husband is the head of the home. This does not mean that he is the dictator, tyrant, or bully of the home. It means that he is the leader of the wife and children. He leads them all...
- in the building of a loving, joyful, and peaceful home
- in the fulfillment of their life's calling and task upon earth

It means that the man is not bossed about or dominated by his wife; that he does not allow his children to disobey, rebel, or talk back to him or their mother; that he takes the lead in controlling his home for Christ and His kingdom.

⇒ Note the word *gravity*. It means dignity. The minister must rule his home with dignity, respect, and love.

> "For if a man know not how to rule his own house, how shall he take care of the church of God?" (1 Ti.3:5).

1 TIMOTHY 3:1-7

QUESTIONS:
1. What does this verse teach about God's order for the home? Are you failing to fully experience God's best in your home? What do you need to do to improve the spiritual climate in your home?
2. Why is it important for the minister or elder to be able to rule his home?
3. What has helped you in the past to bring God's order into your home?

4. SPIRITUAL QUALIFICATIONS (v.6).

The minister or elder must not be a novice, that is, a new convert or a new church member. He must have been a convert or church member for a long time...
- long enough to have become rooted and grounded in the Lord and His Word
- long enough to have become spiritually mature
- long enough to have proven his testimony for Christ
- long enough to be well known and respected by other believers
- long enough to be able to minister to others and to teach them to minister

Note why a novice must not be given a position of leadership in the church: lest he become prideful and "fall into the condemnation of the devil." Satan was expelled from heaven because of pride. It was pride that caused his fall and brought condemnation upon him. When a person is given a great responsibility before he has become rooted and grounded in the faith, he is most likely going to fall and be condemned just as Satan fell and was condemned. We must always remember what Matthew Henry points out: *"Pride...is a sin that turned angels into devils."*[8] We must guard against pride. We must guard against putting a person in a position of leadership that will tempt him to feel more important than he is.

> **"And whosoever shall exalt himself shall be abased; and he that shall humble himself shall be exalted" (Mt.23:12).**

ILLUSTRATION:
A saying that is far too often true is this: more than one spiritual neck has been broken by falling off the platform. How often a new convert is paraded across the platform as a "super" conversion. Here is one example:

> *Al was a successful businessman and middle-aged convert. He had a unique way with words and quickly became the featured speaker at Christian meetings. Less than five years after conversion he became an elder in his church—a position that simply overwhelmed him. He was much more content to be a featured speaker around town than to have to adhere to his biblical responsibilities as an elder. It did not take long for him to burn out and backslide. His previous joy turned into a haunting journey.*

Al's life is a lesson for all believers. If discipleship is omitted, then failure is not far behind.

QUESTIONS:
1. Why are people like Al forced to the front of the pack before they are ready?
2. What dangers lie in wait for the novice? In what ways can they be protected from harm?
3. How does this verse help you to pray for the future leaders in your church?

---

[8] Matthew Henry. *Matthew Henry's Commentary*, Vol.6. (Old Tappan, NJ: Fleming H. Revell Co.), p.815.

1 TIMOTHY 3:1-7

5. COMMUNITY QUALIFICATIONS (v.7).

The minister or elder must meet one very important community qualification. He must have a "good report of them that are without"; that is, he must have a good testimony before the world. Of course, there are some in the world who will criticize and slander any person who has failed and run with the world. Many in the world do not recognize conversion nor repentance and forgiveness—the simple fact that Christ can forgive and change a person. But when a person enters the ministry, he must have experienced such a significant change that it is clearly evident that he is now following Christ. The change in his life must be radical: a radical turning away from the world and self to Christ. The change must be so radical that even the unbelievers can see it. Then and only then can he ever hope to reach the unbelieving world for Christ.

⇒ Note why the minister must have a good testimony before the world: lest he fall into reproach. The unbelievers of the world will reproach, ridicule, and mock him; and he will fall into the snare of the devil. That is, he will hesitate to bear testimony for Christ and to fulfill his duties as a minister. He will tend to withdraw and keep silent and to remain unseen as much as possible. The power of his ministry and testimony will be drastically weakened.

> "First, I thank my God through Jesus Christ for you all, that your faith is spoken of throughout the whole world" (Ro.1:8).
>
> "But sanctify the Lord God in your hearts: and be ready always to give an answer to every man that asketh you a reason of the hope that is in you with meekness and fear" (1 Pe.3:15).

APPLICATION:
A good testimony before the world is essential. The world is not to choose or even have a voice in selecting church leaders. But church leaders must be respected by their day-to-day acquaintances. The point is profession verses possession. You must do more than *profess* the qualities—you must *possess* them. Those outside are the first to notice wrong behavior in a Christian. The Christian believer must behave like a Christian believer before he can serve as an overseer in God's church.

QUESTIONS:
1. Do you worry about having a good testimony in the community? Why?
2. In what ways can your testimony be used to reach the unbelievers in your community?
3. Should the standards for a minister or elder be higher than for other Christians? Why?

SUMMARY:

If anyone sets his heart upon becoming a leader or minister in his local church, God has presented a lofty standard that cannot be compromised. God would have every believer strive to adopt these standards also. How do you check out on these qualifications?

1. The office of overseer or minister.
2. The personal qualifications.
3. The family qualifications: the minister or overseer must manage his own home.
4. The spiritual qualifications.
5. The community qualifications.

1 TIMOTHY 3:1-7

PERSONAL JOURNAL NOTES:
(Reflection & Response)

1. The most important thing that I learned from this lesson was:

2. The area that I need to work on the most is:

3. I can apply this lesson to my life by:

4. Closing Statement of Commitment:

1 Timothy 3:8-13

	D. The Deacons of the Church, 3:8-13	ing found blameless 11 Even so must their wives be grave, not slanderers, sober, faithful in all things.	3. The family qualifications a. Must have a committed wife
1. The personal qualifications	8 Likewise must the deacons be grave, not double-tongued, not given to much wine, not greedy of filthy lucre;	12 Let the deacons be the husbands of one wife, ruling their children and their own houses well.	b. Must have a controlled family & home
2. The spiritual qualifications a. Must have spiritual convictions b. Must be spiritually tested— proven	9 Holding the mystery of the faith in a pure conscience. 10 And let these also first be proved; then let them use the office of a deacon, be-	13 For they that have used the office of a deacon well purchase to themselves a good degree, and great boldness in the faith which is in Christ Jesus.	4. The results or rewards a. Community respect b. Spiritual assurance

Section II
DUTIES AND ORDER IN THE CHURCH
1 Timothy 2:1–3:13

Study 4: **THE DEACONS OF THE CHURCH**

Text: 1 Timothy 3:8-13

Aim: To strive after the qualifications of a deacon.

Memory Verse:
> "For they that have used the office of a deacon well purchase to themselves a good degree, and great boldness in the faith which is in Christ Jesus" (1 Timothy 3:13).

INTRODUCTION:
What if this announcement appeared in your church newsletter?

ANNOUNCEMENT

It has come to the attention of the church leaders that many of our members feel their needs are being neglected. In order to care for these members, the leadership has approved the position of deacon. The candidate who fills this position must have:
- *a great personality*
- *a college education*
- *a 15-passenger van*

For more information about the requirements for this position, contact I. M. Kidding.

Certainly, this "announcement" would never appear in your church newsletter. Deacons are not appointed to serve on the basis of worldly qualifications but on the basis of servant hood—helping and relieving the minister within the church. Deacons are appointed to serve selflessly and to teach others how to serve with them. Therefore, a local church with Spirit-filled deacons is an essential if the life of Jesus Christ is to be seen in the community.

1 TIMOTHY 3:8-13

This passage discusses the second officer of the church, the deacon. The office of deacon is so important that the qualifications required are just as high as those demanded of a minister or elder. In this day and time, when worldliness, immorality, and lawlessness are running so rampant, the qualifications for deacons need to be studied, heeded, and guarded ever so diligently.

OUTLINE:
1. The personal qualifications (v.8).
2. The spiritual qualifications (vv.9-10).
3. The family qualifications (vv.11-12).
4. The results or rewards (v.13).

A CLOSER LOOK:

(3:8-13) **Deacon:** the word deacon means servant, minister. The first reference to deacons is in Acts (Ac.6:1-7). Deacons were appointed to help in the ministerial and administrative duties of the church (Ac.6:2). Their function was to relieve ministers so that ministers could give themselves "continually to prayer and to the ministry of the Word" (Ac.6:4). In particular, they were chosen to minister to the day-to-day needs of believers, to the needs of widows, widowers, the poor, and the sick of a church. They were to relieve ministers so the ministers could concentrate on prayer and preaching.

> "Wherefore, brethren, look ye out among you seven men of honest report, full of the Holy Ghost and wisdom, whom we may appoint over this business. But we will give ourselves continually to prayer, and to the ministry of the word" (Ac.6:3-4).

However, note a significant fact: this does not mean that ministers are never to meet day-to-day needs of believers nor that deacons should never share or preach the Word. In the early church both ministers and deacons served in both areas, but each concentrated upon their primary call and mission.

⇒ Preachers were sometimes called deacons, that is, servants.

> "Who then is Paul, and who is Apollos, but ministers by whom ye believed, even as the Lord gave to every man?" (1 Co.3:5).

⇒ The first deacons preached as well as ministered to the needy of the church.

> "And Stephen [a deacon], full of faith and power, did great wonders and miracles among the people" (Ac.6:8).

⇒ Deacons are closely linked to elders or bishops.

> "Paul and Timotheus, the servants of Jesus Christ, to all the saints in Christ Jesus which are at Philippi, with the bishops and deacons" (Ph.1:1).

⇒ Deacons are to be spiritually equipped for their task.

> "Wherefore, brethren, look ye out among you seven men of honest report, full of the Holy Ghost and wisdom, whom we may appoint over this business" (Ac.6:3; see 1 Ti.3:8-13).

1 TIMOTHY 3:8-13

> ⇒ The office of the deacon was an early development in the church.
>
> "And in those days, when the number of the disciples was multiplied, there arose a murmuring of the Grecians against the Hebrews, because their widows were neglected in the daily ministration. Then the twelve called the multitude of the disciples unto them, and said, It is not reason that we should leave the word of God, and serve tables. Wherefore, brethren, look ye out among you seven men of honest report, full of the Holy Ghost and wisdom, whom we may appoint over this business. But we will give ourselves continually to prayer, and to the ministry of the word" (Ac.6:1-4).

1. THE PERSONAL QUALIFICATIONS (v.8).

1. Deacons must be *grave*: serious, honorable, worthy, revered, highly respected, noble. It is being serious-minded, the very opposite of...
   - being flippant
   - dishonoring oneself
   - being shallow by being over-talkative
   - having little respect because one is not grave or serious enough
   - having a surface religion only

However, note that this does not mean that the deacon is to walk around with a long face, never smiling, joking, or having fun. It simply means that he is serious-minded, committed to Christ and to the mission of the church: the mission of reaching the lost and meeting the desperate needs of the world.

> "For the grace of God that bringeth salvation hath appeared to all men, teaching us that, denying ungodliness and worldly lusts, we should live soberly, righteously, and godly, in this present world; looking for that blessed hope, and the glorious appearing of the great God and our Saviour Jesus Christ" (Tit.2:11-13).

2. Deacons must not be double-tongued: bearing tales, gossiping, saying one thing to a person's face and something else behind his back. No more descriptive word could be chosen than "double-tongued."

The quality of not being double-tongued is important. As a deacon ministers through visitation (going from house to house), he is often tempted to gossip or say one thing to one person and something else to another person. He is also tempted to evade or smooth talk issues. Therefore, he must be a man of integrity, a man who speaks the straight truth, a man who is as honest as the day is long.

> "Where no wood is, there the fire goeth out: so where there is no talebearer, the strife ceaseth" (Pr.26:20).

3. The deacon must not be given to much wine (see 1 Ti.3:2-3 for further discussion).

4. The deacon must not be greedy of worldly gain (see 1 Ti.3:2-3 for further discussion).

ILLUSTRATION:
Talking about living a committed life is one thing, but actually *living it* is quite another.

1 TIMOTHY 3:8-13

An old deacon who used to pray every Wednesday night at prayer meeting always concluded his prayer the same way: "And, Lord, clean all the cobwebs out of my life."

The cobwebs were those things that ought not to have been there, but had gathered during the week. It got too much for one fellow in the prayer meeting, and he heard the old deacon one time too often. So when the man made that prayer, the fellow jumped to his feet and shouted: "Lord, Lord, don't do it! [Don't just clean the cobwebs.] Kill the spider!" [1]

That's good advice for every believer: Go to the source of your sin and kill the spider.

QUESTIONS:
1. Why is it so important for a deacon to be an honorable person?
2. Why is it so important for a deacon not to gossip? For any Christian believer?
3. What would keep a deacon from having an effective ministry?

2. THE SPIRITUAL QUALIFICATIONS (vv.9-10).

Deacons must meet three very important spiritual qualifications.

1. Deacons must hold to the mystery of the faith and hold it in good conscience. The mystery of the faith is given in verse 16:

> **"And without controversy, great is the mystery of godliness:**
>
> ⇒ "God was manifest [revealed] in the flesh
> ⇒ "Justified [vindicated] in the Spirit
> ⇒ "Seen by angels
> ⇒ "Preached [proclaimed] unto the Gentiles
> ⇒ "Believed on in the world
> ⇒ "Received [taken] up into glory."

A deacon must believe in the incarnation, in the glorious gospel that God has come to earth in the Person of the Lord Jesus Christ to preach the love and salvation of God for man. In fact, note what this verse says: a deacon must hold within his own heart the mystery of the faith. He must possess and cling to it, and he must hold it in good conscience. He must believe the whole gospel (mystery) and not deceive the church by being hypocritical about his belief.

There is another point about conscience as well: the deacon must have a good conscience about living and sharing the mystery of the faith. He must not accept the call and office of deacon and then shirk his duties. He must hold the mystery of the gospel of the faith in all good conscience, that is, in sharing it faithfully with both believers and unbelievers.

> **"Holding faith, and a good conscience; which some having put away concerning faith have made shipwreck"** (1 Ti.1:19).

---

[1] Selected from *Gospel Herald*. Cited in *Encyclopedia of 7,700 Illustrations: Signs of the Times.* Paul Lee Tan, Editor. (Rockville, MD: Assurance Publishers, 1985), p.1234.

1 TIMOTHY 3:8-13

2. Deacons must first be proved or tested before they are called to the office of a deacon (see 1 Ti.3:6 for further discussion).
3. Deacons must be "blameless" (see 1 Ti.3:2-3 for further discussion).

QUESTIONS:
1. If a deacon failed to meet God's spiritual qualifications, what would be the result?
2. In what ways should deacons challenge your faith?

3. THE FAMILY QUALIFICATIONS (vv.11-12).

As a deacon visits and ministers to the women of the church, he needs his wife with him if she is able to accompany him. A strong picture of marital and family love and commitment to Christ are needed. Therefore, the deacon's wife must be as strong in the Lord as he is.

1. The deacon must have a wife who is as committed to the Lord and to the church as he is.
   a. The wife of a deacon must be "grave": serious-minded, honorable, respected, and
      noble.
   b. The wife of a deacon must not be a "slanderer": a talebearer, gossiper; a person who goes about talking about others, stirring up mischief and disturbance.

   "Let all bitterness, and wrath, and anger, and clamour, and evil speaking, be put away from you, with all malice" (Ep.4:31).
   "A hypocrite with his mouth destroyeth his neighbor: but through knowledge shall the just be delivered" (Pr.11:9).

   c. The wife of a deacon must be sober.
   d. The wife of a deacon must be faithful in all things: completely trustworthy as a wife and mother and as a believer. She must be faithful to the Lord...
      • in her personal devotion and loyalty to the Lord.
      • in her call as a wife and mother.
      • in her commitment to the church, its services and ministry.
      • in her ministry of serving with her husband.

   "And he said to them all, If any man will come after me, let him deny himself, and take up his cross daily, and follow me" (Lu.9:23).

2. The deacon must be the husband of one wife.
3. The deacon must have a controlled family and home.

QUESTIONS:
1. Do you think it is possible for a deacon to have a successful ministry without the support of his wife?
2. Why do you think God wants deacons and their wives to serve together?
3. In what ways can you pray for the deacon families in your church? What kind of encouragement can you offer them?

1 TIMOTHY 3:8-13

4. THE RESULTS OR REWARDS (v.13).

The faithful deacon experiences two results.
1. He gains a good degree or standing and testimony before both God and man.

> "Even so faith, if it hath not works, is dead, being alone" (Ja.2:17).

2. He gains great boldness and security in the faith. He experiences more and more assurance and freedom in the Spirit of God.

> "Let us therefore come boldly unto the throne of grace, that we may obtain mercy, and find grace to help in time of need" (He.4:16).

ILLUSTRATION:
A person who is full of the Holy Spirit can be a powerful witness. But anyone who tries to do the Lord's work without the provision of God's Spirit will be sorely disappointed.

> *Dr. Paul Brand was speaking to a medical college in India on "Let your light so shine before men that they may behold your good works and glorify your Father." In front of the lectern was an oil lamp, with its cotton wick burning from the shallow dish of oil. As he preached, the lamp ran out of oil, the wick burned dry, and the smoke made him cough. He immediately used the opportunity.*
>
> *"Some of us here are like this wick," he said. "We're trying to shine for the glory of God, but we stink. That's what happens when we use ourselves as the fuel of our witness rather than the Holy Spirit.*
>
> *"Wicks can last indefinitely, burning brightly and without irritating smoke, if the fuel, the Holy Spirit, is in constant supply."* [2]

How much of God's work do you attempt to do without His power?

QUESTIONS:
1. Why do you think that some deacons do not have a good witness?
2. What is the source of a faithful deacon's power? What can you do to secure more and more of the power of God's Spirit in your life?
3. How does trusting God help the deacon's ministry?

SUMMARY:

Service. That should be the key word in the vocabulary of every deacon and believer. In order to be a servant, God has set in place these qualifications...

1. The personal qualifications.
2. The spiritual qualifications.
3. The family qualifications.
4. The results or rewards.

Are you willing to pay the price and serve like a deacon? Think about it...the more servants in your church, the more people will be reached and ministered to in the name of Christ.

---

2 Craig B. Larson, Editor. *Illustrations for Preaching & Teaching*, p.260.

1 TIMOTHY 3:8-13

PERSONAL JOURNAL NOTES:
(Reflection & Response)

1. The most important thing that I learned from this lesson was:

2. The area that I need to work on the most is:

3. I can apply this lesson to my life by:

4. Closing Statement of Commitment:

1 Timothy 3:14-16

	III. BEHAVIOR & RELATIONSHIPS IN THE CHURCH, 3:14–6:21	oughtest to behave thyself in the house of God, which is the church of the living God, the pillar and ground of the truth.	the church a. The house of God b. The church of the living God c. The pillar & support of the truth
	A. The Description of the Church, 3:14-16	16 And without controversy great is the mystery of godliness: God was manifest in the flesh, justified in the Spirit, seen of angels, preached unto the Gentiles, believed on in the world, received up into glory.	3. The truth of the church a. Is confessed by all true believers b. Is the mystery of godliness: Six facts
1. The purpose of the Pastoral Epistles—that men might know how they ought to behave in the church 2. The description of	14 These things write I unto thee, hoping to come unto thee shortly: 15 But if I tarry long, that thou mayest know how thou		

Section III
BEHAVIOR AND RELATIONSHIPS IN THE CHURCH
1 Timothy 3:14–6:21

Study 1: THE DESCRIPTION OF THE CHURCH

Text: 1 Timothy 3:14-16

Aim: To gain a greater understanding of the church, about how you should behave in the church.

Memory Verse:
> "Ye also, as lively stones, are built up a spiritual house, and holy priesthood, to offer up spiritual sacrifices, acceptable to God by Jesus Christ" (1 Peter 2:5).

INTRODUCTION:
If the Apostle Paul were caught in a time warp from the first century and found himself in your church, would he recognize anything familiar? Allow your imagination to wander into this possible conversation as you lead Paul on a tour of your church:

> "Paul, on behalf of all of the Christians from our era, we would like to welcome you to the modern, all-improved church. As you walk around, what do you think so far? Do our numbers impress you? How about the size of our facility? Have you had a chance to browse through our information brochure? It will tell you all about the many programs we offer the people of our community."
>
> Waiting to take a long bow for our accomplishments, we were somewhat disturbed by Paul's response. "In the churches of my time," Paul said, "we spent time building relationships in order to really know each other. Our meeting place was from house to house. And our programs, as you call them, were pretty simplified: Love God. Love one another. Love the lost." "Oh" we sighed in embarrassment.

God is not concerned with how big or pretty your church is, how many programs you have, or how fancy your website. God cares about the behavior of believers and relationships within the church. Would He be pleased with *your* church?

This passage begins a new division of subjects in 1 Timothy—the believer's behavior and relationships in the church. This first passage is one of the greatest discussions

1 TIMOTHY 3:14-16

on the church in all of Scripture. It is a passage that every church and believer needs to study and heed.

OUTLINE:
1. The purpose of the Pastoral Epistles: that men might know how they ought to behave in the church (v.14).
2. The description of the church (v.15).
3. The truth of the church (v.16).

1. THE PURPOSE OF THE PASTORAL EPISTLES: THAT MEN MIGHT KNOW HOW THEY OUGHT TO BEHAVE IN THE CHURCH (v.14).

These two verses explain why Paul was writing to Timothy and why he was later to write to Titus and Philemon. In essence these two verses give the very purpose for all the Pastoral Epistles (First and Second Timothy, Titus, and Philemon). Paul was writing to tell believers how they should behave within the church, that is, within the household or family of God. The word "behave" means the conduct, walk, and behavior of a person; but it especially refers to how a person relates to other people. Therefore, the great concern of the Pastoral Epistles is how believers behave in their relationships to God, to each other, and to the unbelievers of the world.

Remember: Timothy was in Ephesus and Paul was writing from Macedonia. Paul hoped to visit Ephesus and Timothy soon, but he was not quite sure that he would be able to leave Macedonia. Therefore, he was spelling out in some detail...

- how Christian believers are to conduct themselves within the church.
- how Christian believers are to behave and witness to a world that is lost and reeling under the weight of corruption and evil.

ILLUSTRATION:
It should never be assumed that fallen man will naturally gravitate upwards. The Christian believer needs constant reminders to learn how to behave as a Christian should.

> *When the jumble around the starting line of a certain yacht race cleared, the helmsman of the leading yacht remarked rather uneasily, "I never expected to find myself in the lead." He made the same remark several times, but his crew told him it was nothing to complain about. As they rounded the first mark, well ahead, he said, "I think we'll have to let [the] boat [behind] pass us." "No we'll not," said the crew, "we're doing fine." "The trouble is," said the helmsman, "that I don't know where to go next. I was so sure there would be other boats in front that I didn't take the trouble to study the course."*
>
> *There are too many Christians who will have a poor place in heaven because they are living their Christian lives like this helmsman. They were meant to be conquerors, but the last shall be first and the first last because they did not study to show themselves approved unto God—workmen that need not be ashamed.* [1]

If you want to know how to behave in the church, the place to begin is in the Word of God. Are you a good student of Scripture, or have you merely been following the crowd?

---

[1] Donald Grey Barnhouse. *Let Me Illustrate*. (Grand Rapids, MI: Fleming H. Revell, 1967), p.47.

1 TIMOTHY 3:14-16

QUESTIONS:
1. What is the key to knowing how to behave in the church? What would happen to your church if every member applied this answer to their own lives?
2. Why do you think many Christians don't know how to behave in the church?
3. Do you understand what is expected of you in the local church? What areas of behavior need to be further developed in your life?

2. THE DESCRIPTION OF THE CHURCH (v.15).

This verse gives a great description of the church, a description that spells out three great pictures of the church.

1. The church is "the household of God." This does not refer to the building of the church, but to the household of the church, to the people of the church. The church is a body of people who have committed themselves to form a family of people, a family centered around God and His Son, the Lord Jesus Christ.

The church is a family of people...
- who believe in God and in His Son, the Lord Jesus Christ.
- who have committed their lives to live for Christ.
- who have based their lives upon the promise of eternal salvation promised by the Lord Jesus Christ.
- who have committed themselves to live as a family with all other believers.

Simply stated, the church is a body of people who have committed their lives to live as the family of God. God is the Father; Jesus Christ is the only begotten Son of the Father; but we, the followers of God, are the adopted children of God. Every person who truly follows God is a true member of the church, that is, of the family of God (Jn.1:12; 2 Co.6:17-18; Ga.4:4-6).

The point is this:
⇒ How should we behave toward our Father?
⇒ How should we behave toward our brothers and sisters?

The answer is found within the family relationship.
   a. The children of a family are to love, obey, and learn from the Father.

> "**He that hath my commandments, and keepeth them, he it is that loveth me: and he that loveth me shall be loved of my Father, and I will love him, and will manifest myself to him**" (Jn.14:21).
>
> "**And Samuel said, Hath the LORD as great delight in burnt offerings and sacrifices, as in obeying the voice of the LORD: Behold, to obey is better than sacrifice, and to hearken than the fat of rams**" (1 S.15:22).

   b. The children of a family are to love and help each other.

> "**A new commandment I give unto you, That ye love one another; as I have loved you, that ye also love one another. By this shall all men know that ye are my disciples, if ye have love one to another**" (Jn.13:34-35).

2. The church is "the church of the living God." The word *church* means an assembly, a gathering, a company of people who have been called out by God. But note: God is the living God; He is not some dead god. He is not some idol or figment of man's

1 Timothy 3:14-16

imagination. He is the living God who is actually alive and is vitally concerned with how men behave and conduct themselves. This means a most significant thing.

God calls people to His church. He calls them to join His assembly, His gathering, His company of people. He is the living God; therefore, He actually speaks to the human heart and calls people to follow Him and to live for Him. But the decision is up to the individual. God loves the person; therefore, He will not force the person to come to Him.

> "For they themselves show of us what manner of entering in we had unto you, and how ye turned to God from idols to serve the living and true God; and to wait for his Son from heaven, whom he raised from the dead, even Jesus, which delivered us from the wrath to come" (1 Th.1:9-10).

ILLUSTRATION:
The Scriptures clearly teach us that "every joint supplies." That being true, when one part of the body is missing, there is a gap. Listen to this striking story set in rural Europe.

> *A traveler in a European village discovered a beautiful custom. At night she saw the people going to the church, each carrying a little bronze lamp. These lamps [were] placed in sockets by their pews. The soft light of the lamps was the only illumination for the service. If a member was absent, there was a dark space!*
> *We do not carry lamps to church, but we do send forth light. When we are absent there is darkness in our stead. The more people at church, the greater the inspiration. Many small lamps together make a great and beautiful light.*
> *The first Christian church in Jerusalem had no building. It had a small membership; it had no officers; it had no pastor; it had no choir or pipe organ; it had no wealth; and, most startling of all, it had no New Testament.*
> *What made it a successful church? Just this: It had the total attendance of its membership. Pentecost was possible because they were all together in one place.* [2]

God invites you to regularly share your light with His body, the church, to be a faithful family member in your church. Are you part of the great and beautiful light, or is there too often darkness in your place where your light should be shining?

3. The church is the pillar and ground of the truth. The church supports the truth just as pillars and ground support a building. The church props and supports the truth, holds together and binds the truth. William Barclay points out that Paul could also be thinking of the meaning of display.[3] Pillars, whether short and small or towering and large, always appear to have an air of stateliness that attracts attention. Therefore, the church is the pillar, the display, the demonstration of the truth that attracts people to Jesus Christ.

The church holds the truth up before a world that misbehaves and dies, yet does not have to die. The church—the family and company of God—is God's instrument upon earth to proclaim the truth to the world. What truth? The glorious truth of the Incarnation—that God has loved the world and has demonstrated His love by sending His Son

---

[2] Selected from *Rev. Ralph V. Gilbert in Southern Churchmen.* Walter B. Knight. *3,000 Illustrations for Christian Service*, p.135.

[3] William Barclay. *The Letters to Timothy, Titus, and Philemon*, p.102.

to save the world (see v.16). This is the glorious truth that the church supports and holds ever so highly before the world.

APPLICATION:
A piercing question is this: How many within the church are really supporting the truth before the world? How many are really holding up the truth by behaving and conducting themselves as they should? How many are holding up the truth by proclaiming it as they should?

> "Therefore whosoever heareth these sayings of mine, and doeth them, I will liken him unto a wise man, which built his house upon a rock: and the rain descended, and the floods came, and the winds blew, and beat upon that house; and it fell not: for it was founded upon a rock" (Mt.7:24-27).

QUESTIONS:
1. Is your church like a family? Is there love, respect, and close relationships among the members?
2. How does this verse drive home the point that the Church of Jesus Christ is unique from that of secular organizations? Whom does your church serve?
3. Does your church stand for the truth or does it sit on the fence of compromise? What events would cause a church to not stand for the truth?

3. THE TRUTH OF THE CHURCH (v.16).

This is one of the great verses of Scripture; it is the glorious truth of the church—the truth that all true believers confess before the world. It is the truth which the church and its believers must never deny, neglect, ignore, or question. It is the only truth that offers hope and salvation for man beyond the grave. Deny and destroy this truth and all are lost and doomed to death forever. Why? Because all man-made and self-proclaimed truths end in the grave. But this truth will never die, for it is the truth of God's unbelievable love, the great "mystery of godliness." What is the mystery of godliness? This is the only reference to it in the Bible, and note the truth of it: it is "without controversy," that is, indisputable, undeniable, beyond any question. It is the truth that all genuine believers confess. And what is being confessed really happened. God has done six wonderful things for man. This is the mystery of godliness, the mystery that has now been revealed to man.

1. "God was manifest [revealed] in the flesh." God actually became a man in the person of Jesus Christ. He actually partook of flesh and blood.
    a. Jesus Christ identified with man perfectly. By becoming Man, He experienced all the trials and sufferings of men; therefore, He is able to succor and deliver men through all the trials of life.

> "For we have not an high priest which cannot be touched with the feeling of our infirmities; but was in all points tempted like as we are, yet without sin. Let us therefore come boldly unto the throne of grace, that we may obtain mercy, and find grace to help in time of need" (He.4:15-16).

    b. Jesus Christ became man in order to take away the sins of men.

1 Timothy 3:14-16

"Who his own self bare our sins in his own body on the tree, that we, being dead to sins, should live unto righteousness: by whose stripes ye were healed" (1 Pe.2:24).

c. Jesus Christ became Man in order to destroy him who had the power of death, that is, Satan.

"Forasmuch then as the children are partakers of flesh and blood, he also himself likewise took part of the same; that through death he might destroy him that had the power of death, that is, the devil; and deliver them who through fear of death were all their lifetime subject to bondage" (He.2:14-15).

APPLICATION:
The Incarnation (God becoming man in the person of Jesus Christ) is indisputable, undeniable, irrefutable. It is a fact: God did come to earth in the person of Jesus Christ.

"And the Word was made flesh, and dwelt among us, (and we beheld his glory, the glory as of the only begotten of the Father,) full of grace and truth" (Jn.1:14).

2. Christ was justified or vindicated in the Spirit. When Christ walked upon earth, He proclaimed this truth: He was the Son of God who had come to earth to save all who would believe Him. But the vast majority of people did not believe Him. They denied, ignored, neglected, rebuked, mocked, questioned, argued against, and cursed Him. Many tried to use Him in order to get what they wanted, and others plotted to murder Him. But He was truly the Son of God; therefore, the Spirit of God vindicated Him; the Spirit of God proved His claims. How? The Spirit of God did three things.

    a. The Spirit of God enabled Christ to live a sinless and perfect life. The one thing that man knows is this: no man can live a sinless life. If a perfect life could ever be lived, it would have to be lived by God Himself as a Man, and this is exactly the point. Christ proved that He was the Son of God by living a sinless and perfect life.

"For he hath made him to be sin for us, who knew no sin; that we might be made the righteousness of God in him" (2 Co.5:21).

"For we have not an high priest which cannot be touched with the feeling of our infirmities; but was in all points tempted like as we are, yet without sin" (He.4:15).

    b. The Spirit of God vindicated Christ by giving Him the power to do the mighty works of God. Christ worked so many miraculous works of healing and ministry that John could only say that the world itself could not contain the books if they had all been recorded (Jn.21:25). The point is this: no man could do the works that Christ did. Only God Himself could perform the kind of miracles Christ did. Therefore, the very works of Christ were proof that He is who He claimed: the Son of God Himself.

"Believe me that I am in the Father, and the Father in me: or else believe me for the very works' sake" (Jn.14:11).

1 TIMOTHY 3:14-16

c. The Spirit of God vindicated Christ by raising Him from the dead. Men killed Him; they crucified Him upon the cross. But He was truly the Son of God; therefore the Spirit of God proved His claim by raising Him up from the dead.

"And declared to be the Son of God with power, according to the spirit of holiness, by the resurrection from the dead" (Ro.1:4).

3. Christ was seen of angels. The angels are heavenly beings who have always seen and beheld Christ. In fact, they are the very ministers of Christ who have been created to carry out His will in the other world, the spiritual world or spiritual dimension of being. Therefore, it is only natural that the angels were involved when Christ came to earth to save man. They were involved...
- in the preparation for His birth (Lu.1:26f)
- in His birth (Lu.2:8, 13)
- in His temptation (Mk.1:13)
- in His trials (Lu.22:43)
- in His resurrection (Mt.28:2f)
- in His ascension (Ac.1:10-11)

Angels are the ministering spirits of Christ who saw all that happened to Him. They saw Christ secure our salvation. The point is this: angels are living beings who have lived with Christ in a real place throughout all of eternity. Therefore, the promise of Christ—that we too shall live with Him eternally—is true. Heaven and angels are real. There is a real world, a spiritual world and dimension of being where God and Christ actually exist.

QUESTIONS:
1. If asked by an unbeliever, how would you explain why the incarnation (when God became a man) took place?
2. Why was it necessary for the Holy Spirit to prove the ministry of Christ?
3. What is God's purpose for His angels and how should we think of them?

4. Christ was preached to the Gentiles, to all the nations of the world. This is a glorious part of the "mystery of godliness": that Jesus Christ came to save all people, even the heathen—those who know absolutely nothing about God, who are immoral, depraved, and corrupted, who are hopeless and helpless in life. Christ is not the exclusive Savior of the Jews nor of any other nation including America. He is the Savior of all people and all nations, both Jew and Gentile alike.

"And this gospel of the kingdom shall be preached in all the world for a witness unto all nations; and then shall the end come" (Mt.24:14).

5. Christ was believed on in the world. This was the very purpose for the Incarnation, the very reason why Jesus Christ had come to earth: that some might believe on Him and be saved to live with God eternally. Note this: when Christ left earth and ascended into heaven, there were only one hundred and twenty who were following Him and who began to share the gospel. But within fifty years every nation of the world had been touched for Christ. Thousands upon thousands had accepted Christ—so many in fact that Paul declared that the gospel had been carried to the ends of the world.

"But now is made manifest, and by the scriptures of the prophets, according to the commandment of the everlasting God, made known to all nations for the obedience of faith" (Ro.16:26).

1 Timothy 3:14-16

The point is this: what is the difference between the witness of the early believers and our witness today? Why were they able to reach so many and we seemingly reach so few? The answer is the truth of this point: belief. They truly believed on Christ; they rested their past, present, and future upon Him. They cast their souls and lives upon Him. They totally committed their lives to Him. They gave Him all they were and had. This kind of belief is missing today. The belief that so many have is a belief *about* Christ: that He is the Savior of the world. However, a belief *about* Christ is not believing *on* or *in* Christ. It is not turning one's life over to Him; not casting one's being—all that one is and has—upon Him.

The glorious "mystery of godliness" is that a person can be saved by believing on Christ—really believing on Him.

> **"For God so loved the world, that he gave his only begotten Son, that whosoever believeth in him should not perish, but have everlasting life" (Jn.3:16).**

6. Christ was received up to glory. This is a reference to the ascension and exaltation of Christ. He has been exalted as the Supreme Majesty of the universe, as Lord of lords, and King of kings. He is the God of the universe who rules and reigns over the universe in glory and majesty, dominion and power. Jesus Christ has completed the great work of salvation. He has been taken back into heaven, back to the very place from which He had come. He sits at the right hand of the Father, and He shall sit upon the throne of heaven until He chooses to return to earth and bring human history to its climactic consummation,

> **"So then after the Lord had spoken unto them, he was received up into heaven, and sat on the right hand of God" (Mk.16:19).**
>
> **"Saying with a loud voice, Worthy is the Lamb that was slain to receive power, and riches, and wisdom, and strength, and honour, and glory, and blessing" (Re.5:12).**

This is the great mystery and godliness now revealed to men.
- ⇒ God was manifested or revealed in the flesh (in the person of Jesus Christ).
- ⇒ Christ was justified or vindicated in the Spirit.
- ⇒ Christ was seen by angels, actually seen by heavenly beings.
- ⇒ Christ was preached to the Gentiles—to all the nations of the world.
- ⇒ Christ was believed on in the world.
- ⇒ Christ was received up and exalted in heaven.

QUESTIONS:
1. God has done six wonderful things for man. What should be your response to what He has done for you?
2. As you think about the six items above, what are your biggest concerns for the modern church today?
3. Regarding these six doctrinal truths, are you living a life of conviction? What can you do in order to improve and share your knowledge in these areas?

1 TIMOTHY 3:14-16

SUMMARY:

Paul probably had a good idea that future Christians would forget the model of the Church that had gone before them. Through these Scriptures, he still reminds today's believers about...

1. The purpose of the Pastoral Epistles: that men might know how they ought to behave in the church.
2. The description of the church.
3. The truth of the church.

PERSONAL JOURNAL NOTES:
(Reflection & Response)

1. The most important thing that I learned from this lesson was:

2. The area that I need to work on the most is:

3. I can apply this lesson to my life by:

4. Closing Statement of Commitment:

1 TIMOTHY 4:1-5

CHAPTER 4

B. The Warning About False Teachers & Their Apostasy, 4:1-5

1. Their appearance, rising up in the latter days of history
2. Their apostasy
   a. Will abandon the faith
   b. Will follow deceiving spirits
   c. Will be hypocritical liars
   d. Will have consciences burned with guilt
3. Their doctrine
   a. The error: Forbids marriage & certain foods
   b. The truth
      1) God has created all things to be received with thanksgiving
      2) All food created by God is good
      3) All food is consecrated by the Word of God & by prayer

Now the Spirit speaketh expressly, that in the latter times some shall depart from the faith, giving heed to seducing spirits, and doctrines of devils;
2 Speaking lies in hypocrisy; having their conscience seared with a hot iron;
3 Forbidding to marry, and commanding to abstain from meats, which God hath created to be received with thanksgiving of them which believe and know the truth.
4 For every creature of God is good, and nothing to be refused, if it be received with thanksgiving:
5 For it is sanctified by the word of God and prayer.

Section III
BEHAVIOR AND RELATIONSHIPS IN THE CHURCH
1 Timothy 3:14–6:21

Study 2: THE WARNING ABOUT FALSE TEACHERS AND THEIR APOSTASY

Text: 1 Timothy 4:1-5

Aim: To recognize the traits of false teachers and sound the warning.

Memory Verse:
> "Now the Spirit speaketh expressly, that in the latter times some shall depart from the faith, giving heed to seducing spirits, and doctrines of devils" (1 Timothy 4:1).

INTRODUCTION:

What can be done to protect Christian believers from the evil tentacles of false teachers? The answer is simpler than you might think: spend a lot of time handling the truth. Dr. Walter Martin gives this illustration:

> *The American Banking Association has a training program....Each year it sends hundreds of bank tellers to Washington in order to teach them to detect counterfeit money, which is a great source of a loss of revenue to the Treasury Department. "It is most interesting that during the entire two-week training program, no teller touches counterfeit money. Only the original passes through his hands. The reason for this is that the American Banking Association is convinced that if a man is thoroughly familiar with the original, he will not be deceived by the counterfeit bill, no matter how much like the original it appears."* [1]

This is a passage that delivers a serious warning to believers—a passage that must be taken ever so seriously by minister and laymen alike. It is the warning about false teachers and their apostasy.

---

[1] Walter R. Martin. *The Kingdom of the Cults*. (Minneapolis, MN: Bethany House Publishers, 1982), p.16.

1 TIMOTHY 4:1-5

OUTLINE:
1. Their appearance, rising up in the latter days of history (v.1).
2. Their apostasy (vv.1-2).
3. Their doctrine (vv.3-5).

1. THEIR APPEARANCE, RISING UP IN THE LATTER DAYS OF HISTORY (v.1).

The phrase "latter times" means a little later on, not far out in the future. That is, false teachers were to arise within the church almost immediately and continue on through our day and on to the end of time. The point is well made: the church and the genuine believer have to be constantly on guard against false teaching. The terrible danger of false teaching always confronts the church and believer. And note: this is a revelation of the Spirit of God Himself. It is not the idea of some preacher seeking recognition because of his novel idea. It is the warning of God's Spirit. The Spirit has spoken in specific terms so that there can be no question about what is being said. False teachers will arise in the latter times.

ILLUSTRATION:
There is a web of conspiracy that has been inspired by the devil. He has no problem finding willing individuals to do his bidding. The scary thing is that his volunteers look a lot like the real thing, the teachers of truth!

> *The story has been told of a conversation between two fallen angels. "Trickster" and "Tempter" returned to their demonic den after another day of destroying people's lives. Sitting at the table, they began to compare their dastardly notes. "What did you do today?" sneered Tempter. With an evil grin, Trickster spoke in arrogant breaths. "I've had a great day. Several of my projects are finally beginning to bear fruit. Today a pastor made the decision to rationalize the miracles in the Bible. A seminary professor has agreed with our master's agenda and is willing to recruit students to worship anyone but Christ. A Sunday school teacher has turned in his teacher's book and has decided to replace the study of the Bible with an 'issues' class."*
>
> *"Why, that's nothing compared to what I've done today!" responded Tempter. "I've convinced the choir director to cut down on worshipful music and to use popular music instead to appeal to a broader crowd. And he has found a verse in the Bible to justify what he is doing. I've also been at work in the heart of the pastor of another church. I've convinced him that he is the reason for the success of the church and that he can take the church anywhere he wants to go. He is going to be a wonderful pawn in our hands."*
>
> *All of a sudden the door blew open and Satan stood basking in his evil light. "I overheard what you have done. But that is not enough! Get back to work...NOW!"*

Satan stays busy placing false teachers into key places of influence. He never lets up in his war of deception. Neither can we let up in carrying forth the truth.

QUESTIONS:
1. Are there any false teachers living in your generation?
2. What are some characteristics that have brought the false teachers to light?
3. What can you do to guard yourself from the schemes of false teachers?

1 TIMOTHY 4:1-5

2. THEIR APOSTASY (vv.1-2).

The apostasy of the false teachers is serious, so serious that it should make us search our hearts. False teachers commit four tragic errors.

1. False teachers abandon the faith. Note: they are within the church, within the field of religion. This passage is not dealing with the philosophies and false teachings taught by the unbelievers out in the world. It is talking about false teachers within the church itself. The Spirit of God is warning us: some preachers and some teachers will turn away from the faith and become false teachers. They will turn away from the Lord Jesus Christ, away from the death and resurrection of the Lord Jesus.

> "For I delivered unto you first of all that which I also received, how that Christ died for our sins according to the scriptures; and that he was buried, and that he rose again the third day according to the scriptures" (1 Co.15:3-4).

APPLICATION:
There is only one true faith that can save a person. A person can have all kinds of faith and he can have faith in all kinds of people, things, and religions. But only one faith can save a person: the faith in God's Son, the Lord Jesus Christ. This is the faith from which a person must never depart.

> "Jesus saith unto him, I am the way, the truth, and the life: no man cometh unto the Father, but by me" (Jn.14:6).

2. False teachers give attention to seducing spirits and teachings of devils. There are all kinds of evil spirits throughout the world, spirits that are set on seducing and deceiving people. They are set on leading people to follow them and their ideas and teachings. They do all they can to turn people away from the doctrine and faith of Christ. And note: the method they use is not a frontal attack, not a clear or loud declaration against the truth. They mix some truth with error. Their method is to...

- seduce
- deceive
- delude
- lure
- entice
- attract
- persuade
- charm
- appear as light and truth

> "For such are false apostles, deceitful workers, transforming themselves into the apostles of Christ. And no marvel; for Satan himself is transformed into an angel. Therefore it is no great thing if his ministers also be transformed as the ministers of righteousness; whose end shall be according to their works" (2 Co.11:13-15).

3. False teachers speak lies in hypocrisy. Very simply, they teach something different from what the Scripture says, and they know it. They know they are not teaching what Scripture says. In fact, some false teachers take pride in their stand against what they call "a literal interpretation" of Scripture. Some even mock and poke fun at those who believe and hold to the truth of Scripture. But note what is so often overlooked:

⇒ "Speaking lies" means speaking and teaching what is contrary to Scripture. This is exactly what Scripture is declaring. In the eyes of Scripture, a lie is a teaching that is contrary to the teaching of Scripture.

⇒ "In hypocrisy" means the teacher knows that he is teaching contrary to Scripture. He claims to be a minister or teacher of God, Christ, and the Word (Scripture), and yet he teaches something contrary to what Scripture says. A hypocrite is a person who claims to be one thing but he is something else.

1 Timothy 4:1-5

The point is this: the false teacher is a person who speaks lies in hypocrisy. He denies, refutes, or ignores what Scripture says and he knows it; yet he claims to be a minister or teacher of Christ and the gospel. This is the person who is an instrument or tool of some seducing and deceptive spirit, who teaches the doctrines of evil spirits.

> "Ye hypocrites, well did Esaias prophesy of you, saying, This people draweth nigh unto me with their mouth, and honoureth me with their lips; but their heart is far from me. But in vain they do worship me, teaching for doctrines the commandments of men" (Mt.15:7-9).
>
> "They profess that they know God; but in works they deny him, being abominable, and disobedient, and unto every good work reprobate" (Tit.1:16).

APPLICATION:
William Barclay has an excellent statement on men becoming tools of Satan and evil spirits.

> *It was from these evil spirits and demons that...false teaching came. But though it came from the demons, it came through men.... Now here is the threatening and the terrible thing. We know that God and God's Spirit are everywhere looking for men to use. God is always searching for men who will be His instruments, His weapons, His tools in the world. But here we come face to face with the terrible fact that the forces of evil are also looking for men to use. Just as God seeks men for His purposes, the forces of evil seek men for their purposes. Here is the terrible responsibility of manhood. Man can accept the service of God, or the service of the devil. Man can become an instrument of the Supreme Good or the Supreme Evil. Men are faced with the eternal choice—to whom are we to give our lives, to God or to God's enemy? Are we to decide to be used by God, or are we to decide to be used by the devil?* [2]

4. False teachers have consciences that are seared, that is, cauterized, hardened, and insensitive. It does not bother most false teachers to teach contrary to the truth of Scripture. They can ignore and deny the Scripture and present their own ideas and it does not bother them at all. They are totally insensitive to the preachings and convictions of God's Spirit. They have no conscience and no remorse about twisting the Scriptures and the truth about Christ. They are completely past feeling any kind of movement from God's Spirit.

> "For the heart of this people is waxed gross, and their ears are dull of hearing, and their eyes have they closed; lest they should see with their eyes, and hear with their ears, and understand with their heart, and should be converted, and I should heal them" (Ac.28:27).
>
> "He that being often reproved hardeneth his neck, shall suddenly be destroyed, and that without remedy" (Pr.29:1).

QUESTIONS:
1. Where is the most *logical* place for Satan to plant his false teachers?
2. What types of things should believers beware of and look for in its preachers and teachers?
3. What happens to the conscience of a false teacher?
4. Once a false teacher has seared his conscience, is it too late for him to repent? Why?

---

[2] William Barclay. *The Letters to Timothy, Titus, and Philemon*, p.107.

1 TIMOTHY 4:1-5

3. THEIR DOCTRINE (vv.3-5).

The doctrine of the false teachers is also serious, so serious that it too should make us search our hearts.

1. The particular doctrine confronting the church at Ephesus was Gnosticism. The Gnostics felt that what really mattered in life was the spirit of man; the spirit was the only good thing in the world. Everything else in the world—all physical and material substances including the human body—was corruptible and evil. Therefore, man's task upon earth was to deny self and avoid the things of the world and to control the body as much as possible. How? By denying the body as many things as possible. Note: in the church at Ephesus, the two things being denied and forbidden were eating of meat and marriage. Some were teaching that a person could get closer to God and please Him more by being a vegetarian and by remaining single. By being free of family duties, the person could concentrate on God more.

Note one other fact about Gnosticism that is not covered in this passage but is of extreme importance. Some Gnostics took the opposite view. Since the spirit is all that matters, the body and the world do not matter. Therefore, man can do what he likes physically. He can satisfy his passions, lusts, urges, and instincts—just so he takes good care of his spirit.

Every generation has its Gnostics, people who teach the false doctrines of extreme discipline or asceticism and those who teach the false doctrines of loose living (license and indulgence).

⇒ There are those who concentrate upon the body and its health. They seek to overcome the evil, that is, the corruption, disease, aging, and dying of the body as much as possible. Some exercise and exercise and others become vegetarians—all struggling against the aging, weakening, and dying of the body.

⇒ There are even those today who feel they can become closer to God and more spiritual by not marrying and by eating no meat. (But remember what Scripture has just said: it is best for the minister and leaders of the church to be married. See 1 Ti.3:2-13.)

⇒ There are those who live as they please—eating, drinking, partying, indulging, and living extravagantly—all doing their own thing.

The point to see is this: each gives attention to their spirit and worship only as they wish, only as much as they feel is necessary to keep their spirit in tune with God. But note: their concentration is the body and its pleasure. In one case the pleasure is the exhilaration of discipline and control; in the other case the exhilaration is the stimulating of the flesh through partying and possessions.

> **"Wherefore if ye be dead with Christ from the rudiments of the world, why, as though living in the world, are ye subject to ordinances, (touch not; taste not; handle not; which all are to perish with the using;) after the commandments and doctrines of men? Which things have indeed a show of wisdom in will worship, and humility, and neglecting of the body; not in any honour to the satisfying of the flesh" (Co.2:20-23).**

ILLUSTRATION:
To be self-sacrificing sounds very religious. But the real test is found in who or what is being glorified or honored. Is it selfless or selfish? Listen to Aesop's Fable, *The Mouse and the Frog*.

1 TIMOTHY 4:1-5

On an ill-fated day a mouse made the acquaintance of a frog, and they set off on their travels together. The frog pretended to be very fond of the mouse and invited him to visit the pond in which he lived. To keep his companion out of harm's way, the frog tied the mouse's front foot to his own hind leg, and thus they proceeded for some distance by land. When they came to the pond, the frog told the mouse to trust him and be brave as he began swimming across the water. But, no sooner had they reached the middle of the pond than the frog suddenly plunged to the bottom, dragging the unfortunate mouse after him. Now the struggling and floundering mouse made such a great commotion in the water that he managed to attract the attention of a hawk, who pounced upon the mouse and carried him away to be devoured. Since the frog was still tied to the mouse, he shared the same fate of his companion and was justly punished for his treachery.

Beware of false teachers who pretend to look out for your good. When they reap what they sow, you do not want to be part of the harvest!
2. Note how the truth destroys this life-style and teaching.
   a. God has created all things to be received with thanksgiving. And note: all things can be received even by believers, by all who believe and know the truth.
   b. All food that has been created by God is good and is not to be refused, if the believer can give thanks for it.
   c. All food is sanctified or set apart by the Word of God and prayer. If the food is approved by God's Word or can be prayed about and approved by God's Spirit, then the believer can partake of it without any qualm of conscience.

Wycliffe Bible Commentary gives an excellent comment on this point:

The principles governing the right use...of this life are: (a) God is the Creator and his creation is good; (b) He created food for men, and those who believe and know the truth about eternal salvation will have the right attitude toward the necessities of this life, and will neither deify the created thing nor degrade and despise it, but will accept it thankfully as the Father's wise provision.[3]

"Therefore take no thought, saying, What shall we eat? or, What shall we drink? or, Wherewithal shall we be clothed? (For after all these things do the Gentiles seek:) for your heavenly Father knoweth that ye have need of all these things. But seek ye first the kingdom of God, and his righteousness; and all these things shall be added unto you" (Mt.6:31-33).

QUESTIONS:
1. What revealing characteristics can you spot in the teaching of a false teacher?
2. What can you do that will help you to recognize false teaching?
3. As you think about the doctrines of false teachers, what are your biggest concerns for the churches in your nation? For your own church?
4. Can you explain the fallacy of the false doctrine of Gnosticism? What influences has this false doctrine made in the modern Church?

---

[3] *Quoted from First and Second Timothy, Titus.* "The New Testament and Wycliffe Bible Commentary," ed. by Charles F. Pfeiffer and Everett F. Harrison. (Produced for Moody Monthly by the Iversen Associates, NY, 1971), p.854.

1 TIMOTHY 4:1-5

SUMMARY:

The best way to protect yourself from false teachers and their apostasy is to *know* the truth, the truth of God's Holy Word. Once you know the truth, the counterfeit will become apparent. Paul reminds you of the fingerprints of the false teacher and warns you about...

1. Their appearance, rising up in the latter days of history.
2. Their apostasy.
   a. They will abandon the faith.
   b. They will follow deceiving spirits.
   c. They will be hypocritical liars.
   d. They will have their consciences burned with guilt.
3. Their doctrine.
   a. The error: Forbids marriage and certain foods.
   b. The truth.
      1) God has created all things to be received with thanksgiving.
      2) All food created by God is good.
      3) All food is consecrated by the Word of God and by prayer.

PERSONAL JOURNAL NOTES:
(Reflection & Response)

1. The most important thing that I learned from this lesson was:

2. The area that I need to work on the most is:

3. I can apply this lesson to my life by:

4. Closing Statement of Commitment:

1 Timothy 4:6-16

Outline		Scripture	Outline
	C. The Young Minister (Charge 2): To Be a Good Minister, 4:6-16	iour of all men, specially of those that believe.	b. Because God saves
1. He instructs believers concerning false teachers, vv. 1-5	6 If thou put the brethren in remembrance of these things, thou shalt be a good minister of Jesus Christ, nourished up in the words of faith and of good doctrine, whereunto thou hast attained.	11 These things command and teach. 12 Let no man despise thy youth; but be thou an example of the believers, in word, in conversation, in charity, in spirit, in faith, in purity.	7. He commands & teaches these things 8. He is an example to believers a. An example despite his young age b. An example to all believers
2. He nourishes himself in the truths of the faith & of doctrine			
3. He avoids frivolous speculations	7 But refuse profane and old wives' fables, and exercise thyself rather unto godliness.	13 Till I come, give attendance to reading, to exhortation, to doctrine. 14 Neglect not the gift that is in thee, which was given thee by prophecy, with the laying on of the hands of the presbytery.	9. He devotes himself to public worship 10. He does not neglect his gift a. Supernaturally given b. Humanly recognized & ordained
4. He exercises to become more godly a. Physical exercise is good b. Spiritual godliness is better	8 For bodily exercise profiteth little: but godliness is profitable unto all things, having promise of the life that now is, and of that which is to come.	15 Meditate upon these things; give thyself wholly to them; that thy profiting may appear to all.	11. He meditates & is diligent in giving himself wholly to the Scripture
5. He is a man of reason & of purpose	9 This is a faithful saying and worthy of all acceptation.	16 Take heed unto thyself, and unto the doctrine; continue in them: for in doing this thou shalt both save thyself, and them that hear thee.	12. He guards himself & his teaching a. To persevere in the faith b. The purpose: To save himself & the hearers
6. He is a man who works & strives—willingly & laboriously a. Because God lives	10 For therefore we both labour and suffer reproach, because we trust in the living God, who is the Sav-		

(Note: Because of the length of this outline and commentary, you may wish to split the passage into two or three studies.)

Section III
BEHAVIOR AND RELATIONSHIPS IN THE CHURCH
1 Timothy 3:14–6:21

Study 3: THE YOUNG MINISTER (CHARGE 2): TO BE A GOOD MINISTER

Text: 1 Timothy 4:6-16

Aim: To make a strong commitment: To become a good servant of Jesus Christ.

Memory Verse:
> "Take heed unto thyself, and unto the doctrine; continue in them: for in doing this thou shalt both save thyself, and them that hear thee" (1 Timothy 4:16).

1 Timothy 4:6-16

INTRODUCTION:
Exactly what is it that makes a person a *good minister*? Is it the number of degrees that hang on his wall. Is it where he went to school? Does his denominational choice (or lack of a denomination) make him a good minister? Or the books and files in his library? How about his willingness to visit people in the church?

All of these are good things, but in and of themselves they do not have the power to make a minister good. A minister who wants to be good makes a quality decision at the foot of the cross and applies the commands of Scripture to his life. He takes seriously the charge of God to strive for godliness, and that godliness is what makes a minister good.

This is one of the greatest pictures of the minister painted by Scripture. It is an excellent description of just what makes a minister a "good minister" (v.6). Note: this is the second charge given to the young minister Timothy. The minister is given the strong charge: be a good minister.

OUTLINE:
1. He instructs believers concerning false teachers (vv.1-5).
2. He nourishes himself in the truths of the faith and of doctrine (v.6).
3. He avoids frivolous speculations (v.7).
4. He exercises himself to godliness (v.8).
5. He is a man of reason and of purpose (v.9).
6. He is a man who works and suffers reproach—willingly and laboriously (v.10).
7. He commands and teaches these things (v.11).
8. He is an example to the believers (v.12).
9. He devotes himself to public worship (v.13).
10. He does not neglect the gift that is in him (v.14).
11. He meditates and wholly gives himself to the instructions of Scripture—to bear witness (v.15).
12. He guards himself and his teaching (v.16).

1. HE INSTRUCTS BELIEVERS CONCERNING FALSE TEACHERS (vv.1-5).

"These things" (v.6) refers to the previous passage which warns believers to guard against false teachers (v.1-5). A good minister does all he can to lift up Jesus Christ and to warn his flock about false teachers, about those who will try to seduce and lead them astray. The point is this: false teaching is such a threat to the church and believers, the good minister of Jesus Christ will use every method of communication he can to instruct and protect his flock from being seduced by false teachers.

> "Wherefore I will not be negligent to put you always in remembrance of these things, though ye know them, and be established in the present truth. Yea, I think it meet, as long as I am in this tabernacle, to stir you up by putting you in remembrance; knowing that shortly I must put off this my tabernacle, even as our Lord Jesus Christ hath showed me. Moreover I will endeavour that ye may be able after my decease to have these things always in remembrance. For we have not followed cunningly devised fables, when we made known unto you the power and coming of our Lord Jesus Christ, but were eyewitnesses of his majesty" (2 Pe.1:12-16).

1 TIMOTHY 4:6-16

QUESTIONS:
1. Have you been warned in your church about false teachers? What have you done in order to prevent their influence in your life?
2. As you think about false teachers, what are your biggest concerns for the members of your church? For you?
3. How can you be sure that a false teacher will not be able to influence the members of your church?

2. HE NOURISHES HIMSELF IN THE TRUTHS OF THE FAITH AND OF DOCTRINE (v.6).

Note that the Greek uses the definite article "*the* faith." This means the teachings of the Word of God. True doctrines are doctrines which are based upon the Scriptures. No doctrine is true (or Christian) that is not based upon the Scriptures.

Timothy had been nourished upon the Scripture from earliest childhood (2 Ti.3:15), and he had continued to feed upon the Word of God. Paul was now encouraging him to continue the practice, for a good minister is a minister who feeds upon the Scriptures day by day.

> **"Study to show thyself approved unto God, a workman that needeth not to be ashamed, rightly dividing the word of truth" (2 Ti.2:15).**

ILLUSTRATION:
A wise minister, in fact, any believer, should know how to nourish his spirit by feeding on the food that will build him up. Nothing should ever be substituted for the Word of God, not if a person wishes to grow in Christ and minister to the needs of a lost and dying world.

> *The story is told of a cow that grew bored with the fenced-in grazing fields. He thought to himself, "I've fed off this pasture my whole life. I feel like a prisoner in this field...the grass sure does look greener on the other side."*
>
> *As he probed the fence, he discovered a place where he could finally get through. With a hardy shove of his shoulder he was on the other side. Once there, he came eye-to-eye with another cow. "What brings you over here?" said the cow to his visitor. "I've come to try the grass on your side." "That's funny. I was just on my way to try the grass on your side. The grass over here is artificial. It looks real pretty until you try to take a bite!"*

There are a lot of artificial substitutes available on the market today. Don't settle for anything less than the best, the Word of God.

QUESTIONS:
1. What kind of spiritual diet are you on? Which of the following best describes your Bible reading experience?
   ⇒ I've read it from cover to cover.
   ⇒ I'm like a moth; I've put holes in different parts.
   ⇒ I've high-lighted the good parts and ignored the rest
   ⇒ What Bible? It's got to be here somewhere
2. When it comes to feeding on God's Word, what plans do you have to help you grow spiritually?

1 TIMOTHY 4:6-16

3. HE AVOIDS FRIVOLOUS SPECULATIONS (v.7).

The good minister avoids frivolous speculations, rejects profane tales and old wives fables. What a description of false teaching! The good minister rejects all false teachings, which are nothing more than the frivolous speculations and false notions of men.

> "I charge thee therefore before God, and the Lord Jesus Christ, who shall judge the quick and the dead at his appearing and his kingdom; preach the word; be instant in season, out of season; reprove, rebuke, exhort with all longsuffering and doctrine. For the time will come when they will not endure sound doctrine; but after their own lusts shall they heap to themselves teachers, having itching ears; and they shall turn away their ears from the truth, and shall be turned unto fables" (2 Ti.4:1-4).

QUESTIONS:
1. Can you identify an example of frivolous speculation?
2. What does this verse teach you about keeping on course?
3. What can you do to refute someone's false notions and take control of the situation?

4. HE EXERCISES TO BECOME MORE GODLY (v.8).

The minister is compared to an athlete in these two verses. Note two things.

1. The minister is to exercise himself in godliness as much as an Olympic athlete exercises his body. How much energy, effort, time, and dedication does an Olympic athlete put into his training? His sport is his life—unequivocally so. So it is with the minister: godliness is to be his life. All of his energy, effort, time, and dedication are to be given over to godliness. The minister is to know no exercise but the exercise of godliness.

> "Seeing then that all these thing shall be dissolved, what manner of persons ought ye to be in all holy conversation and godliness" (2 Pe.3:11).

2. Bodily exercise is profitable, but godliness is more profitable, far more profitable. The minister should exercise his body regularly; he should keep himself physically fit. But the focus of his life is to be godliness. The reason is clear: godliness bears fruit—great fruit—both in this life and in the life to come. God promises to bless the godly person now while he walks upon this earth, and eternally when he receives the life to come.

> "But godliness with contentment is great gain" (1 Ti.6:6).
>
> "Blessed is the man that walketh not in the counsel of the ungodly, nor standeth in the way of sinners, nor sitteth in the seat of the scornful. But his delight is in the law of the LORD; and in his law doth he meditate day and night. And he shall be like a tree planted by the rivers of water, that bringeth forth his fruit in his season; his leaf also shall not wither; and whatsoever he doeth shall prosper" (Ps.1:1-3).

ILLUSTRATION:
As believers, we live in a constant spiritual tension. On one hand, we need to be good stewards of our bodies, of the temple that God has provided for us to live

1 TIMOTHY 4:6-16

in. But on the other hand, as Martin Luther once said, the believer only *dwells* in the flesh but does not *live* in it. Therefore, we must pursue godliness and inner spiritual maturity.

> *Eric was a professional football player whose body was like granite. From his youth, he was committed to exercise and to excellence on the field of competition. In the eyes of the world Eric had it made. But he wisely knew there was much more to life than scoring touchdowns.*
>
> *Eric's earlier encounter with Jesus Christ had challenged him to work just as hard getting his spiritual life in shape. He later felt a leading from the Lord to become a pastor, and as his spirit matured, so did his witness and boldness. The urban streets of his city became his personal parish. For example, he would often put on a display for the kids in a neighborhood. In a powerful demonstration of physical versus spiritual strength, he would break free from a set of handcuffs. Then he would explain how Jesus Christ gave him the power to break free from the sin that had held him in shackles.*

What is the focus of exercise in your life? You must carefully balance the physical and spiritual to be sure that the fruit you bear is first of all godliness.

QUESTIONS:
1. Is it easier for you to nourish the physical or the spiritual. Why?
2. Are there any areas of your life that need more godly attention? If yes, then which ones?
3. Why do some people not take care of their bodies? What do you do to stay in physical shape?
4. Why do some people not take care of their souls? What do you do in order to keep your soul in shape?

5. HE IS A MAN OF REASON AND OF PURPOSE (v.9).

The good minister knows this:
⇒ the instructions to him are trustworthy.
⇒ the instructions to him deserve his complete acceptance.

Therefore, he commits his life to do exactly what Scripture charges him to do. The good minister is a man of reason and of purpose, a man who understands and knows and commits his life to live as God says. It is the very fact that distinguishes the minister as good.

> **"It is a faithful saying: For if we be dead with him, we shall also live with him: if we suffer, we shall also reign with him: if we deny him, he also will deny us: if we believe not, yet he abideth faithful: he cannot deny himself" (2 Ti.2:11-13).**

QUESTIONS:
1. Have you ever added your own interpretation to what God says in His Word, or are you satisfied that what God says is totally trustworthy?
2. Are you committed to all of God's Word: Committed to do all that God says or to do only what you want to do?
3. Has God ever led you to do anything that was not good for you? Or in your best interest?

1 TIMOTHY 4:6-16

6. HE IS A MAN WHO WORKS AND STRIVES—WILLINGLY AND LABORIOUSLY (v.10).

The word "work" means arduous labor, strenuous work. The good minister labors and works to the point of fatigue and exhaustion, to the point that he can go no further. He exerts every ounce of energy and effort in his body for the sake of God and Christ. And note: he is even willing to suffer reproach for Christ. He continues to minister even when men ridicule, revile, mock, curse, and persecute him. Why?

⇒ Because God is the living God. The minister's work and message are based upon the truth; what he is doing is truth. It is all for the living God.
⇒ Because Jesus Christ is the Savior of all men. All men can be saved, actually delivered from the grip of sin, death, and condemnation.

Therefore the good minister must labor, no matter the reproach. He must share the glorious news: man can now be reconciled to God and live forever.

> "Therefore, my beloved brethren, be ye stedfast, unmoveable, always abounding in the work of the Lord, forasmuch as ye know that your labour is not in vain in the Lord" (1 Co.15:58).
> "And let us not be weary in well doing: for in due season we shall reap, if we faint not. As we have therefore opportunity, let us do good unto all men, especially unto them who are of the household of faith" (Ga.6:9-10).

QUESTIONS:
1. What is the relationship between working for the gospel and suffering for the gospel?
2. Why do some people tend to think that if someone is suffering, that person is out of God's will?
3. Do you ever experience feelings of discouragement when your work for the gospel is opposed? What kind of an attitude are you to keep?

7. HE COMMANDS AND TEACHES THESE THINGS (v.11).

He preaches and teaches with authority. This is the very reason God has called the minister: to command and teach the Word of God with the very authority of God. Therefore, the good minister is a minister who boldly declares the Word of God and the commandments of God. He does not allow the fear of men nor the danger of hardship to stop him. He has been commissioned by the Lord and he stands in the strength of the Lord. Therefore, he knows that the Lord will deliver him through all the dangers of life if he will only be faithful, if he will courageously declare the Word and the commandments of God.

> "Preach the word; be instant in season, out of season; reprove, rebuke, exhort with all longsuffering and doctrine" (2 Ti.4:2).

ILLUSTRATION:
In witnessing, the fear of man is probably the most difficult factor for the Christian to overcome. Will he listen to me? Will he slam the door in my face? Will he laugh at me? Will he be offended? And so on. This timely story is taken from the pages of American history.

1 TIMOTHY 4:6-16

> *Peter Cartwright, a nineteenth-century, circuit riding, Methodist preacher, was an uncompromising man. One Sunday morning when he was to preach, he was told that President Andrew Jackson was in the congregation, and was warned not to say anything out of line.*
>
> *When Cartwright stood to preach, he said, "I understand that Andrew Jackson is here. I have been requested to be guarded in my remarks. Andrew Jackson will go to hell if he doesn't repent."*
>
> *The congregation was shocked and wondered how the President would respond. After the service, President Jackson shook hands with Peter Cartwright and said, "Sir, if I had a regiment of men like you, I could whip the world."* [1]

Are you more interested in guarding your remarks than you are in leading people to Christ?

QUESTIONS:
1. How confident are you when you witness? What is the key to boldness?
2. What causes you to fear the judgment of men? What can you do to overcome these things?
3. What is the authority behind your witness? Why is it important for you to be bound to this authority?

8. HE IS AN EXAMPLE TO BELIEVERS (v.12).

Timothy was a young man; therefore, there was the possibility that some in the church would have difficulty in accepting his ministry. How could he overcome the opposition to his being so young? There was only one way: he had to prove that he was mature well beyond his years. He had to live a mature life, a life that would be an example to the believers.

1. He was to be an example in word: in what he said and in the way he said it. He had to control his conversation and tongue at all times, no matter the opposition.

> **"Let your speech be always with grace, seasoned with salt, that ye may know how ye ought to answer every man" (Co.4:6).**
>
> **"Pleasant words are as a honeycomb, sweet to the soul, and health to the bones" (Pr.16:24).**

2. He was to be an example in behavior. His conduct was to be disciplined and controlled. He was to demonstrate that he was a true follower and leader of the Lord, that he was living for the Lord in all godliness and righteousness.

> **"That ye may approve things that are excellent; that ye may be sincere and without offence till the day of Christ" (Ph.1:10).**

3. He was to be an example in love. The kind of love which the believer is to have for all people is agape love, the great love of God Himself. The meaning of agape love is more clearly seen by contrasting it with the various kinds of love. There are essentially four kinds of love. Whereas the English language has only one word for love to describe all the affectionate experiences of men, the Greek language had a different word to describe each kind of love or affectionate experience.

    a. There is passionate love or *eros* love. This is the physical love between sexes; the patriotic love of a person for his nation; the ambition of a person for

---

[1] Craig B. Larson, Editor. *Illustrations for Preaching & Teaching*, p.42.

1 TIMOTHY 4:6-16

power, wealth, or fame. Briefly stated, eros love is the base love of a man that arises from his own inner passion. Sometimes eros love is focused upon good and other times it is focused upon bad. It should be noted that eros love is never used in the New Testament.

b. There is affectionate love or *storge* love. This is the kind of love that exists between parent and child and between loyal citizens and a trustworthy ruler. Storge love is also not used in the New Testament.

c. There is an endearing love or *phileo* love. Phileo love is the love of a husband and wife for each other, of a brother for a brother, of a friend for the dearest of friends. It is the love that cherishes, that holds someone or something ever so dear to one's heart.

d. There is selfless and sacrificial love or *agape* love. Agape love is the love of the mind, of the reason, of the will. It is the love that goes so far...
- that it loves a person even if he does not deserve to be loved
- that it actually loves the person who is utterly unworthy of being loved

Note four significant points about agape love.

1) Selfless or agape love is the love of God, the very love possessed by God Himself. It is the love demonstrated in the cross of Christ.
   ⇒ It is the love of God for the ungodly.

   "For when we were yet without strength, in due time Christ died for the ungodly" (Ro.5:6).

   ⇒ It is the love of God for unworthy sinners.

   "But God commendeth his love toward us, in that, while we were yet sinners, Christ died for us" (Ro.5:8).

   ⇒ It is the love of God for undeserving enemies.

   "For if, when we were enemies, we were reconciled to God by the death of his Son, much more, being reconciled, we shall be saved by his life" (Ro.5:10).

2) Selfless or agape love is a gift of God. It can be experienced only if a person knows God personally—only if a person has received the love of God into his heart and life. Agape love has to be shed abroad (poured out, flooded, spread about) by the Spirit of God within the heart of a person.

   "And hope maketh not ashamed; because the love of God is shed abroad in our hearts by the Holy Ghost which is given unto us" (Ro.5:5).

3) Selfless or agape love is the greatest thing in all of life according to the Lord Jesus Christ.

   "And Jesus answered him, The first of all the commandments is, Hear, O Israel; The Lord our God is one Lord: and thou shalt love the Lord thy God with all thy heart, and with all thy soul, and with all thy mind, and with all thy strength: this is the first commandment. And the second is like, namely this, Thou shalt love thy neighbour as thyself. There is none other commandment greater than these" (Mk.12:29-31).

4) Selfless or agape love is the greatest possession and gift in human life according to the Scripture (1 Co.13:1-13).

> **"And now abideth faith, hope, charity, these three; but the greatest of these is charity" (1 Co.13:13).**

4. He was to be an example in the spirit. He was to walk being led by the Spirit and keeping his mind upon spiritual things. It means "spiritual-mindedness."[2]

> **"For they that are after the flesh do mind the things of the flesh; but they that are after the Spirit the things of the Spirit" (Ro.8:5).**

5. He was to be an example in faith, that is, in faithfulness. He was to be loyal to the Lord Jesus and the church regardless of the demands, hardships, temptations, trials, or opposition. Imagine! No matter what the circumstance, the good minister is faithful and loyal.

> **"He that is faithful in that which is least is faithful also in much: and he that is unjust in the least is unjust also in much" (Lu.16:10).**

6. He was to be an example in purity. He was to live a moral, clean, just, and honest life. He was to be free—completely free—of coveting, lusting, worldliness, self-seeking, immorality, and all other known sins. He was to live a life of purity that far exceeded the standards of the world. His heart and life were to be pure—perfectly pure.

> **"Blessed are the pure in heart: for they shall see God" (Mt.5:8).**

QUESTIONS:
1. What kind of example do others see in your life? Does your life lead others to Christ?
2. How can you keep your mind on spiritual things?
3. Why is it important for you to be faithful even during hardships?
4. Whose standards should you follow? Whose do you follow? Why?

9. HE DEVOTES HIMSELF TO PUBLIC WORSHIP (v.13).

There are three things in particular to which he publicly devotes himself: the reading, exhortation, and teaching of Scripture and its doctrine. Note what the major task of the minister is as he stands in the pulpit:
- ⇒ He is to read the Scripture.
- ⇒ He is to exhort and teach the doctrines of Scripture.

> **"Holding fast the faithful word as he hath been taught, that he may be able by sound doctrine both to exhort and to convince the gainsayers" (Tit.1:9).**
> **"These things speak, and exhort, and rebuke with all authority. Let no man despise thee" (Tit.2:15).**

---

[2] Matthew Henry. *Matthew Henry's Commentary*, p.821.

1 Timothy 4:6-16

QUESTIONS:
1. Is God's Word preached and taught from the pulpit in your church? What difference does this make in your church? In you?
2. If God's Word is ever compromised from the pulpit, what is the natural result?

10. HE DOES NOT NEGLECT HIS GIFT (v.14).

This refers to the spiritual gift, the special anointing given him by the Holy Spirit to be a minister. Note that the gift had been received through both prophecy and the laying on of hands by other elders or ministers of the church.

To neglect the gift is dangerous, for it means that a minister fails to do his duty. It means that he is unfaithful and stands before God as an unfaithful minister.

> "And he gave some, apostles; and some, prophets; and some, evangelists; and some, pastors and teachers; for the perfecting of the saints, for the work of the ministry, for the edifying of the body of Christ" (Ep.4:11-12).

QUESTIONS:
1. Are you neglecting any gifts that God has given you? How can you cultivate the gifts that He has entrusted to you?
2. Share a time when you used your gift and someone else was blessed, or you were blessed by someone else's gift. How did it make you feel?

11. HE MEDITATES AND IS DILIGENT IN GIVING HIMSELF WHOLLY TO THE SCRIPTURE (v.15).

1. The good minister meditates upon the Word of God. He lives, eats, and drinks the Scripture and its instructions. And he meditates upon the application of the Scripture to his people. He holds the Bible in one hand and the daily newspaper in the other so as to apply the Scripture to the needs of the day. William Barclay has an excellent statement:

> "The great danger of the Christian leader is intellectual sloth and the shut mind. The danger is that he forgets to study and allows his thoughts to run in well-worn grooves. The danger is that he never gets outside the orbit of a limited number of favorite ideas. The danger is that new truths, new methods, the attempt to restate the faith in contemporary terms comes merely to irritate and to annoy him. The Christian leader must be a Christian thinker or he fails in his task; and to be a Christian thinker is to be an adventurous thinker so long as life lasts."[3]

> "Casting down imaginations, and every high thing that exalteth itself against the knowledge of God, and bringing into captivity every thought to the obedience of Christ" (2 Co.10:5).

---

[3] William Barclay. *The Letters to Timothy, Titus, and Philemon*, p.117-118.

1 TIMOTHY 4:6-16

QUESTIONS:
1. On a normal day, how much do you meditate on the Word of God:
    ⇒ Several hours
    ⇒ Several minutes
    ⇒ A few seconds here and there
    ⇒ No, to be truthful, I seldom if ever meditate on the Word of God
2. How can you develop the habit of meditating on God's Word?
3. What benefits await the Christian believer who frequently meditates on the Word of God?

12. HE GUARDS HIMSELF AND HIS TEACHING (v.16).

The words "take heed" mean to keep a strict eye upon or to keep on paying attention to oneself and to one's teaching.
   ⇒ He guards his body, keeps it both morally and physically fit. He flees the temptations that assault and seduce him; he controls his thoughts and keeps them pure from the lusts of the world and flesh. He neither eats too much nor succumbs to immoral thoughts or acts. He neither gives in to greed nor seeks the possessions or wealth of the world.
   ⇒ He guards his spirit and keeps it spiritually fit. He worships God every day and lives in God's Word and prayer all day long; he shares the glorious gospel of Christ, witnessing to and exhorting people as he walks throughout the day.
   ⇒ He guards his study and teaching, avoiding the profane doctrines, teachings, notions, philosophies, ideas, and fables of men.

Note what he does. He continues in the instructions of the Word of God. Why? Because by continuing in them, he saves both himself and those who hear him.

> **"He that endureth to the end shall be saved" (Mt.10:22).**
> **"But I keep under my body, and bring it into subjection: lest that by any means, when I have preached to others, I myself should be a castaway" (1 Co.9:27).**

ILLUSTRATION:
We seldom take the time to look in the mirror to examine our lives. While caring for others is important, taking care of ourselves is just as essential. Remember that a part of the greatest commandment is to love your neighbor as you love yourself.

> *Jim, a young Christian businessman, planned for success and was pretty close to fulfilling his desire before he turned 30. During his quest, sleep did not matter. Eating right did not matter. Physical exercise was only an inconvenience. God, church, prayer, and personal Bible study did not matter. But in his "busyness," he almost lost his grip on life.*
>
> *Subtle things began to crop up in Jim's life: depression took the place of joy...slackness replaced discipline...a sharp, critical tongue quenched his normally friendly personality. Jim's thought-life began to wander...his job performance began to slip and to draw his employer's attention.*
>
> *Staring into the bathroom mirror, he examined the pathetic figure in the reflection. His marriage was on the rocks and his love for God was lukewarm at best. "Where did I go wrong?" he asked himself. The truth is that Jim had been more concerned about success than about anything or anyone else on earth. He had become enslaved by the passion to succeed at any cost. The result: he was on the brink of destroying his life and ripping his family apart.*

1 Timothy 4:6-16

But Jim was fortunate. Some Christian friends rallied around to help restore him both physically and spiritually. From the ashes of his brokenness evolved a man who was better able and more willing to serve the Lord and to care for his family and himself.

Are you guarding your physical fitness, your spiritual fitness, and remaining true to God's Word in your lifestyle? Remember that you cannot effectively influence others for Christ if you do not first take care of yourself.

QUESTIONS:
1. What would you say to believers who equate "busyness" with godly behavior?
2. What do you do in order to stay spiritually fit? Are you satisfied with your spiritual health? What changes do you need to make in your spiritual life today?

SUMMARY:

Would you like to have the traits of a good minister as your very own? Then the following qualities must become a part of your testimony—a testimony that Paul charged Timothy to keep as a good minister:

1. He instructs believers concerning false teachers.
2. He nourishes himself in the truths of the faith and of doctrine.
3. He avoids frivolous speculations.
4. He exercises himself to become more godly.
5. He is a man of reason and of purpose.
6. He is a man who works and strives—willingly and laboriously.
7. He commands and teaches these things.
8. He is an example to believers.
9. He devotes himself to public worship.
10. He does not neglect his gift.
11. He meditates and is diligent in giving himself wholly to the Scripture.
12. He guards himself and his teaching.

PERSONAL JOURNAL NOTES:
(Reflection & Response)

1. The most important thing that I learned from this lesson was:

2. The area that I need to work on the most is:

3. I can apply this lesson to my life by:

4. Closing Statement of Commitment:

1 TIMOTHY 5:1-2

CHAPTER 5

D. The Spirit & Discipline of Relationships, 5:1-2

1. Older men: To be treated as fathers	Rebuke not an elder, but intreat him as a father; and the younger men as brethren;
2. Younger men: To be treated as brothers	
3. Older women: To be treated as mothers	2 The elder women as mothers; the younger as sisters, with all purity.
4. Younger women: To be treated as sisters	

Section III
BEHAVIOR AND RELATIONSHIPS IN THE CHURCH
1 Timothy 3:14–6:21

Study 4: **THE SPIRIT AND DISCIPLINE OF RELATIONSHIPS**

Text: 1 Timothy 5:1-2

Aim: To develop the right spirit toward every age group in the church.

Memory Verse:
"And be ye kind one to another, tenderhearted, forgiving one another, even as God for Christ's sake hath forgiven you" (Ephesians 4:32).

INTRODUCTION:
A joke is told that asks this question: What do you get when an elephant sits on a fence? The answer is a broken fence. We can take some liberty with this joke and ask another question: What do you get when a Christian with a critical spirit "sits on" or attempts to correct another Christian? The answer is a broken relationship. Do not be mistaken: there is a duty to correct and discipline various age groups. But how?

> *The instructions are clear: the members of a church are to treat each other as family members. In no sense is any member to be rebuked. "Rebuke" means to be severely censured, angrily reprimanded, violently reproached. When a family church member needs to be corrected, there is to be no severity, anger, or violence involved; no contempt or disgust. A church member is to be corrected and disciplined through entreaty, that is, through exhortation and encouragement, through appeal and pleading.*

Healthy relationships within the church are vital. When damaged, they hinder the work of the Holy Spirit. We must do all we can to restore fellowship with Christian brothers and sisters. Remember, restoration—not reproach—is the goal.

1 Timothy 5:1-2

OUTLINE:
1. Older men: to be treated as fathers (v.1).
2. Younger men: to be treated as brothers (v.1).
3. Older women: to be treated as mothers (v.2).
4. Younger women: to be treated as sisters (v.2).

1. OLDER MEN: TO BE TREATED AS FATHERS (v.1).

Elderly men are to be treated as fathers. Older men who are true Christian believers have more experience and wisdom in dealing with life. This is not to say they are always right; sometimes they are not. But they do have the wisdom of experience. Therefore, they are not to be ignored, neglected, bypassed, overlooked, or set aside as useless. They are to be treated as a father, with affection, respect, and honor. Their ideas, opinions, counsel, and direction are to be sought. They are to be a part of the life and ministry of the church.

One other point is important as well. Because of their experience, older men sometimes hold strong opinions and become set in their ways. They can become close-minded to new ideas, ministries, and methods. The end result is sometimes tragic: misbehavior, grumbling, complaining, criticism, opposition, and division.

The point is this: if an older man ever needs to be corrected, he is to be corrected and disciplined as a father, not as an enemy. He is to be approached and exhorted, appealed to and pleaded with just as we would our earthly father.

> **"Children, obey your parents in the Lord: for this is right" (Ep.6:1).**

QUESTIONS:
1. What attitude should younger Christians have toward elderly men in the church? What things make it hard to have a good relationship with an older man?
2. What do you think your role is when you know that an older man is wrong and you are right?
3. What is the best relationship you have ever had with an older man? What made the relationship so good? How can you apply those same points to relationships within the church?

2. YOUNGER MEN: TO BE TREATED AS BROTHERS (v.1).

Younger men are to be treated as brothers. The young are sometimes thought to know too little and be too inexperienced to have a part in the decisions and ministry of the church. Therefore, there is the tendency to ignore and bypass them. But this is never to be. Young men are to be treated as brothers; they are to be accepted and invited and given a part in the life and ministry of the church. The older members of a church are not to show an air of superiority in dealing with young men. They are to show brotherly affection: consideration, respect, and care.

There is another need that also sometimes arises among younger men. They need direction: there are times when younger men need to be taught, corrected, and disciplined—no matter their age. When these times arise, there is to be no air of superiority, severe reaction, contempt, or disgust. There is to be a brotherly spirit: affection and care, exhortation and direction, guidance and teaching.

1 Timothy 5:1-2

"We then that are strong ought to bear the infirmities of the weak, and not to please ourselves. Let every one of us please his neighbour for his good to edification" (Ro.15:1-2).

ILLUSTRATION:
One of the greatest challenges in the field of human relationships is to cross over generational lines and relate to older or younger people. Here is one example of an older man who found a way to bridge the gap.

> *Everyone knew him as Papa K. He was a very busy person, but he always had time for young people searching for the meaning to life. What made Papa K. so unique was his willingness to trust teenagers with ministry responsibilities. He trained kids to do everything from running a Christian coffeehouse to sharing their personal testimonies.*
>
> *Not once did he compromise. The young people could count on his unconditional love. Because they knew he was genuine, the kids accepted Papa K.'s direction and even his constructive criticism. Once their mistakes or flaws were addressed, the young people would repent and then move on towards a greater maturity in their Christian journey. As a result of his personal touch, many young people went on to become faithful husbands and wives, loving fathers and mothers, hard-working and honest employees. And just as important, he taught them by example to get involved in the lives of other believers, discipling them just as he had done.*
>
> *Sure, Papa K. took risks. Some kids failed to handle their responsibilities. But the fruit of his ministry affected thousands of lives.*

Whether you are in the younger group or the older group, what can you do to bridge the generation gap?

QUESTIONS:
1. What kinds of things does your church do to involve younger men in the life of the church?
2. Who do you know like the man in the above story? What traits do they have which helps them to relate to the younger generation?
3. What is the end result of a church that has a brotherly spirit? How can this kind of spirit be cultivated in your church? In you?

3. OLDER WOMEN: TO BE TREATED AS MOTHERS (v.2).

Elderly women are to be treated as mothers. Just think what a mother gives to a family and you can see what the older women can contribute to the church:

⇒ love	⇒ affection	⇒ protection	⇒ direction
⇒ warmth	⇒ compassion	⇒ provision	⇒ teaching
⇒ care	⇒ nourishment	⇒ kindness	⇒ instruction
⇒ tenderness	⇒ concern	⇒ guidance	⇒ discipline
⇒ energy	⇒ perseverance	⇒ giving	⇒ understanding

A church is totally irresponsible if it ignores its elderly women who are true Christian believers. Their potential contribution to the lives and fellowship of believers is immeasurable. Therefore, the church is instructed to treat its elderly women as mothers. They are to be loved and protected, and their softness, tenderness, guidance, understanding, instruction, and energy are to be sought and used by the church.

Again, if an elderly woman needs correction and discipline, it must not be done in contempt and disrespect, but rather by the appeal and pleading of encouragement.

1 TIMOTHY 5:1-2

"Honor thy father and thy mother: that thy days may be long upon the land which the LORD thy God giveth thee" (Ex.20:12).

QUESTIONS:
1. What role do older women have in your church? Do they have the same role in your life?
2. What is the best way to give correction to an older woman?
3. Are you comfortable with the relationship you have with the older women in your church? What can you do to cultivate your relationship with them?

4. YOUNGER WOMEN: TO E TREATED AS SISTERS (v.2).

Younger women are to be treated as sisters. But note the added exhortation: in all purity. Lust, immoral thoughts, sex—thinking about physical attractiveness and the bodies of the younger women—none of this is to have a place in the church. The men and women of the church are all to keep themselves pure and to treat the young Christian women as sisters. They are to be protected and guarded, nourished and taught within the church. And their energy, tenderness, understanding, and compassion are to be sought and used by the church in its ministry.

In the matter of correction and discipline, young women are not to be treated with severity or disgust, but in love, encouragement, and exhortation.

"Blessed are the pure in heart: for they shall see God" (Mt.5:8).

(But note: a woman must guard how she dresses and makes herself up. Although not covered in this passage, other passages cover this subject. See 1 Ti.2:9-10.)

ILLUSTRATION:
How important is personal purity? If your sin can affect others, then certainly your purity can do the same. The following story illustrates this point:

> Hugh Martin in The Parables of the Gospels, *tell[s] the story of a rather rough, uncultured man who fell in love with a beautiful vase in a shop window. He bought the vase and put it on the mantelpiece in his room.*
> *There it became a kind of judgment on its surroundings. He had to clean up the room to make it worthy of the vase. The curtains looked dingy beside it. The old chair with the stuffing coming out of the seat would not do. The wallpaper and the paint needed renewing. Gradually the whole room was transformed.* [1]

Does your life transform others around you for good? Or is your example one to be avoided?

QUESTIONS:
1. Are you living a life of purity and morality?
2. What can you do to maintain your own personal purity? What kinds of protective measures do you have in place? What else can you do?
3. What happens to the Christian when purity is compromised?
4. How does trusting God help you to live a pure life?

---

[1] O.R. Powell. Cited in: *Encyclopedia of 7,700 Illustrations: Signs of the Times.* Paul Lee Tan, Editor, pp.1105-1106.

1 TIMOTHY 5:1-2

SUMMARY:

How solid are the relationships in your church? They can be strong and enduring if believers learn how to relate to each other with the right spirit and discipline. Remember, there are four different types of people who must be esteemed. They are...

1. Older men: to be treated as fathers.
2. Younger men: to be treated as brothers.
3. Older women: to be treated as mothers.
4. Younger women: to be treated as sisters.

PERSONAL JOURNAL NOTES:
(Reflection & Response)

1. The most important thing that I learned from this lesson was:

2. The area that I need to work on the most is:

3. I can apply this lesson to my life by:

4. Closing Statement of Commitment:

1 TIMOTHY 5:3-16

	E. Christian Widows, 5:3-16		
1. The church & Christian widows: Are to help widows in real need	3 Honour widows that are widows indeed.	children, if she have lodged strangers, if she have washed the saints' feet, if she have relieved the afflicted, if she have diligently followed every good work.	2) Must be known for good works
2. The children & their widowed parents	4 But if any widow have children or nephews, let them learn first to show piety at home, and to requite their parents: for that is good and acceptable before God.	11 But the younger widows refuse: for when they have begun to wax wanton against Christ, they will marry;	4. The church & younger widows & idleness
a. Children are to care for their widowed parents			a. Should not be counted permanent widows
b. Widows are to live above reproach	5 Now she that is a widow indeed, and desolate, trusteth in God, and continueth in supplications and prayers night and day.	12 Having damnation, because they have cast off their first faith.	1) Can desire to be remarried
1) Trusting God & praying		13 And withal they learn to be idle, wandering about from house to house; and not only idle, but tattlers also and busybodies, speaking things which they ought not.	2) Can bring judgment upon themselves
			3) Can become idle, gossips, & busybodies
2) Not living for pleasure	6 But she that believeth in pleasure is dead while she liveth.		
c. Both widows & children are to obey these instructions	7 And these things give in charge, that they may be blameless.	14 I will therefore that the younger women marry, bear children, guide the house, give none occasion to the adversary to speak reproachfully.	b. Should remarry
			1) Lest they cause gossip due to immorality
d. Children are accountable to God for relatives, especially for immediate family	8 But if any provide not for his own, and specially for those of his own house, he hath denied the faith, and is worse than an infidel.		
		15 For some are already turned aside after Satan.	2) Lest they turn to Satan
3. The church & its organization of widows	9 Let not a widow be taken into the number under threescore years old, having been the wife of one man,	16 If any man or woman that believeth have widows, let them relieve them, and let not the church be charged; that it may relieve them that are widows indeed.	5. The believer is to take care of the widows in his own family
a. The required age to be a member: 60			
b. Their reputation	10 Well reported of for good works, if she have brought up		
1) Must remain unmarried, v. 9			

Section III
BEHAVIOR AND RELATIONSHIPS IN THE CHURCH
1 Timothy 3:14–6:21

Study 5: **CHRISTIAN WIDOWS**

Text: 1 Timothy 5:3-16

1 TIMOTHY 5:3-16

Aim: To actively honor Christian widows, to make sure they receive adequate care.

Memory Verse:
   "Honour widows that are widows indeed" (1 Timothy 5:3).

INTRODUCTION:
Do you know someone who has recently been widowed? How is that person doing? Do you even know?

> *It took only a split second for Linda to lose her husband and become the sole surviving parent for their two young children. The grief and open-ended questions were very much a part of her devastated world. But even though the pain was great, she experienced an even greater sense of comfort as her church rallied to her side.*
>
> *The Christian believer is not exempt from the pain of a loved one's death. But there is a major difference. The believer has a valuable membership in the body of Christ, a group of people who have been given specific instructions on how to treat those who are hurting.*

If you are hurting, do not withdraw into your pain. God has someone in mind who is ready to reach out to help you. But if you see someone else hurting, be alert. Maybe God has *you* in mind to do the reaching out.

What is the children's responsibility to their widowed parents? What is the believer's and the church's responsibility to the Christian widows under their care? These are the all important questions of this passage.

OUTLINE:
1. The church and Christian widows: are to help widows in real need (v.3).
2. The children and their widowed parents (vv.4-8).
3. The church and its organization of widows (vv.9-10).
4. The church and younger widows and idleness (vv.11-15).
5. The believer is to take care of the widows in his own family (v.16).

1. THE CHURCH AND CHRISTIAN WIDOWS: ARE TO HELP WIDOWS IN REAL NEED (v.3).

Honor means to respect and esteem, but it also means to consider and give due care. It has the idea of looking after and caring for, of giving material help. All Christian widows are to be honored, respected, and esteemed by the church. But note the term "widows indeed." This limits the material support of the church. Not all widows need help. Some widows have family and estates that can help them. The widows who have no family and inadequate finances are those who are to be helped and supported by the church. They are the widows who are to be honored with the material support of the church.

ILLUSTRATION:
Many people are indifferent to caring for the Christian widow. But look at how one particular church takes a practical and Biblical approach.

> *As Jane buried her precious husband, the crushing reality of his absence began to overwhelm her. During the forty-five years of their marriage, Sam paid the bills, balanced the checkbook, kept the cars running, and maintained their home with his "handy-man" talents. Now, all of his contribu-*

1 TIMOTHY 5:3-16

tions were gone. "What on earth will I do?" Jane tossed this question back and forth against the walls of her broken heart.

What Jane did not know, but would soon come to realize, is that her church family was aware of her needs. They were committed to care for their widows. Bob was a professional auto mechanic who pledged to keep her car in running condition. Larry's position as a banker would prove to be an answer to Jane's prayers. He took responsibility for her financial affairs. The men's fellowship included her home in their out-reach as they took care of her household repairs and yard care.

None of this care escaped the attention of her younger sister Linda. Linda was also a widow but was not a Christian and had always mocked Jane for her naiveté. But because of the quality care these Christians gave her sister, Linda's closed heart began to open up and she eventually received Christ as her Savior. All because Christians cared.

How does your church care for widows?

QUESTIONS:
1. How are widows honored in your church?
2. What can you personally do to honor the widows in your church?
3. What is the purpose of honoring widows?

2. THE CHILDREN AND THEIR WIDOWED PARENTS (vv.4-8).

Note four significant points.

1. Children are to care for their parents and grandparents. This is a strong statement. In fact, the very first duty of a child is to be pious at home, that is...
- to live for Christ in the home
- to be responsible in caring for his own family

A true believer is a Christian at home before he is a Christian anyplace else. His first duty as a Christian is to love and care for his own family, and this includes his parents and grandparents. His parents and grandparents loved and took care of him when he was a child; therefore, he is to return the love and care when they are no longer able to take care of themselves.

Note the declaration: this is "good and acceptable before God." No other action is good or acceptable with God. A Christian child must love and take care of his widowed parents or else he receives the disapproval of God (see v.8).

2. Widowed parents who are true Christians are to live above reproach. Who are "widows indeed," the persons who are to be cared for by the church?

⇒ The person who is "desolate": left completely alone; without husband, children, or close kin.
⇒ The person who trusts in God; the person who "has set her hope on God," who has "placed her hope [and keeps it] on God."[1] Note what God declares:

"Let thy widows trust in me" (Je.49:11).

⇒ The person who continues in supplications (earnest seeking) and prayers night and day.

---

[1] A.T. Robertson. *Word Pictures in the New Testament*, Vol.4, p.584.

1 TIMOTHY 5:3-16

The widow who really trusts God and focuses her life and attention upon praying day and night—that widow is a true Christian, a person who is focused upon Christ and His mission just as the church is. Therefore, the church is to look after and take care of this dear saint of God. But note the contrast: some widows live in pleasure; that is, they give themselves over to the flesh and the world. They party, get drunk, and live immoral lives. These are not to be supported by the church. The church's energy and resources are not to be used to indulge and give license to worldliness and sin. Such a woman is "dead while she lives." She is dead to God and to the things of God. Her mind is upon her clubs and parties, the world and the flesh, not upon the Lord and His church and the desperate needs of a dying world.

3. Both widowed parents and children are to obey these instructions. The reason is clearly stated: so that they can be blameless before God. We shall all be held accountable:

⇒ children: for how they treat their widowed and aged parents.
⇒ widowed parents: for how they live when widowed and aged, whether righteous or immoral, godly or ungodly.

We must both live obeying God and doing exactly what He says. We shall either be declared blameless and acceptable to God or else guilty of sin and unacceptable to God.

4. Children are accountable to God. This is a frightening declaration. It clearly shows just how important God considers our treatment of widows. If a child does not take care of his family, especially those within his own household (meaning immediate family—wife, children, parents, and grandparents), two things are true of him.

⇒ He denies the faith.
⇒ He is worse than an infidel or an unbeliever.

An infidel is a person who rejects Christ and sometimes even opposes Christ. He denies God and everything about God. The point is this: a person who does not take care of his parents (or anyone else of his household) stands opposed to God. He even denies the very existence of God by his behavior, for he shows that he does not fear God nor God's command to respect and care for his parents. How we treat our aged parents is of critical importance to God. God holds us accountable and will judge us for how we treat our fathers and mothers when they become old.

> "Honour thy father and thy mother: that thy days may be long upon the land which the Lord thy God giveth thee" (Ex.20:12).
>
> "Pure religion and undefiled before God and the Father is this, To visit the fatherless and widows in their affliction, and to keep himself unspotted from the world" (Ja.1:27).

QUESTIONS:
1. Who has the first responsibility in the care of widows? What is behind God's reasoning for this order?
2. What is the first duty of a Christian in relation to his family? Why do many Christians put more of an effort into ministry outside their homes rather than in their homes?
3. What consequences can be expected if an adult child fails to care for his parents?

3. THE CHURCH AND ITS ORGANIZATION OF WIDOWS (vv.9-10).

Apparently, the early church did what any wise church does: organized its most spiritual widows for ministry. Widows who are committed to Christ have a great potential for ministry. Once they have recovered from the loss of their spouse, their commitment, energy, time, and talents can concentrate upon Christ and the ministry of the

1 TIMOTHY 5:3-16

church. The early church recognized this fact and organized the widows for a very special ministry to the needy. But note: the ministry of organization had high spiritual standards.

⇒ The widow had to be at least sixty years old. This would mean that she had probably walked with Christ and proven her faith for some years.
⇒ The widow must have been the wife of only one husband. By this, she would be a strong example of purity and trustworthiness.
⇒ The widow must have had a strong testimony of good works.
⇒ The widow must have reared and nourished her children as she should have: in love and care, correction and discipline, in Christ and in His church.
⇒ The widow must have been a hospitable person, opening and using her home as a ministering center for Christ. The inns of that day were "notoriously dirty, notoriously expensive, and notoriously immoral."[2] Therefore, Christians who were willing to open their homes to strangers traveling about showed an open heart for ministry.
⇒ The widow must have washed the saints' feet. The people of that day wore sandals and the roads and paths were dirty. Therefore, it was the common practice to have a bowl of water at the entrance of the home for guests to wash their feet. The idea is that the spiritual woman would have a humble spirit. She would have never allowed a servant to welcome other Christians into her home; she would have done that herself. She would have humbly met them and cleaned their feet herself. This would show that she was willing to do the most humble and menial task in ministering to people.
⇒ The widow must have helped the afflicted and distressed, the suffering and troubled. This would show that she was tender and compassionate.
⇒ The widow must have devoted herself to all good work.

APPLICATION:
Every church needs to organize its widows for ministry, especially those who love the Lord, have lived for Him, and are committed to the church. They can...
- be a strong example in purity and trustworthiness
- provide a strong testimony of good works
- minister to the children of the church and community, both the orphans and those with parents
- minister enormously through hospitality using their homes as an outreach center
- serve in the most humble and menial tasks of the church
- minister to the suffering and distressed
- be used in all the works and ministries of the church

> **"Let your light so shine before men, that they may see your good works, and glorify your Father which is in heaven" (Mt.5:16).**
>
> **"And let us consider one another to provoke unto love and to good works" (He.10:24).**

QUESTIONS:
1. Does your church have an organization to use widows in ministry? If so, how close does it match up with these Scriptures?
2. What special roles can widows play in the life of the church?
3. What is the secret to getting widows to join in the ministry of the church?
4. Are you a widow or widower? If so, how are you involved in the church? How could you become more involved?

---

[2] William Barclay. *The Letters to Timothy, Titus, and Philemon*, p.128.

1 TIMOTHY 5:3-16

4. THE CHURCH AND THE YOUNGER WIDOWS AND IDLENESS (vv.11-15).

Two significant things are said here about young widows and the early church.

1. Young widows were not allowed to serve in the church's order of widows. The reason given is that they might wish to marry again. This tells us that the church's order of widows made a vow to serve God and His church for the remainder of their lives, never again marrying.

The picture is this: a young Christian lady whose husband had just died would be gripped with bitter sorrow. She would find her most comforting solace in God Himself and in her friends at church. She could be subject to the hasty impulse of dedicating her life to God as a widow—and requesting that she be added to the church's order of widows. The exhortation to refuse her request is to prevent a hasty and impulsive decision. Such a decision would bring criticism to the young widow at a later date when she might wish to break her vow to God and marry again. (See 1 Co.7:8-9; 7:39-40.) If she broke her vow, she would displease God, stir criticism, and lower the meaning of making vows to God and to the ministry of the church.

Another problem might also arise. Young widows have not had time to become all that mature in the Lord. Therefore, as they went from house to house in their ministry, they might tend...
- to idle time away
- to gossip
- to be busybodies
- to say "things they should not say and [talk] of things they should not mention" (Amplified New Testament)

> **"For we hear that there are some which walk among you disorderly, working not at all, but are busybodies" (2 Th.3:11).**

2. Young widows should, therefore, marry.
   a. They should marry lest they cause immoral gossip.

   > **"I will therefore that the younger women marry, bear children, guide the house, give none occasion to the adversary to speak reproachfully" (v.14).**

   APPLICATION:
   It is not wrong for a young widow to remain single if she can live for Christ and the church. But if she cannot dedicate her life to Christ and the ministry, then she should marry.

   b. They should marry lest they turn aside to Satan (v.15). Note that this verse says that some in Ephesus had turned aside and gone after the world and its immoral and unclean life-style.

   > **"Love not the world, neither the things that are in the world. If any man love the world, the love of the Father is not in him. For all that is in the world, the lust of the flesh, and the lust of the eyes, and the pride of life, is not of the Father, but is of the world" (1 Jn.2:15-16).**

1 TIMOTHY 5:3-16

QUESTIONS:
1. What warnings do these Scriptures give the young widow? What explanations for these warnings are given?
2. If a young woman just widowed makes a vow to God, how could it be a bad thing? Have you ever regretted making a decision under duress that you later came to regret?
3. What counsel does Paul give to the young widow? Why do you think he gives such counsel?

5. THE BELIEVER IS TO TAKE CARE OF THE WIDOWS IN HIS OWN FAMILY (v.16).

The church is not to be charged with the care of widows if there are living relatives. The responsibility is that of the families.

> **"Learn to do well; seek judgment, relieve the oppressed, judge the fatherless, plead for the widow" (Is.1:17).**

ILLUSTRATION:
When adult children face the challenge of caring for a widowed parent, it does not have to be a one-way street. Granny is a good example.

> *Granny was Mary's mother. Mary's father had died years earlier and until recently her mother was doing just fine on her own. But with advancing age, she either had to move her mother to a retirement home or move her into her own home with herself and her family. It was obvious to Mary and her husband Dan that Granny needed to be brought into their home and be made a part of their family.*
>
> *Having Granny in the home gave the grandchildren memories they would never forget. Did she put a strain on the family? Sure. But the blessings from having Granny live with them far outweighed any sacrifice that was made by Mary and Dan.*
>
> *When Granny finally went home to be with the Lord, she did not leave an empty room behind. Instead, she left an abundance of great memories in the hearts of Mary's family.*

Who can you reach out to today and touch with God's love?

QUESTIONS:
1. How does trusting God help an adult child care for a widowed parent?
2. How does having an understanding of the commands of Scripture help the Christian care for the widow?
3. Why do you think God wants adult children to take up this responsibility?

SUMMARY:

God has given the church a wonderful opportunity to witness to the world. It is a witness of loving care for Christian widows. Paul has reminded us with these five major points how it is to be done:
1. The church and Christian widows: Are to help widows in real need.
2. The children and their widowed parents.
3. The church and its organization of widows.
4. The church and younger widows and idleness.
5. The believer is to take care of the widows in his own family.

1 TIMOTHY 5:3-16

PERSONAL JOURNAL NOTES:
(Reflection & Response)

1. The most important thing that I learned from this lesson was:

2. The area that I need to work on the most is:

3. I can apply this lesson to my life by:

4. Closing Statement of Commitment:

1 TIMOTHY 5:17-20

	F. The Elders, Officials, or Ministers, 5:17-20	muzzle the ox that treadeth out the corn. And, The labourer is worthy of his reward.	paid (see De.25:4; Lu.10:7; 1 Co.9:9, 14)
1. The honor & pay of an elder a. Is conditional: Must manage the church well b. Scripture commands that they be	17 Let the elders that rule well be counted worthy of double honour, especially they who labour in the word and doctrine. 18 For the Scripture saith, Thou shalt not	19 Against an elder receive not an accusation, but before two or three witnesses. 20 Them that sin rebuke before all, that others also may fear.	2. The discipline of an elder a. To be accused by several witnesses b. To be rebuked publicly (before other elders or officials)

Section III
BEHAVIOR AND RELATIONSHIPS IN THE CHURCH
1 Timothy 3:14–6:21

Study 6: **THE ELDERS, OFFICIALS, OR MINISTERS**

Text: 1 Timothy 5:17-20

Aim: To give due respect to the ministers of God.

Memory Verse:
> "Let the elders that rule well be counted worthy of double honour, especially they who labour in the word and doctrine" (1 Timothy 5:17).

INTRODUCTION:
How do you feel when you hear about an animal being abused? Anyone with a tender heart is sickened when a pet has been mistreated. Animal abuse occurs daily: everything from kicking a cat to starving a dog. Would any true animal lover do these kinds of things? Of course not.

On the other hand, what emotions fill your heart when you hear about one of God's servants being mistreated—whether through neglect or a direct attack? Would a person who professes to follow Christ ever criticize one of God's servants? Is it possible that a church would do this? Unfortunately, it happens far too often.

This is a day in which the minister of God is being attacked, attacked not only by the world but, most unfortunately, by those within the church. The attackers are causing a loss of respect for Christ and a persecution of the ministry that has seldom been experienced in civilization. Because of this, ministers are being neglected when it comes to meeting their financial needs and quickly deserted when gossip and rumors swirl about. Whether the rumors are true or not is often not even considered. Prayer and financial support for the minister of God are simply dropped. This is the work of the devil. The Christian believer must not take part in such diabolical abuse.

This passage deals with both prayer and financial support for the minister—critical subjects for any day and age.

OUTLINE:
1. The honor and pay of an elder (vv.17-18).
2. The discipline of an elder (vv.19-20).

1 Timothy 5:17-20

1. THE HONOR AND PAY OF AN ELDER (vv.17-18).

The church is to honor its minister—esteem, respect, acknowledge, and recognize him. He is to be held within the heart of the believer and held ever so closely, and he is to be esteemed ever so highly. In fact, note what Scripture says: he is to be "counted worthy of double honor."

But note: there is a condition attached to honoring the minister. The minister to be honored is one who "rules well." The word *rule* is a general word meaning to oversee, supervise, and look after. The minister who is worthy of double honor is the minister who labors and works arduously. If he is to receive double honor, then he must demonstrate a double commitment to Christ and the church.

Note also that the whole ministerial staff is covered by this charge. All the ministers of a church staff are to be counted worthy of double honor. But there is one minister who is singled out: the minister who labors in the Word and doctrine, that is, who preaches and teaches. It is he upon whom so much responsibility lies: he is the minister who takes the lead in edifying and building up the believer and the church. He is the one who has to spend hours on his face before God and in the Word in order to preach and teach—this in addition to taking the lead in all the other duties and ministries of the church. If he is a committed minister, a minister who truly labors for Christ and diligently works for the church, then he is worthy of double honor.

Now, one other significant fact. The word *honor* means more than just esteem and respect. It means to pay and bestow what is due. A minister is due an honorarium; he is due compensation, some pay, some wage for his labor. And if he performs his duty well, then he is due double honor. Is this to be taken literally? Is the church to pay him a double salary? A.T. Robertson states that there are "numerous examples of Roman soldiers who received double pay for unusual services."[1] One thing is sure: double pay means adequate, ample, sufficient, and generous financial support.

The oxen used to grind out the corn is an example. In the East, oxen have been used to pull a millstone around and around over grain. The oxen was never muzzled. He was allowed to eat as much grain as he wished, for he was considered to have earned all the grain he wished. So it is to be with the minister of God. He is worthy of his labor. As he grinds and grinds away at the harvest of souls for God and His church, the minister is to be given more than enough financial support.

> **APPLICATION:**
> Scripture has already deplored money-grabbing (1 Ti.3:3). God equally deplores inadequate compensation. The point is: if God ordained that working oxen should be cared for, how much more has He ordained the church to adequately care for the working minister!
>
> **"Thou shalt not muzzle the ox when he treadeth out the corn" (De.25:4).**
> **"And in the same house remain, eating and drinking such things as they give: for the labourer is worthy of his hire. Go not from house to house. And into whatsoever city ye enter, and they receive you, eat such things as are set before you" (Lu.10:7-8).**
>
> **ILLUSTRATION:**
> There is probably no more awkward time for the minister than when he has to negotiate his salary. Some churches live by the adage, "Keep 'em humble. Keep 'em poor." Here is one story to illustrate this point.

---

[1] A.T. Robertson. *Word Pictures in the New Testament*, Vol.4, p.588.

1 TIMOTHY 5:17-20

> *A pastor's search committee was interviewing one particular candidate for their church. They were impressed by what the man brought to the table as a minister. He could preach, teach, and fulfill all the other pastoral duties in a professional manner.*
>
> *As the interview came to a close, the chairman of the committee tossed out one final question, "Approximately how much money will it take for you to make it financially?" The minister gave him a very reasonable figure that his denomination had suggested to him. The committee chairman took a deep breath and said, "That's a little bit more than we had in mind. We feel that a preacher can live off what we offer and then let faith do the rest."*
>
> *At first, the minister did not say a word. But under his breath he prayed for wisdom. When he felt confident that God had given him a word to share, he looked each person in the eye and said, "Would you be willing to work for what you just offered me and let faith do the rest?"*

Is your church being fair financially to your pastor, or is it trying to pay him as little as possible?

QUESTIONS:
1. Why is it important to God that His ministers are fairly compensated for their labor?
2. Why do some churches try to take the cheap way out?
3. What kind of an impact would it make upon your thinking if you spent a week with your pastor? Would you be willing to do his job for what he is being paid?

2. THE DISCIPLINE OF AN ELDER (vv.19-20).

A very practical and warm position on this verse is given by Oliver Greene:

> *It is possible for even a godly, separated, God-appointed elder to commit sin....It is possible even for those who live very near to the heart of God to be caught off guard and commit sin that will bring shame and disgrace upon the church. But we are not to accuse an elder unless there are two or more witnesses to testify that the accusation is an accomplished fact. We should never repeat anything we hear about a minister, deacon, steward, elder, Sunday school teacher or any leader in the church. If we hear reports of evil, we should investigate in the right way, through the right people—and certainly we should not discuss the situation with unbelievers. It is very clear in verse 19 that an elder must not be accused unless there are at least two or three witnesses who can prove the truth of the accusation.*[2]

The discipline is clearly stated: the elder or minister is to be rebuked. The words "before all" most likely mean before all the elders rather than before the whole church.[3] To go before the whole church would only add fuel to the flame of the immature and carnal believers within the church. It would make a public spectacle before the outside world. Such would naturally damage the church's testimony—even if an attempt was made to balance the damaged image by claiming disciplinary action. Note

---

2 Oliver Greene. *The Epistles of Paul the Apostle to Timothy and Titus.* (Greenville, SC: The Gospel Hour, Inc., 1966), p.202.
3 A.T. Robertson. *Word Pictures in the New Testament*, Vol.4, p.589.

1 Timothy 5:17-20

that the point of the discipline is the correction of the sinning minister and the prevention of other ministers from sinning: that they may fear exposure and embarrassment.

William Barclay has an excellent exposition of this verse that merits being read by all believers:

> *"Those who persist in sin are to be publicly rebuked. That public rebuke had a double value. It sobered the sinner into a consideration of his ways, and wakened him into a sense of shame; and it made others have a care that they did not involve themselves in a like humiliation. The threat of publicity is no bad thing, if it keeps a man in the right way, even from fear. A wise leader will know when there is a time to keep things quiet, and a time for public rebuke. But whatever happens, the Church must never give the world the impression that it is condoning sin."*[4]

In conclusion, making charges against a minister or anyone else is one of the most serious acts a person can do. Barclay states it as well as it can be stated:

> *This would be a happier world, and the Church would be a happier Church, if people would realize that it is nothing less than a sin to spread and to repeat stories about people of whose truth they are not, and cannot be, sure. Irresponsible, slanderous and malicious talk does infinite damage and causes infinite heartbreak, and such talk will not go unpunished by God....*[5]

> **"Moreover if thy brother shall trespass against thee, go and tell him his fault between thee and him alone: if he shall hear thee, thou hast gained thy brother. But if he will not hear thee, then take with thee one or two more, that in the mouth of two or three witnesses every word may be established. And if he shall neglect to hear them, tell it unto the church: but if he neglect to hear the church, let him be unto thee as an heathen man and a publican" (Mt.18:15-17).**

ILLUSTRATION:
The Christian believer has a very sober charge to make certain that an elder receives the protection or discipline that Scripture demands. Here is one story that shows the right way to bring discipline to an elder.

> *Bruce was the minister of an independent church whose past finally caught up with him. For years, he was able to cover his illicit sexual excursions. Those on his staff went out of their way to defend his reputation in the community. They believed the church's business did not belong in the tabloids. The church's business belonged in the church.*
>
> *At first, Len, his associate pastor, came to him in confidence and told him of the news he was hearing. He pleaded for the sake of Christ for Bruce to turn from his immoral affairs. But instead of thanking his associate for his concern, Bruce lashed out at Len and said, "You have no right to judge me. Furthermore, if my sex-life becomes public, this church and your position will go down the tubes. It would be best for you to be quiet...or else."*
>
> *Because Len was a man of integrity, he refused to be intimidated by Bruce's threat. His next step was to assemble the other staff ministers and meet with Bruce once more. All of these ministers loved Bruce and wanted to protect his reputation. They offered him confidentiality and restoration. They wanted him*

---

[4] William Barclay. *The Letters to Timothy, Titus, and Philemon*, p.135.
[5] ibid, p.135f.

1 TIMOTHY 5:17-20

to take a sabbatical and fidget some counseling. But, again, instead of being grateful for their offer of grace, Bruce verbally attacked them all.

Refusing to repent, Bruce saw his staff resign one by one. As the church began to sink in the icy waters of gossip and rumor, Len finally submitted his resignation. Less that a year later, the church dissolved and Bruce lost his ministry.

Scriptural discipline has never been popular in the church, but withholding it will create a church perverted by sin. The alternative? A church living according to the principles of Scripture and perfected in holiness.

QUESTIONS:
1. How can you do a better job of protecting your pastor from false accusations?
2. If an elder is living in sin, what is your responsibility to him?
3. Do you believe that God can use a church of loving people to restore a fallen elder?
4. What thoughts come to your mind when you hear the word *rebuke*? What do you think comes to God's mind?

SUMMARY:

Do you now have a better understanding of how to treat elders and ministers? Remember, they are men who have feet of clay just like the rest of us. If you want to obey God's Word, then you must be willing to know about...

1. The honor and pay of an elder.
2. The discipline of an elder.

PERSONAL JOURNAL NOTES:
(Reflection & Response)

1. The most important thing that I learned from this lesson was:

2. The area that I need to work on the most is:

3. I can apply this lesson to my life by:

4. Closing Statement of Commitment:

1 TIMOTHY 5:21-25

	G. The Young Minister (Charge 3): To Be An Impartial Minister, 5:21-25		
		of other men's sins: keep thyself pure.	& keep yourself pure
		23 Drink no longer water, but use a little wine for thy stomach's sake and thine often infirmities.	4. Charge 4: Care for the body & its weaknesses
1. Charge 1: Live in the presence & sight of God, Christ, & the holy angels	21 I charge thee before God, and the Lord Jesus Christ, and the elect angels, that thou observe these things without preferring one before another, doing nothing by partiality.	24 Some men's sins are open beforehand, going before to judgment; and some men they follow after.	5. Charge 5: Leave the judgment of others to God
2. Charge 2: Minister without partiality			a. Because sin is not always clearly seen
3. Charge 3: Guard against ordaining people too quickly	22 Lay hands suddenly on no man, neither be partaker	25 Likewise also the good works of some are manifest beforehand; and they that are otherwise cannot be hid.	b. Because good is not always clearly seen

Section III
BEHAVIOR AND RELATIONSHIPS IN THE CHURCH
1 Timothy 3:14–6:21

Study 7: **THE YOUNG MINISTER (CHARGE 3): TO BE AN IMPARTIAL MINISTER**

Text: 1 Timothy 5:21-25

Aim: To strive after a balanced life, serving with impartiality.

Memory Verse:
> "I charge thee before God, and the Lord Jesus Christ, and the elect angels, that thou observe these things without preferring one before another, doing nothing by partiality" (1 Timothy 5:21).

INTRODUCTION:
As believers we must do our duty—no matter what the circumstance. American history gives us a stirring and powerful example of objectivity under stressful conditions, as seen in the movie *Gods and Generals*.

> *During the Civil War, three deserters from the Southern armies were captured in Virginia. The adjutant to General Thomas "Stonewall" Jackson reported the capture. Worse yet was the news that the deserters were from Jackson's own brigade.*
>
> *Without hesitation, the general ordered that they were to be tried for their crimes and, if found guilty, to be executed. The younger commander hesitated, but Jackson explained that soldiers cannot choose when to be in the army and when to go their own way. He further instructed his lesser experienced adjutant that the rest of the army depends on the faithful, unswerving, impartial service of every member. The general went on to instruct, "Duty is ours; the consequences are God's."*[1]

---

[1] *Gods and Generals.* Warner Bros., 2003.

1 Timothy 5:21-25

We are in a spiritual battle, a battle for our lives. The rules do not change with our whims and pleasures. We must serve God without partiality.

Keeping your life balanced and serving impartially is no easy task, but it must be done. This is the third personal charge given to Timothy, a charge that desperately needs to be heeded by all believers and all ministers and teachers of God's Word.

OUTLINE:
1. Charge 1: live in the presence and sight of God, Christ, and the holy angels (v.21).
2. Charge 2: minister without partiality (v.21).
3. Charge 3: guard against ordaining people too quickly and keep yourself pure (v.22).
4. Charge 4: care for the body and its weaknesses (v.23).
5. Charge 5: leave the judgment of others to God (vv.24-25).

1. CHARGE 1: LIVE IN THE PRESENCE AND SIGHT OF GOD, CHRIST, AND THE HOLY ANGELS (v.21).

This is a strong charge, a command that opens the eyes and awakens the mind. The charge is directed to the minister of God, and it is given...

"*Before God, and the Lord Jesus Christ, and the elect angels,*" that is, the angels who obeyed God.

The mention of all three—God, Christ, and the elect angels—shows how important these instructions are to God. He wants the message of 1 Timothy preached and taught. Timothy was not only to appear before God, he was also to appear before the Lord Jesus Christ and the elect angels. He was to be held accountable for the way he discharged his duty to preach and teach these things. So is every other minister—whether preacher or layman. We shall all be held accountable for the way we preach and teach the Scripture.

ILLUSTRATION:
Are you the kind of person who pays close attention to details? As a believer in God's service you *should* be. You should respond in obedience to all the instructions that come from the Head of the Church, the Lord Jesus.

> *When he was only a boy, French physician Alexis Carrel, Nobel Prize winner and one-time head of the Rockefeller Institute in New York, determined that he was going to be a surgeon. At a very early age he began to prepare his hands for the flexibility and suppleness necessary to perform delicate operations. One means was to secure the cover of a matchbox, place it over the two smallest fingers of either hand, and with a needle and suture...stitch the edges of cigarette paper together. Then he tied a fine knot in the suture to finish off the "operation"—all this in the narrow confines of that box top. As a surgeon he later amazed the medical world with his manipulative skill in the narrow recesses of the human body. Dr. Carrel's head was in complete mastery of his fingers.*
>
> *In the domain of the spiritual life we are frequently awkward because we have not allowed the Head, the Lord Jesus, to control our coordination and to teach us the possibilities of complete domination by our Lord....The world will never look at clumsy handlers of the problems of life, but will stop in some awe before the life that has trained itself...in the craft of Christian living. Men*

1 TIMOTHY 5:21-25

did not admire Carrel's fingers, they admired his head; men will not admire the man, but the Lord Jesus when they see your good works. 2

You may be the only exposure some have to the gospel and the Christian life. Do others see Jesus in you? Do your actions point others to Christ?

QUESTIONS:
1. This verse is a very serious charge. What do you think your role is?
2. How familiar are you with the essential elements of God's Word? Can you preach or teach them with authority and conviction?
3. What difference does it make in your daily routine knowing that God is holding you accountable for how you share His Word?
4. The Christian believer is held accountable by God. What does this mean?

2. CHARGE 2: MINISTER WITHOUT PARTIALITY (v.21).

Timothy faced the temptation that every minister faces:
⇒ being prejudiced against some people—judging some people because they have a different color skin, belong to a different race, are poor, live in a different section of town, are less educated, move in different social circles, and so on.
⇒ showing partiality and favoritism to other people—seeking, listening, recognizing, and spending more time with certain people while ignoring others.

Scripture is clear in its warning to us about partiality, yet we continue to be prejudiced and to show partiality. As believers of the Lord—servants, teachers, and ministers of Christ—we must heed the following instructions of God.
⇒ We must not make decisions because we fear the face of some men, that is, their position and power.

> **"Ye shall not respect persons in judgment; but ye shall hear the small as well as the great; ye shall not be afraid of the face of man; for the judgment is God's: and the cause that is too hard for you, bring it unto me, and I will hear it" (De.1:17).**

⇒ We must not make decisions because some leader or powerful person desires it.

> **"Ye shall do no unrighteousness in judgment: thou shalt not respect the person of the poor, nor honor the person of the mighty: but in righteousness shalt thou judge thy neighbor" (Le.19:15).**

⇒ We must not preach and teach the Word of God with partiality; we must not hold back, fearing the face of man. We must fearlessly share the truth for the sake of people's salvation—all people. The wealthy and powerful must repent as much as the poor and unknown.

> **"I charge thee before God, and the Lord Jesus Christ, and the elect angels, that thou observe these things without preferring one before another, doing nothing by partiality" (1 Ti.5:21).**

---

2 Donald Grey Barnhouse. *Let Me Illustrate*, p.66.

1 Timothy 5:21-25

⇒ We must not accept and favor people because of their social standing, wealth, position, or power.

> "My brethren, have not the faith of our Lord Jesus Christ, the Lord of glory, with respect of persons. For if there come unto you assembly a man with a gold ring, in goodly apparel, and there come in also a poor man in vile raiment; and ye have respect to him that weareth the gay clothing, and say unto him, Sit thou here in a good place; and say to the poor, Stand thou there, or sit here under my footstool: are ye not then partial in yourselves, and are become judges of evil thoughts?" (Ja.2:1-4).

⇒ We must not admire or give more attention to some people because they have a greater advantage in looks, society, position, or popularity.

> "These are murmurers, complainers, walking after their own lusts; and their mouth speaketh great swelling words, having men's persons in admiration because of advantage" (Jude 16).

⇒ We must not secretly show partiality.

> "He will surely reprove you, if ye do secretly accept persons" (Jb.13:10).

⇒ God clearly says: it is not good to have respect of persons.

> "These things also belong to the wise. It is not good to have respect of persons in judgment" (Pr.24:23).

QUESTIONS:
1. Why do you think God wants you to minister and serve without prejudice or partiality?
2. What is the source of prejudice?
3. What things do you need to overcome in your struggle to serve with impartiality and without prejudice?

3. CHARGE 3: GUARD AGAINST ORDAINING PEOPLE TOO QUICKLY AND KEEP YOURSELF PURE (v.22).

The laying on of hands here can refer to ordaining men to the ministry of the Lord Jesus Christ or to restoring the ministers who had fallen into sin and been disciplined. The charge is certainly meant for both situations, for ordaining men to the ministry of Christ is of critical importance.

1. Note the word "suddenly." We must not rush to ordain men. The reason is clearly understood.

⇒ Young believers have not yet grown enough in the Lord. They have not yet learned to conquer the temptations and sins of the world and of their former lives (through Christ). They can easily slip back and disgrace the name of Christ and of the ministry. Therefore, all young believers must be given time to grow in Christ before they are ever ordained.

⇒ New church members must also be given time to prove their profession and call before being ordained. A person is not always what he professes to be. Ordaining someone before we know for sure that he is going to continue on

1 TIMOTHY 5:21-25

for Christ and is definitely called by Christ can lead to devastating results. A novice, a new church member, often returns to the world and its sinful ways. If he has been ordained, he brings reproach upon Christ, the church, and the ministry.

> *Undue haste in Christian appointments has...led to unworthy men bringing havoc to the cause of Christ.*[3]
>
> *Before a man gains promotion in business, or in teaching, or in the army or the navy or the air force, he must give proof that he has earned it and that he deserves it. No man should ever start at the top. A man must give proof that he deserves a position of responsibility and leadership. This is doubly important in the Church; for a man who is raised to high office, and who then fails in it or brings discredit on it, brings dishonour, not only on himself, but also on the Church. In a critical world the Church cannot be too careful in regard to the kind of men whom she chooses as her leaders.*[4]

> **"And the saying pleased the whole multitude: and they chose Stephen, a man full of faith and of the Holy Ghost, and Philip, and Prochorus, and Nicanor, and Timon, and Parmenas, and Nicolas a proselyte of Antioch: whom they set before the apostles: and when they had prayed, they laid their hands on them" (Ac.6:5-6).**

2. The minister who has fallen into sin can take great heart from this passage (see vv.19-22). It definitely teaches that the fallen minister can be restored to the ministry—just as effectively as he was before, perhaps even more because of the praise to Christ that results through God's mercy. It is God's eternal mercy and eternal grace that reaches out and saves the fallen minister; therefore, when the minister is reached, God's mercy and grace are seen to be ever so wonderful and glorious, beyond imagination. God is praised—gloriously praised. But note the Scripture:

> **"Lay hands suddenly on no man."**

The fallen minister is not to be re-ordained or replaced in the pulpit immediately after his repentance. Ministers are to wait until he has proven...
- that his repentance is genuine
- that his rededication and recommitment to follow Christ sticks
- that he is being conformed and molded into the image of Jesus Christ
- that he is committed to serving Christ and His church, being actively involved in reaching people for Christ and in ministering to the needs of the needy

But note a critical point: this does not mean that we do not embrace the dear brother, that we withdraw fellowship from him, that we look upon him with distrust and suspicion. Contrariwise, we reach out and embrace him, love and care for him, nourish and nurture him. In fact, we do this immediately upon hearing about his fall. We go after him immediately, for he is too precious to lose to the world.

> **"To wit, that God was in Christ, reconciling the world unto himself, not imputing their trespasses unto them; and hath committed unto us the word of reconciliation. Now then we are ambassadors for**

---

[3] Donald Guthrie. *The Pastoral Epistles*, p.107.
[4] William Barclay. *The Letters to Timothy, Titus, and Philemon*, p.136.

1 TIMOTHY 5:21-25

> Christ, as though God did beseech you by us: we pray you in Christ's stead, be ye reconciled to God" (2 Co.5:19-20).
> "Brethren, if a man be overtaken in a fault, ye which are spiritual, restore such an one in the spirit of meekness; considering thyself, lest thou also be tempted" (Ga.6:1).

3. Note that ministers are held responsible for those they ordain. The minister who lays hands on an unworthy man for ordination bears equal responsibility for his sins. In God's eyes, the minister himself becomes guilty of the man's sins—just as guilty as the man himself. This is the meaning of the exhortation: when ordaining men do not "be partaker of other men's sins: keep thyself pure."

> "For with what judgment ye judge, ye shall be judged: and with what measure ye mete, it shall be measured to you again" (Mt.7:2).

QUESTIONS:
1. What cautions should be applied to ordaining Christian believers to the ministry?
2. Have you ever personally known of a fallen minister? Is it possible that God may want the fallen minister restored? What guidelines does God provide for this important ministry?
3. What is the relationship between those who ordain and those who are ordained? What warning is given to the ordaining minister? Why should this important warning be heeded?

4. CHARGE 4: CARE FOR THE BODY AND ITS WEAKNESSES (v.23).

Timothy was having stomach problems of some sort and had been drinking water exclusively. Wine was used as a mild medicine in that day and time, but apparently Timothy had refused to drink it because of the Scriptural commands that a priest or minister of God must not touch the fruit of the vine when it had fermented (Nu.6:3-4; Je.35:5-7). However, Paul assures him that he is not violating the Scripture by taking a little wine as medicine. The word "little" would be what we would refer to as a tablespoon or two.

The point is this: we must take care of our bodies. Health must not be neglected. There is no excuse...
- for overeating and being flabby
- for lying around and not exercising or being physically alert
- for eating junk food and not eating healthy food
- for not having periodic checkups from a physician if physicians are available in our communities

No matter what we may think or claim, we must always remember and never forget...
- if the body is sluggish, the mind and spirit are sluggish
- if the body is not fed oxygen, the mind is not fed oxygen
- if the body is not energetic, the mind and spirit are not energetic

> "What? know ye not that your body is the temple of the Holy Ghost which is in you, which ye have of God, and ye are not your own? For ye are bought with a price: therefore glorify God in your body, and in your spirit, which are God's" (1 Co.6:19-20).

1 TIMOTHY 5:21-25

QUESTIONS:
1. Do you ever feel physically out of shape? What do you need to do in order to be a better steward of your body?
2. What practical difference does taking care of your body make in your life?
3. Who keeps you accountable in the area of taking care of your physical body?

5. CHARGE 5: LEAVE THE JUDGMENT OF OTHERS TO GOD (vv.24-25).

A minister's task is to deal with people and their sins. In fact, he is always involved with people, dealing with their weaknesses and strengths, their sins and virtues. Because of this he is often tempted to pass judgment upon people; he is tempted to look upon some as being weak and non-committal and others as being strong and decisive. But this point is an eye-opener. Judgment is to be left up to God, for only God knows the whole truth about a person. Only God knows...

- the genes and heritage and childhood of a person that affect a person so much
- every day, hour, minute and breath the person has lived
- every trial and temptation the person has experienced
- every thought, longing, and hope the person has had

Only God knows all this and the multitudes of ramifications of each of these. Therefore, only God can judge. But as stated, we are tempted to judge when we see a person commit open sin and another person do good works. But we must not judge, for only God sees and knows everything about a person. Note how clearly Scripture states this fact.

⇒ We do not clearly see the sins of people—not always. The sins of some people are clearly seen and they make no attempt to hide them. These people shall suffer judgment; their sins definitely point to judgment. But some people are secret sinners; they hide their sins behind closed doors and in the dark. Their sins and judgment will be exposed later—in the terrible day of judgment.

⇒ Likewise, the good works of some people are clearly seen, but the good works of others are not seen.

The point is this: we have no way to tell what is in a person's heart and life, what he is doing and thinking every moment of every day. We cannot even know our spouses or children or parents that well—not well enough to judge them. Judgment is to be left up to God, not to men—not even to ministers. In fact, the minister himself is charged: leave the judgment up to God.

> "Be ye therefore merciful, as your Father also is merciful. Judge not, and ye shall not be judged: condemn not, and ye shall not be condemned: forgive, and ye shall be forgiven" (Lu.6:36-37).

ILLUSTRATION:
Some Christians appear to be "gifted" with judging the faults of others. Those who do so usually do and say the most foolish things. The following story illustrates this point:

> *John Killinger tells about the manager of a minor league baseball team who was so disgusted with his center fielder's performance that he ordered him to the dugout and assumed the position himself. The first ball that came into center field took a bad hop and hit the manager in the mouth. The next one was a high fly ball, which he lost in the glare of the sun—until it bounced off his forehead. The third was a hard line drive that he charged with outstretched arms; unfortunately, it flew between his hands and smacked his eye.*

1 Timothy 5:21-25

Furious, he ran back to the dugout, grabbed the center fielder by the uniform, and shouted, "You idiot! You've got center field so messed up that even I can't do a thing with it!" [5]

When you assume God needs your help in judging others, you put yourself in a position to be judged!

QUESTIONS:
1. Why do some Christians want to judge others?
2. What attitude are you to have when someone you know is walking in sin?
3. Why is God better qualified to render judgment?

SUMMARY:

As you strive to be an impartial servant, stay focused on the things that will keep your life and ministry in balance. Remember that the believer has a God-given duty:

1. Charge 1: live in the presence and sight of God, Christ, and the holy angels.
2. Charge 2: minister without partiality.
3. Charge 3: guard against ordaining people too quickly and keep yourself pure.
4. Charge 4: care for the body and its weaknesses.
5. Charge 5: leave the judgment of others to God.

PERSONAL JOURNAL NOTES:
(Reflection & Response)

1. The most important thing that I learned from this lesson was:

2. The area that I need to work on the most is:

3. I can apply this lesson to my life by:

4. Closing Statement of Commitment:

---

[5] Craig B. Larson, Editor. *Illustrations for Preaching & Teaching*, p.16.

1 Timothy 6:1-2

CHAPTER 6

H. The Believing Slaves or Employees, 6:1-2

1. **Duty toward any master (employer)**
   a. Duty: Respect
   b. Reason: To avoid reproach to God's name & His teaching

Let as many servants as are under the yoke count their own masters worthy of all honour, that the name of God and his doctrine be not blasphemed.

2 And they that have believing masters, let them not despise them, because they are brethren; but rather do them service, because they are faithful and beloved, partakers of the benefit. These things teach and exhort.

2. **Duty toward the Christian master (employer)**
   a. Duty 1: Do not show disrespect—they are brothers
   b. Duty 2: Give greater service—faithfulness bears fruit

Section III
BEHAVIOR AND RELATIONSHIPS IN THE CHURCH
1 Timothy 3:14–6:21

Study 8: THE BELIEVING SLAVES OR EMPLOYEES

Text: 1 Timothy 6:1-2

Aim: To use your work as a positive Christian witness; to eliminate all hypocrisy in your employment.

Memory Verse:
> "Let as many servants as are under the yoke count their own masters worthy of all honour, that the name of God and his doctrine be not blasphemed" (1 Timothy 6:1).

INTRODUCTION:

How real is your Christian witness at work? Should your witness even be evident in a secular setting? In many cases, a believer's witness is most powerful when it permeates the workplace. Remember, the best sermons are the ones that are *seen*, not heard. The Christian believer must, therefore, be a diligent worker and be on his best behavior at work, respecting and obeying what his employer says and requires. He must be appreciative for having work to do.

The instructions to slaves and masters in the New Testament are applicable to every generation of workmen. As Francis Foulkes says, "...*the principles of the whole section apply to employees and employers in every age, whether in the home, in business, or in the state.*" [1]

What impact or impression are you making on your employer and your co-workers?

OUTLINE:
1. Duty toward any master (employer) (v.1).
2. Duty toward the Christian master (employer) (v.2).

A CLOSER LOOK:

(6:1-2) **Slavery:** William Barclay points out that there were millions and millions of slaves in the Roman Empire during the days of Paul. He says that there were over sixty

---

[1] Francis Foulkes. *The Epistle of Paul to the Ephesians.* "Tyndale New Testament Commentaries." (Grand Rapids, MI: Eerdmans Publishing Company, n.d.), p.167.

1 TIMOTHY 6:1-2

million.² The gospel was bound to reach many of these, and the churches all over the Empire were bound to be filled with slaves. For this reason the New Testament has much to say to slaves (1 Co.7:21-22; Co.3:22; 4:1; 1 Ti.6:1-2; Tit.2:9-10; 1 Pe.2:18-25 and the whole book of Philemon is written to a slave). However, slavery is never directly attacked by the New Testament. If it had been, there would probably have been so much bloodshed the scene would have been unimaginable! The slave owners and government would have...
- attacked the church, its preachers and believers, seeking to destroy such a doctrine.
- imprisoned and executed any who refused to be silent about such a doctrine.
- reacted and killed all the slaves who professed Christ.

The Expositors Greek Testament has an excellent statement on how Christianity went about destroying slavery. It is found in the commentary on Ep.6:5.

Here, as elsewhere in the NT, slavery is accepted as an existing institution, which is neither formally condemned nor formally approved. There is nothing to prompt revolutionary action, or to encourage repudiation of the position...the institution is left to be undermined and removed by the gradual operation of the great Christian principles of...
- *the equality of men in the sight of God*
- *a common Christian brotherhood*
- *the spiritual freedom of the Christian man*
- *the Lordship of Christ to which every other lordship is subordinate.*³

1. DUTY TOWARD ANY MASTER (EMPLOYER) (v.1).

The word "yoke" means to be under bondage, enslaved, weighed down ever so heavily. Paul does not hesitate to call slavery just what it is: a yoke that does not belong upon any man. Paul is expressing a heartfelt compassion for the slaves.

Now, note the specific instructions of this passage. The duty of the slave or workman is to count his master (employer) worthy of all honor. That is...
- to respect, comply, obey, and do what the employer says and requires.
- to do a job and to do it well.
- to be thankful and appreciative for having work to do.

This is especially true when a workman commits his life to Christ. If the workman does not give a full day's work for a full day's wage, he dishonors the name of Christ. If the workman is lazy, slothful, and beating time, or if he is disrespectful, the employer knows something: the God of the new convert is a laugh, for He is inactive and dead. God has made no difference in the life of the workman. Therefore, the superior blasphemes the name of God and the teachings of the gospel.

APPLICATION:
An excellent application of this point is given by Oliver Greene that merits quoting in full.

I personally know dear men today who have been fired by their employer because they talked too much about Jesus while they were on the job; and I

---

2   William Barclay. *The Letters to the Philippians, Colossians, and Thessalonians.* "The Daily Study Bible." (Philadelphia, PA: Westminster Press, 1957), p.141.
3   S.D.F. Salmond. *The Epistle to the Ephesians.* "The Expositor's Greek Testament, Vol.3, ed. by W. Robertson Nicoll. (Grand Rapids, MI: Eerdmans, 1970), p.377.

1 Timothy 6:1-2

have also known professing Christians who did not give their employer a good day's work for the salary received, and that is not right. It is not right for Christians to use company time to witness on the job. If one can witness without robbing his employer, that is fine; but a Christian's testimony will be hurt by his being seen talking when he should be working, even though he may be talking with an unsaved person about the grace of God and the saving power of Jesus. In Romans 14:16 Paul tells us, "Let not then your good be evil spoken of." Christians must be "wise as serpents and harmless as doves." Any Christian who has an employer must render to that employer a good day's work and proper respect, lest reproach be brought upon the Gospel.

Young man, young woman—if you are a Christian, do not be any less alert and on the job when the boss is absent than you are when he is looking at you. Your earthly master may not always be watching you, but the Heavenly Master sees and knows all that you do. So whether your job is that of superintendent in a huge plant or janitor in a small office, never forget that if you do not give your employer a good day's work in the right spirit, you are bringing reproach upon the name of Jesus.[4]

ILLUSTRATION:
The believing employee has a unique opportunity to turn his or her employer to Christ by what he does—and doesn't do—on the job and how he does it.

Russ was a crusty man who prided himself on pushing people until they quit or struck out against him. As store manager, he had a pretty good bark and held the power to bite when it served his purpose.

Harold was a mild-mannered fellow who got along with everybody. When he started his job, every employee warned him about Russ. Nevertheless, Harold decided to let the quality of his work speak for itself. Harold loved Jesus a lot. And he knew the thing that would please Christ the most would be to give his best effort to Russ.

At first, Russ ignored Harold's work. But that did not bother Harold. For in reality, Harold was not working for Russ but for the Lord. Over the course of time, Harold proved to be a very valuable employee. The quality of his work did not taper off. In fact, with added experience, his work actually improved.

Being a man whose chief interest was results, Russ began to take a serious interest in Harold. One day Russ said to Harold, "Harold, what is it that makes you tick?" Seeing an open door Harold responded, "Russ, I'm a Christian." Russ just scoffed. "I've hired and fired a bunch of Christians and they have not impressed me one little bit. What makes you so different?"

Harold thought about his question for a few moments. He squinted his eyes as if that would squeeze out a good answer. "Russ, I guess the difference is that I not only love the Lord and want to please Him, but I also want to love and please you. I figure that if I please Him, He will take care of pleasing you."

Do you work to please the Lord? The quality of your work should say so—loud and clear. It should be good enough that others will take notice.

QUESTIONS:
1. What can you do at work to become a valuable employee?
2. How can you keep from destroying your Christian witness at work?
3. What differences are there between you and non-Christians where you work?

---

[4] Oliver Greene. *The Epistles of Paul the Apostle to Timothy and Titus*, p.212f.

1 TIMOTHY 6:1-2

2. DUTY TOWARD THE CHRISTIAN MASTER (EMPLOYER) (v.2).

It is a wonderful thing when a Christian workman can have a Christian employer, for the workman can expect to be treated justly, fairly, and in a brotherly spirit. However, the workman faces a serious danger, the danger of feeling that he...
- should be given special treatment
- should be allowed to slack off some
- should be treated with more leniency
- should be given more consideration
- should not be as readily corrected or rebuked for inefficiency or mistakes

In the case of slaves in the Roman empire, or for that matter anywhere else, the slave would have faced the temptation to despise or be disrespectful of his master. He could have easily felt that a master, upon becoming a believer, should grant his freedom or at least show some favor. However, the fact that a master became a Christian did not mean that a believing slave was to appeal for better and easier treatment. On the contrary, the believing slave was to become the best worker he could because the master was now a Christian believer.

Once the believing slave became the best worker possible—once he began to work diligently as though he was working for Christ—then he could expect to reap some benefits from having a Christian master. He could expect to reap benefits such as fair and decent and brotherly treatment. Believing slaves were to treat believing masters as brothers, faithful and beloved, and there was to be a greater testimony because of greater production, efficiency, and fruitfulness.

The point is this: the Christian workman is to give great service to a Christian employer because faithfulness bears fruit. Both the workman and employer doing the best they can will bear more fruit of the Spirit and a greater production of work. Thereby they will together bear a greater testimony for Christ.

APPLICATION:
In reality, being a slave or a master has nothing to do with your commitment to life and work. As a believing Christian, whether employer or employee, you are to do the very best you can at whatever you are doing. Your environment or circumstance have nothing to do with faithfulness to your work. You are to do your very best no matter who or where you are.

> **"Servants [workmen], obey in all things your masters according to the flesh; not with eyeservice, as menpleasers; but in singleness of heart, fearing God: and whatsoever ye do, do it heartily, as to the Lord, and not unto men; knowing that of the Lord ye shall receive the reward of the inheritance: for ye serve the Lord Christ. But he that doeth wrong shall receive for the wrong which he hath done: and there is no respect of persons" (Co.3:22-25).**

ILLUSTRATION:
If you as a believer have a Christian employer, there may be a temptation to take advantage of the situation because of your common faith. This is, of course, completely unfair to the employer. The following example helps illustrate the point.

> *John was a college student on the dorm's "bowling team"; that is, his job was to clean toilet bowls for an hour and a half once a week. Like most busy people, John was always looking for ways to cut corners and save time. In his eagerness to have time for more fun things, he turned in a false time card.*
>
> *It did not take John's supervisor long to discover the deception and call John to task. "John, why did you lie about the time you spent on the job?" asked his*

1 TIMOTHY 6:1-2

supervisor, who was a Christian. John was immediately repentant and truly sorry for what he had done. Seeing his change of heart, his supervisor told John to see him the next day to receive his discipline.

Knowing John's desire to become a financial counselor, the supervisor realized how vital integrity was for that kind of work. As he prayed, he came to the conclusion that John's discipline would be to do a study of the word integrity. But the basic source for his study had to be the Bible, how the word integrity is used in the Bible, and how it applied to John's life.

John took his discipline well. By the end of the year, he was by far the best member of the "bowling team." After graduation, the Lord took a man who understood the meaning of integrity and placed him in a position that required unqualified trust.

If you are ever tempted to cheat or to take unethical shortcuts at work, remember God's challenge to the believer in Ephesians 6:7: "With good will doing service as to the Lord, and not to men."

QUESTIONS:
1. Can you relate to John's experience? How and why would a Christian take advantage of his Christian employer?
2. What can you do to be a greater blessing to your employer?
3. What attitude are you to have toward a Christian employer?

SUMMARY:

As a believer, you must be aware of your Christian witness where you work. Imagine what would happen if every believer decided to eliminate any hypocrisy in his Christian witness and work by fulfilling his...

1. Duty toward any master (employer).
   a. Duty: Respect
   b. Reason: To avoid reproach
2. Duty toward the Christian master (employer).
   a. Duty 1: Despise not—they are brothers
   b. Duty 2: Give greater service—faithfulness bears fruit

PERSONAL JOURNAL NOTES:
(Reflection & Response)

1. The most important thing that I learned from this lesson was:

2. The area that I need to work on the most is:

3. I can apply this lesson to my life by:

4. Closing Statement of Commitment:

1 TIMOTHY 6:3-5

	I. The False Teacher, 6:3-5	ing nothing, but doting about questions and strifes of words, whereof cometh envy, strife, railings, evil surmisings,	3. He has a sick interest in controversial questions

1. He teaches a false doctrine
  a. Does not agree to the sound teachings of Christ
  b. Does not agree to godly teaching
	3 If any man teach otherwise, and consent not to wholesome words, even the words of our Lord Jesus Christ, and to the doctrine which is according to godliness;	5 Perverse disputings of men of corrupt minds, and destitute of the truth, supposing that gain is godliness: from such withdraw thyself.	4. He has a corrupt mind & is ignorant of the truth
			5. He thinks religion leads to financial gain

2. He is conceited	4 He is proud, know-		

Section III
BEHAVIOR AND RELATIONSHIPS IN THE CHURCH
1 Timothy 3:14–6:21

Lesson 9: THE FALSE TEACHER

Text: 1 Timothy 6:3-5

Aim: To expose false teachers, to protect yourself from their web of deceit.

Memory Verse:
"Beware of false prophets, which come to you in sheep's clothing, but inwardly they are ravening wolves" (Mt.7:15).

INTRODUCTION:
How can you tell if someone is a phony or a counterfeit? Simply put, when he fails to tell the truth. But what is the truth and where is it found? The Christian believer's best guard against falsehood is knowing for himself what the Bible says. With God's Word available, there is no excuse for ignorance. Ignorance is like a welcome mat at the door inviting the wolf to come in to destroy God's precious lambs.

This is a most serious and critical passage, a passage that the church must constantly study in order to keep its message and ministry pure. It deals with those who fill the pulpit and classrooms of the church, whether the positions are filled by true teachers or false teachers. Every minister, teacher, leader, and member must heed and search his heart over this description of the false teacher.

OUTLINE:
1. He teaches a false doctrine (v.3).
2. He is conceited (v.4).
3. He has a sick interest in controversial questions (v.4).
4. He has a corrupt mind and is ignorant of the truth (v.5).
5. He thinks religion leads to financial gain (v.5).

1. HE TEACHES A FALSE DOCTRINE (v.3).

He does not teach the words of the Lord Jesus Christ. This is a terrible indictment. Imagine being in the pulpit of a Christian church and claiming to be a teacher of the Lord Jesus Christ yet not teaching His words. How many of us are guilty of this indictment? How many of us are guilty of teaching a different doctrine? Two reasons are given as to why the false teacher teaches a different doctrine.

1 TIMOTHY 6:3-5

1. The false teacher does not consent to the words of our Lord Jesus Christ. The word "consent" means approach and has the sense of "attaching oneself to" Christ.[1] The false teacher is just not willing to attach himself to the Lord Jesus Christ. He is...
   - not willing to confess that Jesus is the Lord God from heaven, the very Son of God Himself
   - not willing to confess that Jesus is the Christ, the Messiah and Savior of the world

2. The false teacher does not consent to the teachings of godliness. He is...
   - not willing to accept the righteousness of God revealed in Jesus Christ
   - not willing to separate himself from the world nor to set his life wholly apart unto God

One or both of these reasons are why the false teacher does not teach the wholesome words of Christ but rather chooses to teach a different doctrine and way of life. He has committed his life to the profession of the ministry...
- as a way to serve mankind
- as a way to earn a livelihood

But he is not committed to represent Christ and His Word. As a result, the person is called a false teacher by both the Holy Scriptures and Christ.

> "I marvel that ye are so soon removed from him that called you into the grace of Christ unto another gospel: which is not another; but there be some that trouble you, and would pervert the gospel of Christ. But though we, or an angel from heaven, preach any other gospel unto you than that which we have preached unto you, let him be accursed. As we said before, so say I now again, If any man preach any other gospel unto you than that ye have received, let him be accursed" (Ga.1:6-9).

QUESTIONS:
1. What motivates a false teacher to teach a different doctrine?
2. What is the relationship between a false teacher and his commitment to the ministry of Christ?
3. What attitude are you to have toward a false teacher?

2. HE IS CONCEITED (v.4).

The word "proud" means puffed up and conceited. But note: the word includes the idea of folly; it lacks good sense. Rejecting the evidence that Jesus is the Lord—the Lord Jesus Christ—is the height of pride and folly. Such rejection just lacks good sense.

The false teacher takes pride in...
- his views and ideas
- his rejection of certain portions of the Bible
- his knowledge that some of the stories and events in the Bible are what he calls fables
- his intellectual ability to dissect the truth from the falsehood about Christ
- his enlightenment—that he knows better than to believe in such things as the miracles, deity, virgin birth, incarnation, resurrection, ascension, and the personal return of Christ to earth
- his new and novel concepts and ideas about Christ

---

[1] Daniel Guthrie. *The Pastoral Epistles*, p.110f.

1 Timothy 6:3-5

The list could go on and on, but all believers have detected this pride in discussions with other believers. And, tragically, we have all been guilty of feeling pride over our own ideas before. William Barclay has an excellent comment on the pride of the false teacher:

> *His first characteristic is conceit. His first aim is self-display. His desire is not to display Christ, but to display himself. There are still preachers and teachers who are more concerned to gain a following for themselves than for Jesus Christ. They are more concerned to press their own views upon people than they are to bring to men the word of God. When people meet together for worship they are not concerned to listen to what any man thinks; they are eager to hear what God says. The great preacher and teacher is not a purveyor of his own ideas; he is an echo of God.*[2]

ILLUSTRATION:
A false teacher thinks that he is God's gift to the world. Instead of true humility, his arrogant pride exposes his true motives—fame and glory. Al Bryant shares an example of a man who allowed pride to ruin his ministry.

> *One of [Charles] Spurgeon's students went into a pulpit with every expression of confidence, but he had an extremely difficult time. He came down distressed, almost brokenhearted, and he went to Spurgeon about it. The words of Spurgeon to him were these, "If you had gone up as you came down, you would have come down as you went up."*[3]

The same thing that is true of physical gravity is true of spiritual pride: What goes up must come down.

QUESTIONS:
1. What is the source of pride? Why is this such a difficult hurdle for so many Christians to overcome?
2. How can you guard against pride replacing humility in your life?
3. Can a person be prideful about his humility? What dangers can arise from these feelings?

3. HE HAS A SICK INTEREST IN CONTROVERSIAL QUESTIONS (v.4).

When preparing to preach and teach, the false teacher does not rely upon the primary source, the Word of God itself. He relies upon secondary sources, that is, books about the Bible.

The Bible just is not the basis for his life nor for his preaching and teaching. The false teacher rejects the primary source (the Bible) and turns to secondary sources about the Bible. In some cases, he does not even know how to study the Bible. His interest lies...
- in trying to discover the truth in the Bible not in proclaiming the truth of the Bible
- in questioning what is true and not true instead of living out what the Bible says

---

[2] William Barclay. *The Letters to Timothy, Titus, and Philemon*, p.146.
[3] Paul Lee Tan, Editor. *Encyclopedia of 7,700 Illustrations: Signs of the Times*, p.1100.

1 TIMOTHY 6:3-5

The result, of course, is what we so often see written on the faces and minds of the false teacher and those who sit under him: many thoughts and moments of...
- disturbance and lack of peace
- emptiness and lack of purpose
- questioning and lack of meaning
- wondering if God really does exist
- wondering if there is really any meaning to religion and worship
- wondering if there really is a world or life beyond this earth

Why? Because what the human heart craves is God and His Word, the knowledge and assurance of Him and His guidance.

This is only reasonable and to be expected, for God is bound to have put within man a deep, natural hunger for Him and His Word. Therefore, what the human heart craves, even the heart of the false teacher, is not controversial questions and arguments over the "words of our Lord Jesus Christ" or of the Bible. What the heart craves is to hear from God, to hear the authoritative proclamation of the Word of God itself.

> "For our exhortation was not of deceit, nor of uncleanness, nor in guile: but as we were allowed of God to be put in trust with the gospel, even so we speak; not as pleasing men, but God, which trieth our hearts" (1 Th.2:3-4).
>
> "All scripture is given by inspiration of God, and is profitable for doctrine, for reproof, for correction, for instruction in righteousness: that the man of God may be perfect, throughly furnished unto all good works" (2 Ti.3:16).

QUESTIONS:
1. What do false teachers use as their primary sources for teaching? Name some examples. Why are these wrong?
2. Why do some people have such a low respect for God's Word? What can be done to raise their level of respect for God's Word?
3. What are some of the eventual consequences of those who sit under a false teacher?
4. God has created within every man a Christ-shaped vacuum. How is this to be filled?

4. HE HAS A CORRUPT MIND AND IS IGNORANT OF THE TRUTH (v.5).

His mind is corrupt in that it is not centered upon teaching the "words of our Lord Jesus Christ and the doctrine...of godliness" (the Word of God, the Scriptures, the Bible. v.3). His mind...
- focuses upon the doctrines and theologies of men.
- focuses upon the psychologies and philosophies of men.
- focuses upon man's own energy and self-improvement, upon building up man's ego and self-image.
- focuses upon the latest religions or theological ideas.
- focuses upon the popular religious discussions that please and tickle men's ears.

ILLUSTRATION:
It is sad to say, but our culture has been infected with an epidemic of mental corruption. For example...

1 TIMOTHY 6:3-5

> *Ron was a popular university professor whose favorite pastime was confusing Christians in his philosophy class. The course was advertised in the college catalog as "Understanding the New Testament," but it was renamed by believing Christians who took the course as "Misunderstanding the New Testament."*
>
> *His twisting of the Scriptures would have been a little more bearable if he were simply a practicing pagan. But the tragedy was compounded because he was an ordained minister. Under the guise of the cloth, he spoke as one who had authority on two levels: both the academic and the spiritual.*
>
> *One semester Ron met his match. Two Christian students refused to follow the path of deception and confusion. Ron's aggressive and confrontational teaching style drove these two Christians into an even deeper relationship with the Lord. With each point of deception, they went right to God's Word, and in a kind and gracious spirit, they corrected the professor.*

Did Ron cave in and see things their way? No, but note what happened: other Christian students who were teetering on the fence jumped off and landed on a firmer faith because of the witness of their two classmates.

The point is this: the false teacher does not focus upon the truth, the Word of God. He is destitute and empty of the truth. He does not possess nor teach the truth. He is bankrupt when it comes to the truth. However, note this: what the false teacher teaches often helps us do better, but only temporarily. It often helps to build our ego and self-image and to achieve more in this life. Some self-help preaching is just like some self-help programs, clinics, and seminars conducted all across the nation: they are excellent in so far as they go. But they have one serious flaw: they do not go far enough. They do not show...
- that God is really with us and looking after us as we walk upon earth
- that Jesus Christ has really died for our sins and risen to give us life—life that goes on forever
- that God has really forgiven our sins and accepted us in Christ
- that when we die, God will immediately transfer us into His presence to live with Him forever

This kind of absolute, deep, intense assurance is missing in the false teacher and in anyone else whose mind is not focused upon "the words of our Lord Jesus Christ and the doctrine...of godliness," that is, the Word of God (v.3).

> **"And even as they did not like to retain God in their knowledge, God gave them over to a reprobate [depraved] mind, to do those things which are not convenient [immoral]" (Ro.1:28).**

QUESTIONS:
1. Are you prone to sit on the fence and allow a false teacher sway you over to his side? Or are you prepared to fight for the truth?
2. Do you believe a false teacher can make people feel better about themselves? Give an example.
3. Why do students of a false teacher walk away with an empty feeling?

5. HE THINKS RELIGION LEADS TO FINANCIAL GAIN (v.5).

This means at least three things.

1. Some false teachers are concerned with morality and virtue and with man being the best and achieving the most that he can. They believe in God, not necessarily in

1 TIMOTHY 6:3-5

Christ, but in God. Therefore, they know the answer to making man and his world better is religion. Hence, they commit their lives to God and religion, to getting men to do the works of religion and to living more righteous and moral lives. They want people to be good and to do good. They think that "godliness is gain," that it helps and benefits man and his world.

APPLICATION:
Note that the false teacher is right on this point: the moral teaching of religion—living moral and upright lives—is good for man. But as pointed out above, works and self-help ministers do not go far enough. They do not focus upon God's Son, the Lord Jesus Christ. And God will never accept anyone who does not honor His Son, for He has only one Son who is begotten of Him. That Son, the Lord Jesus Christ, is loved by God. God loves His Son with His whole being, for His Son has the very nature of God Himself. Christ has always obeyed the Father—has always lived a perfectly godly life just as the Father willed. Therefore, anyone who honors Christ shall be honored and accepted by the Father. But the converse is also true: anyone who does not honor Christ will not be honored by the Father. The craving of man's heart for God and His Word—for the deep, intense knowledge and assurance of God—comes only through Christ. Therefore, as good as they are, religion and good works do not go far enough. They do not make a person acceptable to God. God accepts only one thing: faith in Christ, His only Son.

"Therefore being justified by faith, we have peace with God through our Lord Jesus Christ" (Ro.5:1).

2. Some false teachers enter the ministry as a profession and as a means to make a living. They probably have some concern for the religious welfare of people, but the major consideration in choosing to enter the ministry was this: they thought it would be a good and commendable profession, providing a good livelihood for them and their present or future family.

ILLUSTRATION:
A person does not choose the ministry; God chooses the minister. A person should only enter the ministry if he has been truly called by the Lord.

A middle-aged farmer who had been desiring for years to be an evangelist was out working in the field one day when he decided to rest under a tree. As he looked into the sky he saw that the clouds seemed to form into the letters P and C. Immediately he hopped up, sold his farm, and went out to P-reach C-hrist, which he felt was God's leading. Unfortunately, he was a horrible preacher. After one of his sermons, a neighbor came forward and whispered in his ear, "Are you sure God wasn't just trying to tell you to P-lant C-orn?"[4]

A person who hears God's call needs to be sure it is not his *own* selfish voice he is hearing!

3. Some false teachers have commercialized religion. The false teacher is *"out for profit. He looks on his teaching and preaching, not as a vocation, but as a career. He is in the business, not to serve others, but to advance himself."*[5]

---

[4] Michael P. Green. *1500 Illustrations for Biblical Preaching.* (Grand Rapids, MI: Baker Books, 2000), #1460.

[5] William Barclay. *The Letters to Timothy, Titus, and Philemon,* p.148.

1 TIMOTHY 6:3-5

The exhortation of Scripture to the believer is clear, direct, and forceful: "from such withdraw." We must not sit under, associate, or have anything to do with the person who is a false minister and teacher. The church is not the place for professionalism nor for the doctrine of human effort and works (humanism).

APPLICATION:
Man-centered and self-help teaching is sometimes helpful, but it does not belong in the pulpit of God's church; it belongs in the conference rooms and halls of the secular world. The church must be kept pure and free in proclaiming the gospel and the supreme love of God demonstrated in His Son, the Lord Jesus Christ. If the human race fails to keep the pure Word of God flowing from the pulpits of God's church, then the human race is doomed. Why? Because when we die, that will be it. We shall be separated from God eternally. For God will only accept us if we approach Him in Christ. Therefore, the critical hour for man will always be when he sits under the preaching of the Word of God—the preaching of "the words of our Lord Jesus Christ and the doctrine…of godliness." When man hears the Word of God preached, he must respond and do as God says.

> **"If there come any unto you, and bring not this doctrine, receive him not into your house, neither bid him God speed: for he that biddeth him God speed is partaker of his evil deeds" (2 Jn.10-11).**

QUESTIONS:
1. Is it enough for a preacher or teacher of the gospel to promote being good and doing good works without preaching Christ?
2. It is a fact that some people enter the ministry for the wrong reasons. What is the right reason to enter the ministry? What are some wrong reasons and motives?
3. In these days of mass media, there has been an unfortunate rise in commercialization of religion. What can Christians do to combat this trend?

SUMMARY:
If it looks like a false teacher, sounds like a false teacher, and Acts like a false teacher, then it must be a false teacher. If you come across these traits, then you have found one:

1. He teaches a false doctrine.
2. He is conceited.
3. He has a sick interest in controversial questions.
4. He has a corrupt mind and is ignorant of the truth.
5. He thinks religion leads to financial gain.

Do not let ignorance be your undoing. KNOW what you believe and why!

1 TIMOTHY 6:3-5

PERSONAL JOURNAL NOTES:
(Reflection & Response)

1. The most important thing that I learned from this lesson was:

2. The area that I need to work on the most is:

3. I can apply this lesson to my life by:

4. Closing Statement of Commitment:

1 TIMOTHY 6:6-10

	J. The Secret of Contentment, 6:6-10		
1. The secret to contentment is godliness			
a. At birth—brought nothing into the world	6 But godliness with contentment is great gain.	be rich fall into temptation and a snare, and into many foolish and hurtful lusts, which drown men in destruction and perdition.	**ment is not money**
b. At death—take nothing out of the world	7 For we brought nothing into this world, and it is certain we can carry nothing out.		a. Money tempts & enslaves
			b. Money causes many foolish & harmful desires
c. Conclusion: Be content with necessities	8 And having food and raiment let us be therewith content.	10 For the love of money is the root of all evil: which while some coveted after, they have erred from the faith, and pierced themselves through with many sorrows.	c. Money plunges men into destruction
2. The secret to content-	9 But they that will		d. Money—the love of money—is the root of all evil
			1) Causes wandering
			2) Causes acute mental anguish

Section III
BEHAVIOR AND RELATIONSHIPS IN THE CHURCH
1 Timothy 3:14–6:21

Study 10: THE SECRET OF CONTENTMENT

Text: 1 Timothy 6:6-10

Aim: To seek true contentment, contentment that comes from God alone.

Memory Verse:
> "But godliness with contentment is great gain" (1 Timothy 6:6).

INTRODUCTION:
Think for a moment. What would make you perfectly content? Every person strives for contentment. Contentment is the one thing we all want. We want to be fulfilled, complete, satisfied, completely self-sufficient. But when we look around, this is not what we see. What we see is a society and a world discontented, about as unfulfilled, incomplete, dissatisfied, empty, lonely, and restless as they can be. Why? Why are so many people discontented? Why are few people truly contented? There is a secret to contentment, but in order to learn it, you must be willing to look at what God's Word has to say. This is the importance of this passage: the secret of contentment.

OUTLINE:
1. The secret to contentment is godliness (vv.6-8).
2. The secret to contentment is not money (vv.9-10).

1. THE SECRET TO CONTENTMENT IS GODLINESS (vv.6-8).

"Contentment" means to be completely sufficient, to need absolutely nothing. It means to be fulfilled, satisfied, and complete. Imagine a person who feels wholly complete and sufficient, who lacks absolutely nothing. This is what Scripture means by contentment. What makes a person content? What brings such contentment to the human soul?

1 Timothy 6:6-10

Scripture pulls no punches; it unequivocally states that it is godliness. Godliness alone can make a person content. Godliness alone can take a person and make him...
- fulfilled
- satisfied
- complete
- sufficient

Godliness alone can give man the sense that he lacks absolutely nothing. Imagine being so contented—so fulfilled, so satisfied, so completed, so sufficient—that you sense no lack. You just sense no need whatsoever within your innermost being and soul. This is exactly what godliness does for the human soul. This is the reason Scripture declares that godliness with contentment is great gain. No greater gain could ever come to a person than contentment.

Note that Scripture wants us to think about the three stages of life for a moment:
⇒ There is the stage of birth. At birth we brought nothing into this world. When we entered the world, we came with only two things: our bodies and life. Beyond these we were stark naked. We had nothing else.
⇒ There is the stage of death. Note that the fact of death is an absolute certainty. At death, we carry nothing—absolutely nothing—out of this world. We leave this world just as we entered it, with nothing.
⇒ There is the stage between birth and death—the stage of life. Life is entirely different from birth and death. There are some things that we need during life: necessities that we must have to sustain life. In order to live and complete our lives upon earth, we need food, clothing, and shelter. But note: we need nothing else. We can live and sustain life if we have these things. Therefore, a person is to be content with these. Remember the point of these verses: the secret of contentment is godliness. Godliness with contentment is great gain.

The point is driven home by a series of statements taken from Matthew Henry:
⇒ *"If a man [has]...enough to carry him through [this world], he needs...no more, his godliness...will be his great gain."*
⇒ *"Wherever there is true godliness, there will be contentment."*
⇒ *"He that is godly is sure to be happy in another world."*
⇒ *"A Christian's gain is great: it is not like the little gain of worldlings, who are so fond of a little worldly advantage."*

"Not that I speak in respect of want: for I have learned, in whatsoever state I am, therewith to be content" (Ph.4:11).

ILLUSTRATION:
A popular American expression speaks of "keeping up with the Joneses," that is, having as many material possessions as your neighbors. In the race to see who can outdo whom, contentment is becoming extinct even in the lives of many Christians. See if you can find yourself in this amusing story.

As a new family was moving in across the street, an observant neighbor was struck by the amount of things one family could accumulate. The stream of boxes unloaded from the moving van was seemingly endless. Their four cars were parked on the lawn out of the way. The new family lived by the popular adage, "If you've got it, flaunt it." He couldn't be sure, but he thought he counted at least five television sets unloaded and taken into the house. "Maybe they have a few spare ones in case one breaks," he thought to himself.

1 TIMOTHY 6:6-10

> *Despite all the commotion, the man decided to go and greet his new neighbor. "Hi there! Good to meet you." While pointing to the moving van, he remarked, "Do you think all of your stuff is going to fit into the house?" With a sense of pride, the new neighbor responded, "I doubt it. I've just got too much. If you ever need to borrow anything, let me know—I'm sure to have it."*
>
> *Thinking to himself he could use some of the items, the old neighbor responded pointedly, "If you need help getting rid of some things, I'll be glad to take them off your hands."*

Both of these men, in their own way, were focusing on the material. But material things cannot give anyone contentment—not permanently, not perfectly. It is through God and God alone that man finds a contentment that leaves him wanting for nothing.

QUESTIONS:
1. What is the secret to godliness? Why is this so hard for some people to obtain?
2. Where did you find yourself in the above story? What are some ways you can avoid trying to keep up with 'the Joneses.'
3. Describe your reaction to those who try to find contentment by filling their lives with material goods? What advice would you give someone who was caught in the trap of materialism?

2. THE SECRET TO CONTENTMENT IS NOT MONEY (vv.9-10).

This is shocking, for the rich cling to and hoard their money, and the rest of mankind is forever seeking to get more and more money. But God is clear about the matter: money and wealth do not bring contentment. There are four reasons why this is true.

1. Money tempts and enslaves. How can money tempt and enslave? The answer is clearly seen. A person with money...
- can buy anything he wants when he wants
- can go wherever he wants when he wants
- can do just about anything he wants when he wants

This is power within the world—what we might call worldly power. A person who has the power to buy anything, go anywhere, and do whatever he wants has worldly power.

The point is this: a person who has such power—the money to buy anything, go anywhere, and do anything—is always tempted. He is tempted to live selfishly and to hoard what he has. He is always tempted...
- to keep on buying
- to keep on going
- to keep on doing

The rich are far more tempted to indulge the flesh and to live extravagantly—far more tempted to live selfishly, controlling and dominating people through the power of their wealth.

The rich and they who would be rich are never free from the bombardment of temptation. Therefore, the rich person never has peace. He never possesses contentment, not inward completeness and satisfaction. He never feels completely fulfilled and sufficient. This is the first reason money does not bring contentment. Money brings a bombardment of temptation, and it ensnares men in sin.

1 Timothy 6:6-10

2. Money can cause many foolish and hurtful lusts. Think how foolish and hurtful some of these things are.
⇒ How foolish are closets full of clothing that we can seldom wear?
⇒ How foolish is extravagance in clothes? Labels on clothes? An expensive store and an inexpensive chain store will carry the very same clothing made by the same manufacturer. Is it wise or foolish to buy the expensive clothing because of a small label with a different name?
⇒ How foolish is extravagance in eating? Eating and eating and eating—training our bodies to crave more and more food. Is it foolish or wise to damage the body?
⇒ How foolish is indulgence in smoking? Walking around like a smoke-stack damaging our bodies.
⇒ How foolish and hurtful is selling and giving our bodies over to intoxicating drink, drugs, immorality, and greed?
⇒ How foolish and hurtful is it to continually...
- crave?
- lust?
- hoard?
- indulge?
- secure?
- possess?

How foolish and hurtful is it to feed our desires and lusts with the things, possessions, and niceties of this world when millions upon millions are hopeless and helpless and going to bed hungry, cold, and sick—all dying from disease and lack of food, clothing, and shelter? And, most tragic of all—dying without Christ and without any hope of living eternally with God. As stated, money can cause many foolish and hurtful lusts.

3. Money drowns men in destruction and perdition. The word "drown" is a descriptive picture of wealth being *"a personal monster, which plunges its victims into an ocean of complete destruction."*[1] The idea is this: the person who falls into the foolish and hurtful lusts of this world shall be utterly destroyed and ruined, both in body and soul. And the destruction and ruin shall be for eternity.[2]

> **"For many walk, of whom I have told you often, and now tell you even weeping, that they are the enemies of the cross of Christ: whose end is destruction, whose God is their belly, and whose glory is in their shame, who mind earthly things" (Ph.3:18-19).**

ILLUSTRATION:
If someone offered you a sack of gold, would you take it? Before you answer too quickly, listen to this story and then give your answer.

> *"The voyage home to Spain has been a long time coming, but after a very successful gold strike in the New World, it is time to cash in on our good fortune," thought Carlos, the ship's captain, as he relaxed on the deck of his ship. Sitting there, Carlos imagined what he would do with his share of the treasure. But then off in the distance he saw dark clouds rising over the horizon.*
>
> *Carlos and his crew had made the trans-Atlantic trip several times and were considered to be sea-worthy sailors. But this time, they sailed into the storm of the century. They had never seen waves like the ones that rocked their ship back and forth. As the water flooded the hold, Carlos gave the order to throw everything of significant weight overboard.*

---
1 Donald Guthrie. *The Pastoral Epistles,* p.113.
2 A.T. Robertson. *Word Pictures in the New Testament,* Vol.4, p.593.

1 TIMOTHY 6:6-10

> *With hearts heavier than their gold fortune, they began to throw bags of gold overboard. It was to no avail. The ship continued to sink. The captain ordered the men to lower lifeboats and to abandon the ship. During all of the confusion, one of the sailors took a bag of gold and stuffed it in his shirt. "Those poor suckers. They've lost everything," he thought to himself.*
>
> *Yet as he stepped into the lifeboat, he was thrown off balance and fell into the angry sea. "Swim to us!" shouted his shipmates. But the weight of the gold pulled the man under, never to be seen again. The sailor's greed formed his grave, one that showed no respect for the material possessions.*

Is the love of the world dragging you down? Let it go. Let the Savior rescue you before it is too late.

4. Money—that is, the love of money—is the root of all evil. Note the three reasons why:

⇒ The love of money causes people to covet, and covetousness is idolatry.

⇒ The love of money causes people to wander away from the faith. It causes people to lust after the things of this world.

⇒ The love of money causes people to pierce themselves through with many sorrows. The things, possessions, and lusts of this world do not satisfy nor fulfill a person's heart and life. Money cannot bring contentment to a person. The love of money only consumes and eats a person with grief.[3] It pierces the heart with a void—the void of emptiness, worry, anxiety, and insecurity. Money cannot buy love, health, and deliverance from death. Money cannot buy God; it cannot buy assurance, not the assurance and confidence of living forever.

The point is this: a person craves the necessities of life; his very nature craves them. However, once man has the necessities of life, he discovers that he still craves for more. The necessities do not satisfy his inner craving and emptiness—his void, hunger, and thirst—for something more. Therefore, man seeks to satisfy his craving by getting more and more food, clothing and everything else he desires. He eats and eats, buys and buys, and goes after more and more comfort, ease, pleasure, wealth, money, and everything else he wants. But what man overlooks is this: the craving within his heart—the void, the hunger, the thirst—is not for more material possessions. It is for spiritual satisfaction, the filling up of another part of his being. His craving is for godliness. Therefore, once he has food and raiment, he has satisfied his physical craving. Enough food and raiment for today brings contentment today—but only physical contentment. What he needs after that is spiritual food, the satisfaction of his spiritual hunger. Man's contentment comes from having his physical and spiritual needs met. One without the other leaves him with some emptiness, some void (Co.2:8-9). True contentment comes only from godliness.

APPLICATION:
William Barclay makes an excellent point that is worthy of note:

> *Money in itself is neither good nor bad; it is simply dangerous in that the love of it may become bad. With money a man can do much good; and with money he can do much evil. With money a man can selfishly serve his own desires; and with money he can generously answer to the cry of his neighbour's need. With money a man can buy his way to the forbidden things and facilitate the path of wrong-doing; and with money he can make it easier for someone*

---

[3] A.T. Robertson. *Word Pictures in the New Testament*, Vol.4, p.594.

1 TIMOTHY 6:6-10

else to live as God meant him to live. Money is not an evil, but it is a great responsibility.[4]

QUESTIONS:
1. What are some ways you can keep the power of money from controlling your life?
2. Why do money and wealth not bring contentment?
3. If money does not bring contentment, then why do so many Christians live like it does?
4. What were your thoughts as you read the story about the gold-filled ship that was sinking? What would you take with you if you were running for your life? Why?

SUMMARY:

If you want to be content, then your desire is no different from anyone else's. The big difference is how to get there from here. God's Word provides the key:

1. The secret to contentment is godliness.
2. The secret to contentment is not money.

Godliness or gold. Which one do you want the most?

PERSONAL JOURNAL NOTES:
(Reflection & Response)

1. The most important thing that I learned from this lesson was:

2. The area that I need to work on the most is:

3. I can apply this lesson to my life by:

4. Closing Statement of Commitment:

---

[4] William Barclay. *The Letters to Timothy, Titus, and Philemon*, p.152.

1 Timothy 6:11-16

K. The Young Minister (Charge 5): To Be a Man of God, 6:11-16

1. Flee the passion for wealth, vv. 9-10
2. Pursue, follow after the things of God
3. Fight the good fight for the faith & lay hold of eternal life
   a. You are destined for eternal life
   b. You have been good witnesses before many
4. Keep this charge—keep this commandment, v. 14
   a. Because of God's power to quicken,

   to give life
   b. Because of Christ's example

   c. Because Christ is to come again: He is to be exalted as King of kings & Lords of lords

   d. Because Christ alone is immortal: He lives in the eternal dimension or world
   e. Because Christ alone lives in the unapproachable light of God's glory

11 But thou, O man of God, flee these things; and follow after righteousness, godliness, faith, love, patience, meekness. 12 Fight the good fight of faith, lay hold on eternal life, whereunto thou art also called, and hast professed a good profession before many witnesses. 13 I give thee charge in the sight of God, who quickeneth all things, and before Christ Jesus, who before Pontius Pilate witnessed a good confession; 14 That thou keep this commandment without spot, unrebukeable, until the appearing of our Lord Jesus Christ: 15 Which in his times he shall show, who is the blessed and only Potentate, the King of kings, and Lord of lords; 16 Who only hath immortality, dwelling in the light which no man can approach unto; whom no man hath seen, nor can see: to whom be honour and power everlasting. Amen.

Section III
BEHAVIOR AND RELATIONSHIPS IN THE CHURCH
1 Timothy 3:14–6:21

Study 11:   THE YOUNG MINISTER (CHARGE 4): TO BE A MAN OF GOD

Text: 1 Timothy 6:11-16

Aim: To seek one thing above all else: To become a man (or woman) of God.

Memory Verse:
"Fight the good fight of faith, lay hold on eternal life, whereunto thou art also called, and hast professed a good profession before many witnesses" (1 Timothy 6:12).

INTRODUCTION:
In the mid-1950's there was a popular American television program called "To Tell the Truth." Three guests on the show would claim to be the same person. Four panelists would then ask the guests questions to determine who was telling the truth. After a set time was up, each panelist voted for his or her choice as to who was telling the truth. Then the host of the show asked, "Will the real...[John Doe or whoever] please stand up?"

In many ways, this game is being played out in churches throughout the world. People are presenting themselves or claiming to be godly. Is there a sure way to know who is telling the truth? How can we know who is truly a godly person? If we know the right questions to ask, we will be able to pick the right person, the godly man or woman who will stand up and be counted as such. Where are those questions to be

1 TIMOTHY 6:11-16

found? Right in God's Word. There is a straightforward charge to the Christian believer to be a "man of God." What a dynamic challenge!

OUTLINE:
1. Flee the passion for wealth (v.11).
2. Pursue, follow after the things of God (v.11).
3. Fight the good fight for the faith and lay hold of eternal life (v.12).
4. Keep this charge—keep this commandment (vv.13-16).

1. FLEE THE PASSION FOR WEALTH (v.11).

A person is to flee the love of money—run away from all that has just been covered in verses 9-10. Note a shocking fact (shocking because so many people love money and the things it can buy):
⇒ the man who loves money is not a man of God. The man of God is the person who flees the love of money.

The man of God does not love the world nor seek after the things of the world. He flees from the love and passion of this world.

> "Love not the world, neither the things that are in the world. If any man love the world, the love of the Father is not in him. For all that is in the world, the lust of the flesh, and the lust of the eyes, and the pride of life, is not of the Father, but is of the world" (1 Jn.2:15-16).

QUESTIONS:
1. If you were to be described by others, would they say you had a passion for wealth or a passion for the Lord?
2. Is it possible to love money and love God at the same time? Why or why not?

2. PURSUE, FOLLOW AFTER THE THINGS OF GOD (v.11).

The word "follow" is strong. It means to run after; to run swiftly after; to hotly pursue; to seek eagerly and earnestly. It has the idea of aiming at and pursuing until something is gained, of never giving up until we have reached our goal. There are six things the man of God is to pursue.
1. The man of God pursues righteousness. Righteousness means two things.
   a. Righteousness means *being right* with God.
      ⇒ It is having a heart that is right with God, that has approached God exactly like He says: through His Son, the Lord Jesus Christ.
      ⇒ It is having a heart that has allowed God to recreate and remake it in righteousness: through the Lord Jesus Christ.
      ⇒ It is having a heart that has partaken of the divine nature of God (2 Pe.1:4).

   > "Blessed are they which do hunger and thirst after righteousness: for they shall be filled" (Mt.5:6).

   b. Righteousness means *doing right*, that is, living exactly as God says to live. Simply stated, a righteous person is a person who does his duty both to God and to man. He walks righteously before God and man day by day. As a result, he is free from guilt and has a free conscience and a strong self-image. The man of God follows and runs after righteousness.

1 TIMOTHY 6:11-16

"Awake to righteousness, and sin not; for some have not the knowledge of God: I speak this to your shame" (1 Co.15:34).

2. The man of God pursues godliness. Godliness means to live in the reverence and awe of God; to be so conscious of God's presence that one lives just as God would live if He were walking upon earth. It means to live seeking to be like God; to seek to possess the very character, nature, and behavior of God. The man of God follows and runs after godliness. He seeks to gain a consciousness of God's presence—a consciousness so intense that he actually lives as God would live if He were on earth.

Note: godliness means to be Christ-like, to live upon earth just as Christ lived.

"But we all, with open face beholding as in a glass the glory of the Lord, are changed into the same image from glory to glory, even as by the Spirit of the Lord" (2 Co.3:18).

3. The man of God pursues faith. Faith means both to believe and to be faithful.
   ⇒ The man of God seeks faith: to learn to trust God more and more; to be a man of great faith and belief. He wants to believe, trust, and depend upon God—to grow more and more in believing God.
   ⇒ The man of God seeks to be faithful: be faithful to God more and more. He wants to be loyal, obedient, and attached to God. He wants to please God in all that he does.

"Moreover it is required in stewards, that a man be found faithful" (1 Co.4:2).

4. The man of God pursues love. The kind of love which the believer is to have for all people is agape love, the great love of God Himself.

5. The man of God pursues patience. The word "patience" means to be stedfast, to endure, and to persevere. The Thessalonian believers endured and held fast to their faith in Christ through all the persecutions and tribulations thrown against them.
   ⇒ The word "tribulations" is a more general word than persecutions and refers to any kind of trial or trouble.[1]

6. The man of God pursues meekness. Meekness means to be gentle, tender, humble, mild, considerate, but strongly so. Meekness has the strength to control and discipline, and it does so at the right time.
   a. Meekness has a humble state of mind. But this does not mean the person is weak, cowardly, and bowing. The meek person simply loves people and loves peace; therefore, he walks humbly among men regardless of their status and circumstance in life. Associating with the poor and lowly of this earth does not bother the meek person. He desires to be a friend to all and to help all as much as possible.
   b. Meekness has a strong state of mind. It looks at situations and wants justice and right to be done. It is not a weak mind that ignores and neglects evil and wrong-doing, abuse and suffering.
      ⇒ If someone is suffering, meekness steps in and does what it can to help.
      ⇒ If evil is being done, meekness does what it can to stop and correct it.
      ⇒ If evil is running rampant and indulging itself, meekness actually strikes out in anger. However, note a crucial point: the anger is always at the right time and against the right thing.

---

[1] Leon Morris. *The Epistles of Paul to the Thessalonians.* "Tyndale New Testament Commentaries." (Grand Rapids, MI: Eerdmans Publishing Company, Began in 1958), p.115.

c. Meekness has strong self-control. The meek person controls his spirit and mind. He controls the lusts of his flesh. He does not give way to ill-temper, retaliation, passion, indulgence, or license. The meek person dies to himself, to what his flesh would like to do, and he does the right thing—exactly what God wants done.

In summary, the meek person walks in a humble, tender, but strong state of mind. He denies himself and gives utmost consideration to others. He shows a control and righteous anger against injustice and evil. A meek man forgets self and lives for others because of what Christ has done for him.

⇒ God is meek.

"But the fruit of the Spirit is love, joy, peace, longsuffering, gentleness, goodness, faith, meekness, temperance: against such there is no law" (Ga.5:22-23).

⇒ Jesus Christ was meek.

"Take my yoke upon you, and learn of me; for I am meek and lowly in heart: and ye shall find rest unto your souls" (Mt.11:29).

⇒ Believers are to be meek.

"Brethren, if a man be overtaken in a fault, ye which are spiritual, restore such an one in the spirit of meekness; considering thyself, lest thou also be tempted" (Ga.6:1).

APPLICATION:
Dr. J. Wilbur Chapman was asked this question,

"What do you consider a good rule of life?" He replied, "This rule governs my life—anything that dims my vision of Christ, or takes away my taste for Bible study, or cramps my prayer life, or makes Christian work more difficult, is wrong for me and I must, as a Christian, turn away from it."[2]

How many Christians can honestly say that this is the motto they live by? Unfortunately, not many. And yet this is what it takes to truly follow after the things of God.

QUESTIONS:
1. What things is a man of God to pursue? Why is he to pursue them?
2. What hinders believers from pursuing these things?
3. Picture yourself getting this letter from Paul. What things would challenge you to do better?

3. FIGHT THE GOOD FIGHT FOR THE FAITH AND LAY HOLD OF ETERNAL LIFE (v.12).

This is a picture of an athletic contest. The word fight means to agonize, struggle, battle, contend, and fight for the prize. It is the idea of a desperate effort and struggle.

Note: the believer is in a desperate struggle for eternal life. Laying hold of the prize of eternal life is the struggle. Eternal life is the goal for which the man of God is fighting. Matthew Henry described it well:

---

[2] Selected from *Pilgrim Holiness Advocate.* Walter B. Knight. *Knight's Treasury of 2,000 Illustrations*, p.443.

1 Timothy 6:11-16

> *Those who will get to heaven must fight their way there. There must be a conflict with corruption and temptations and...the power of darkness. Observe. It is a good fight, it is a good cause, and it will have a good [end and purpose]...*
> *Eternal life is the crown proposed to us...*
> *We must lay hold [of eternal life], as those that are afraid of coming short of it and losing it. Lay hold, and take heed of losing your hold.*[3]

Note an extremely significant point: what the profession of a minister is. When a man commits his life to the ministry, he is professing...
- that he believes in eternal life—that eternal life is a reality
- that he and all others who trust Christ shall live forever

He professes the reality of eternal life before "many witnesses"—all who know him and come in contact with him.
⇒ The point is this: the man of God must live up to his profession. He must do exactly what he professes: fight the good fight of faith and lay hold of eternal life.

"No man that warreth entangleth himself with the affairs of this life; that he may please him who hath chosen him to be a soldier" (2 Ti.2:4).

ILLUSTRATION:
Many distractions seek to pull you as a Christian believer off course. But you are in a race—the race of your life—and the question is, how will you run?

> *On March 6, 1987, Eamon Coughlan, the Irish world record holder at 1500 meters, was running in a qualifying heat at the World Indoor Track Championships in Indianapolis. With two and a half laps left, he was tripped. He fell, but he got up and with great effort managed to catch the leaders. With only 20 yards left in the race, he was in third place—good enough to qualify for the finals.*
> *He looked over his shoulder to the inside, and, seeing no one, he let up. But another runner, charging hard on the outside, passed Coughlan a yard before the finish, thus eliminating him from the finals. Coughlan's great comeback effort was rendered worthless by taking his eyes off the finish line.*[4]

Are you concentrating on the finish line, eternal life? Or are you giving up before the race of life is over?

QUESTIONS:
1. What motivates you to run the Christian race?
2. As you think about running the race—the trials, the temptations, the struggles—what are your biggest concerns?
3. Have you ever wanted to quit the race? What can you do to keep yourself aroused and motivated for Christ?

---

3 Matthew Henry. *Matthew Henry's Commentary*, Vol.6, p.830.
4 Craig B. Larson, Editor. *Illustrations for Preaching & Teaching*, p.178.

1 TIMOTHY 6:11-16

4. KEEP THIS CHARGE—KEEP THIS COMMANDMENT (vv.13-16).

What commandment? The commandment just covered in vv.11-12. Five reasons are given for keeping these commandments.

1. God has the power to quicken all things. The word "quicken" means to give life; to bring forth alive.[5] God is life; He possesses the very energy and power of life within Himself. Therefore, God actually has the power to inject and infuse eternal life into us. There is no greater reason for keeping the commandments of God. If we keep His commandments, He will quicken us to live forever; He will give us eternal life.

2. Christ has set the example of a good profession before us. When Christ stood before Pilate, He said:

> "My kingdom is not of this world: if my kingdom were of this world, then would my servants fight, that I should not be delivered to the Jews: but now is my kingdom not from hence. Pilate therefore said unto him, Art thou a king then? Jesus answered, Thou sayest that I am a king. To this end was I born, and for this cause came I into the world, that I should bear witness unto the truth. Every one that is of the truth heareth my voice" (Jn.18:36-37).

The man of God is to make the very same profession that Christ made: Jesus Christ is King, the Supreme majesty of the universe, the "blessed and only Potentate, the King of kings, and Lord of lords" (v.15). This is the second reason for keeping the commandments of God.

3. Christ is to come again and be exalted as King of kings and Lord of lords. The point is judgment. Every one of us must confront Christ: we will be called forth and be forced to stand face to face with Him. We will have to give an account of how well we kept His commandments.

⇒ *"Keep [the commandment] with an eye to His second coming, when we must all give an account of the talents we have been entrusted with...*
  - *"The Lord Jesus Christ will appear; and it will be a glorious appearing....Ministers [all servants] should have an eye to this appearing of the Lord Jesus Christ in all their administrations...*
  - *"Till his appearing, they are to keep this commandment without spot, unrebukeable."*[6]

Jesus Christ shall return to earth and be exalted:

> "In his times he shall show, who is the blessed and only Potentate, the King of kings, and Lord of lords" (1 Ti.6:15).

This is the third reason why we must keep the commandments of God.

4. Christ alone possesses immortality and dwells in the transcendent and unapproachable light of God's glory. This is one of the magnificent doxologies of the Bible. Its message is powerful.

  a. Christ alone has immortality: no person shall ever live forever apart from Jesus Christ.

> "Verily, verily, I say unto you, If a man keep my saying, he shall never see death" (Jn.8:51).

---

[5] A.T. Robertson. *Word Pictures in the New Testament*, Vol.4, p.594.
[6] Matthew Henry. *Matthew Henry's Commentary*, Vol.6, p.831.

1 Timothy 6:11-16

b. Christ alone dwells in the light which no man can approach unto, the glorious light of God's presence. No person shall ever approach God or dwell in the light of God's presence apart from Jesus Christ.

"For there is one God, and one mediator between God and men, the man Christ Jesus" (1 Ti.2:5).

5. Christ alone has seen and can see the light of God's presence and glory. No person shall ever be allowed to see the light of God's presence and glory apart from Christ.

"No man hath seen God at any time; the only begotten Son, which is in the bosom of the Father, he hath declared him" (Jn.1:18).

Therefore, to God and Christ alone belong honor and power everlasting. Amen.

ILLUSTRATION:
Sometimes we treat God's commandments as options on a menu instead of as orders or instructions. But a failure to keep God's commandments is sin. What is sin? *Moody Monthly* makes this contribution:
- "Man calls it an *accident*; God calls it an *abomination*.
- "Man calls it a *blunder*; God calls it a *blindness*.
- "Man calls it a *defect*; God calls it a *disease*.
- "Man calls it *chance*; God calls it a *choice*.
- "Man calls it an *error*; God calls it an *enmity*.
- "Man calls it a *fascination*; God calls it a *fatality*.
- "Man calls it an *infirmity*; God calls it an *iniquity*.
- "Man calls it a *luxury*; God calls it a *leprosy*.
- "Man calls it a *liberty*; God calls it *lawlessness*.
- "Man calls it a *trifle*; God calls it a *tragedy*.
- "Man calls it a *mistake*; God calls it a *madness*.
- "Man calls it a *weakness*; God calls it *willfulness*." [7]

What do you call a failure to keep God's commandments?

QUESTIONS:
1. Are you prone to pick and choose which of God's commandments you want to obey?
2. Why is it imperative to keep all of God's commandments? What is the greatest challenge to you in being totally obedient?
3. What does disobedience say to God about your reverence and respect for Him?

SUMMARY:
For Christ, you must set your sights on the finish line and focus on a life of godliness:

1. Flee the passion for wealth.
2. Pursue, follow after the things of God.
3. Fight a good fight for the faith and lay hold of eternal life.
4. Keep this charge—keep this commandment.

---

[7] *Moody Monthly*. Walter B. Knight. *Knight's Treasury of 2,000 Illustrations*, p.363.

1 TIMOTHY 6:11-16

PERSONAL JOURNAL NOTES:
(Reflection & Response)

1. The most important thing that I learned from this lesson was:

2. The area that I need to work on the most is:

3. I can apply this lesson to my life by:

4. Closing Statement of Commitment:

	L. The Rich Man & the Minister: The Final Charge, 6:17-21	store for themselves a good foundation against the time to come, that they may lay hold on eternal life.	e. Must lay up wealth for the world to come

1. The charge to the rich man
a. Must not be arrogant
b. Must not trust in riches
c. Must hope & trust in the living God
d. Must do good & be rich in good deeds: Be generous & share sacrificially
	17 Charge them that are rich in this world, that they be not highminded, nor trust in certain riches, but in the living God, who giveth us richly all things to enjoy;
	18 That do good, that they be rich in good works, ready to distribute, willing to communicate;
	19 Laying up in
		20 O Timothy, keep that which is committed to thy trust, avoiding profane and vain babblings, and oppositions of science falsely so called:
		21 Which some professing have erred concerning the faith. Grace be with thee. Amen.
			2. The charge to the minister
			a. Guard the faith, God's trust
			b. Avoid, flee false teaching
			  1) Godless & empty words
			  2) False knowledge
			  3) Some have turned away from the faith

Section III
BEHAVIOR AND RELATIONSHIPS IN THE CHURCH
1 Timothy 3:14–6:21

Study 12: THE RICH MAN AND THE MINISTER: THE FINAL CHARGE

Text: 1 Timothy 6:17-21

Aim: To trust in God and to keep the faith entrusted to you.

Memory Verse:
> "O Timothy, keep that which is committed to thy trust, avoiding profane and vain babblings, and oppositions of science falsely so called" (1 Timothy 6:20).

INTRODUCTION:
In October of 1987, the Stock Market crashed in America. The day was called "Black Friday." Some investors lost thousands of dollars. A great number of individuals were putting their trust in stocks in order to fund their retirement days. Those who trusted in their riches were disappointed. Now, where do you place your trust?

This is the final lesson and study in the book of First Timothy. The lessons have been helpful and stirring. This last lesson and study is no exception. It is a strong charge both to the rich of this world and to the ministers of the gospel.

OUTLINE:
1. The charge to the rich man (vv.17-19).
2. The charge to the minister (vv.20-21).

1. THE CHARGE TO THE RICH MAN (vv.17-19).

The word "charge" is a strong word. It has the force of a military command, yet it has the tenderness of an appeal to it. It means to beg and beseech a person—strongly so—to the point that the person is commanded to act. In this charge, God is appealing to and begging the rich person, but He is doing it so strongly that it is a command. The rich person is approached in love and tenderness and an appeal is made to him, but he is expected to do exactly what God says. Five strong charges are given to the rich.

1. The rich person is not to be high-minded, proud, or arrogant. The world honors money. Practically everyone in the world wants more money, and most are actually seeking more money. Few persons would turn down money. Money—the thought of riches and wealth—is so interwoven in the fabric of this world that it is probably the most honored thing in this world. The result is that the rich person is lifted up in the minds of most people. Most people want to be like the rich person. Most people put the rich person upon a pedestal. This makes it extremely difficult for a rich person to keep a proper perspective of himself.

⇒ There is great danger that the rich person will begin to think too highly of himself. There is the danger that he will become high-minded, prideful, and arrogant; that he will begin to feel above other persons and to esteem himself better than others. There is the danger that he will begin to look down upon others and downplay others. The rich person—just because of his riches—must guard against feeling more important than other people. Riches and possessions do not make a person a good person; they do not make a person a quality person. Therefore, riches and possessions do not make a person better, of more quality than anyone else.

The charge is forceful: "Charge them that are rich in this world, that they be not high minded." The temptation is there—always confronting the rich—because of the world's attitude toward riches. But the charge of God is clear: "Be not high minded."

> "For I say, through the grace given unto me, to every man that is among you, not to think of himself more highly than he ought to think; but to think soberly, according as God hath dealt to every man the measure of faith" (Ro.12:3).

2. The rich person is not to trust in the uncertainty of riches. Riches are about the most uncertain thing in life. The world's economy is never certain, fluctuating up and down every few years; crisis follows crisis in world affairs and the markets respond and react to each crisis. Even if a person can keep his wealth in this life, disease or accident can happen overnight, and the person's wealth does him no good whatsoever. The value and benefit of riches may be here today, but they are just as easily gone tomorrow.

The charge is forceful:

> "Charge them that are rich in this world, that they...trust not in the uncertainty of riches." (1 Ti.6:17).
>
> "And the disciples were astonished at his words. But Jesus answereth again, and saith unto them, Children, how hard is it for them that trust in riches to enter into the kingdom of God!" (Mk.10:24).

3. The rich person is to trust in God. The word "trust" means to fix and set one's heart and life upon God. God is; He actually exists. He is living and He is the only Person who possesses every good and perfect gift. Therefore, He alone can give us...
- the good and perfect gifts necessary for this life
- the good and perfect gifts necessary for the next life

In fact, every good gift that we receive now, including riches, has come from God. This fact is not to be missed; it bears repeating: every good gift that we now have has come from God. Therefore, if we want more and more of the good things of this life, we must trust in God.

> "But seek ye first the kingdom of God, and his righteousness; and all these things shall be added unto you" (Mt.6:33).

4. The rich person is to do good and to be rich in good works. What works? The works of a rich man are clearly stated: he is to distribute his wealth and be generous in it. Too many rich people shut their ears when they hear this. They turn their attention elsewhere, for they do not want to think about giving large amounts of money. They reject the fact that God expects them to give—to give to the point of sacrifice just like God did when He gave His Son and just like God's people do. But think about something; think honestly and realistically.

⇒ First, literally millions of people are hurting and dying every day from hunger, disease, and lack of fresh water; from ignorance, sin, loneliness, and emptiness. When God looks down upon earth and sees someone hurting and dying, and He sees us—the rich of the earth—what do you think God expects us to do? The world is one community; God expects us to meet the needs of the earth, to sacrificially meet the needs.

⇒ Second, why do you think a person has wealth? To hoard it? To bank and store it up and just let it lie around, never being used? Every one of us knows better. God expects the rich to do good and be rich in good works. He expects the rich to distribute and to be generous and sacrificial in meeting the needs of the lost and poor and dying of this world.

> "Sell that ye have, and give alms; provide yourselves bags which wax not old, a treasure in the heavens that faileth not, where no thief approacheth, neither moth corrupteth" (Lu.12:33).

5. The rich person is to lay up wealth for the world to come. How does a rich person do this?

⇒ By distributing and giving generously and sacrificially (v.18).
⇒ By using "their wealth to do good [and being]...ready to share...[remembering] that a Christian is essentially a man who is a member of a fellowship."[1]

> "But lay up for yourselves treasures in heaven, where neither moth nor rust doth corrupt, and where thieves do not break through nor steal" (Mt.6:20).

Again, think of all the desperate needs of the world and of our own communities and cities. Any example of any need could be taken, but consider a person who is starving to death. If a rich person does not reach out and save the starving person and give life to him, how can the rich person expect God to give life to him in the next world? The only way we can lay hold of eternal life is to give life to those who are dying in the sins and deprivations of their world.

The charge is militarily strong: charge them that are rich in this world, that they lay up in store for themselves a good foundation against the time to come.

ILLUSTRATION:

---

1 William Barclay. *The Letters to the Philippians, Colossians, and Thessalonians*, p.159.

There is no question that God allows certain believers to become materially rich. However, it is never for their gain; it is always for the gain of His Kingdom. Here is an inspiring example of channeling God's resources to do God's work.

> *Mr. Wilson was a successful businessman in the orange juice business. He was on the cutting edge of the production, shipping, and marketing of his product. In fact, he was so successful that he became a dominant player in the juice industry.*
>
> *From humble beginnings, he became a very rich man. Mr. Wilson was never one to count his money except for the purpose of giving to the work of God. He tithed and gave huge sums to help meet the ministry and building needs of his church. In addition, he was led by the Lord to become involved in financing a Bible college. He helped the college build its buildings, but he also did something that every student at the Bible college appreciated: provided free orange juice for breakfast through his company.*
>
> *When Mr. Wilson visited the campus, he had breakfast in the cafeteria that he had provided, had a glass of juice that he had paid for, sat with a student body that he had provided with scholarships; but he was never recognized by anyone. But for Mr. Wilson, that was acceptable. Recognition was not his motivation. He gave because God had gripped his heart. He gave out of thanksgiving for God's salvation. And because God saved him, Mr. Wilson invested in the lives of people, people who would take the gospel, the good news, to the nations of the earth.*

No matter how much or how little you have, are you using God's blessings to further God's Kingdom or your own?

QUESTIONS:
1. Why is it hard for some rich people to get into heaven?
2. What should be your attitude toward any rich person?
3. What is the most tempting thing about trusting in riches? Why is it dangerous?

2. THE CHARGE TO THE MINISTER (vv.20-21).

The charge is twofold.
1. Keep that which is committed to your trust. What is it that has been committed to the minister? What is the trust committed to him?
    ⇒ *"It is the deposit of truth delivered to him....It is the teaching which Paul imparted to Timothy, 'the sound words' [of the truth]."*[2]
    ⇒ *"The truths of God, the ordinances of God, keep these."*[3]
    ⇒ *"Let nothing cause you to deviate from the Gospel message of the grace of God."*[4]

The great trust committed to the minister of God is...
- the faith.
- the glorious truth of God which God has revealed to men in His Word and in the Lord Jesus Christ.
- the wonderful gospel of God—the gospel that is revealed in the sending of God's Son to earth in order to save men.

---

2 Kenneth Wuest. *The Pastoral Epistles.* "Word Studies in the Greek New Testament," Vol.2. (Grand Rapids, MI: Eerdmans Publishing Co., 1953), p.102f.
3 Matthew Henry. *Matthew Henry's Commentary*, Vol.5, p.831.
4 Oliver Greene. *The Epistles of Paul the Apostle to Timothy and Titus*, p.241.

The picture here is that of a deposit, of a faithful and diligent banker who looks after the money deposited into his care. The minister of God is to guard and keep, look after and care for the faith and truth of God, His Son, His Word, His Revelation, and His gospel. The minister must never forget that God has deposited—actually laid—the truth of God into his hands. The minister has been entrusted with the gospel of God, the glorious message of His Son, the Lord Jesus Christ.

William Barclay's comments are worthy of quote:

> *If in our day the Christian faith were to be twisted and distorted, it would not only be we who were the losers; those of generations still to come would be robbed of something infinitely precious. We are not only the possessors, we are also the trustees of the faith. That which we have received, we must also hand on.*[5]

"For if I do this thing willingly [serve], I have a reward: but if against my will, a dispensation [trust] of the gospel is [still] committed unto me" (1 Co.9:17).

APPLICATION:
How would you feel if you received a nice inheritance from a dear loved one who passed away? For instance if you were to receive a valuable antique car, would you be excited, anxious to hear about it, see it, and use it? Of course you would. But what if the car had been neglected, abused, and left to rust in the rain? You would be disappointed, hurt, and disenchanted with the car and the loved one who gave you this so-called 'treasure.' Why? Because it was not properly taken care of. It was not what it was supposed to be - something to be admired and taken care of, to be passed on in excellent condition to someone else who would love it and cherish it and take care of it.

Likewise, the gospel is the most valuable inheritance anyone could ever receive. But it must be guarded, taken care of, passed on in truth. If it is neglected, abused, and distorted, it will not serve its purpose. It will never be passed on from one person to another with total effectiveness. Just like a valuable heirloom, we must cherish the gospel and protect it for the Lord to honor it.

You have the inheritance of the gospel in your possession now. Are you taking good care of it, or is it stashed away somewhere and not even being used?

2. The minister is to turn away from false teaching. The description of false teaching is graphic.
   a. False teaching is described as profane and vain babblings.
   ⇒ The word "profane" means common, irreverent, and godless talk.
   ⇒ The word "vain" means empty and meaningless.
   ⇒ The word "babbling" means "empty voices."[6]

Therefore, the charge is to take all empty talk and turn away from it. Have absolutely nothing to do with common, irreverent, godless, and empty voices—no matter who is sounding forth the words. This would, of course, include:

⇒ false claims to truth   ⇒ all forms of false teaching
⇒ worldly philosophy   ⇒ novel ideas of religion
⇒ cursing   ⇒ gossip
⇒ criticism   ⇒ off-colored jokes
⇒ suggestive talk

---
5 William Barclay. *The Letters to Timothy, Titus, and Philemon*, p.161.
6 Kenneth Wuest. *The Pastoral Epistles*, Vol.2, p.103.

b. False teaching is described as "science," but as "science falsely called."
   ⇒ The word "science" means knowledge.
   ⇒ The word "oppositions" means antithesis, that is, to stand against some thesis, truth, or fact. What is being condemned is the false knowledge of men, the things that men teach that are contrary to God's glorious revelation in Christ and in the Word of God. The minister of God—in fact, any person—is a fool to stand against truth and fact, whether of God or of true science.

The charge is strong, very strong: turn away from men and their teachings when they stand against Christ and the teachings of God's Word. Have nothing to do with the false science or false knowledge of men. The men and their false teachings may concern philosophy, psychology, education, sociology, religion—any area of science or knowledge—but turn away from them if they are false. How do you tell if it is false? By the Word of God, the revelation and record of Christ and of the truth of God. If the science or knowledge stands in opposition to the Word of God, turn away from it.

Note that some professing church members had turned to false teaching. The seriousness of the situation is seen in that these are the last words of this letter. The very last thing that Paul says to Timothy is to turn away from false teaching. What a warning to us!

"Nevertheless I have somewhat against thee, because thou hast left thy first love" (Re.2:4).

ILLUSTRATION:
It is critical that anyone who speaks for Jesus Christ be listened to clearly—and with discernment. Listen closely to this example.

The setting was a Bible conference where a variety of speakers were invited to address the participants. One of the speakers was a man noted for his deep scholarship and quick wit. Popular across the country as a Christian keynote speaker, his address shocked the people who heard him. His opinion was that God had changed His mind about a few things since the Bible was written thousands of years ago. For example...
- *Certain sins are really not a problem anymore. After all, our cultural values have been up-dated.*
- *Homosexuality is simply an issue of sexual preference.*
- *There are errors in the Bible. We need an inner-guide to show us what is true and to understand the wisdom of the great writers down through the ages.*

One by one, people began to whisper. "Did you hear what I heard?" "What should we do?" "Would it be rude to get up and leave?" "Do you think he could be right? After all, he is a respected authority on the Bible." Before long, the brave ones began to close their notebooks and make their way to the exits. But many more sat in their seats, soaking up the deception of the false teacher.

How clearly are you listening to the messenger of the gospel?

QUESTIONS:
1. What did God entrust to Paul and Paul in turn entrust to Timothy?
2. Are you aware of this fact: as a Christian believer, you have been entrusted with the same commitment? Do you take it as seriously as you should? If not, why not?
3. When you pass along the gospel to others, is it passed in truth, without being distorted?
4. How can you have a clearer picture of the gospel? How can you present a clear picture of the gospel?

SUMMARY:

Do you trust in God instead of riches and the things of this world? Can God trust *you* with the gospel, to protect it and pass it along in truth? For Christ, you must heed this final charge:

1. The charge to the rich man.
2. The charge to the minister.

Remember...GUARD THE WORD OF GOD!

PERSONAL JOURNAL NOTES:
(Reflection & Response)

1. The most important thing that I learned from this lesson was:

2. The area that I need to work on the most is:

3. I can apply this lesson to my life by:

4. Closing Statement of Commitment:

Outline & Subject Index

1 Timothy

OUTLINE & SUBJECT INDEX

1 TIMOTHY

REMEMBER: When you look up a subject and then turn to the Scripture reference, you have not only the Scripture but also *an outline and a discussion* (commentary) of the Scripture and subject.

This is one of the *GREAT VALUES* of *THE TEACHER'S OUTLINE & STUDY BIBLE*™. Once you have all the volumes, you will have not only what all other Bible indexes give you, that is, a list of all the subjects and their Scripture references, *BUT* you will also have...

- an outline of *every* Scripture and subject in the Bible
- a discussion (commentary) on every Scripture and subject
- every subject supported by other Scriptures or cross-references

DISCOVER THE GREAT VALUE for yourself. Quickly glance below to the very first subject of the Index of *First Timothy*. It is:

ACCUSERS, FALSE
Meaning. 3:2-4

Turn to the reference. Glance at the Scripture and the outline of the Scripture, then read the commentary. You will immediately see the GREAT VALUE of the INDEX of *THE TEACHER'S OUTLINE & STUDY BIBLE*™.

OUTLINE AND SUBJECT INDEX

ACCEPTANCE - ACCEPTABLE
Who - what is **a**.
Children caring for parents. 5:4-8; 5:16
Prayer. 2:1-8

ADAM
And Eve. Function of each in God's creation. 2:12-14
Fact.
Bore greater sin than Eve. 2:14
Sinned willfully. Was not deceived. 2:14
Illustrates orderly function in the family. 2:13
Sinned willfully. 2:14

ADORN
Meaning. 2:9-10

ALCOHOL (See DRUNKENNESS)

ALEXANDER
Discussed. A believer with shipwrecked faith. 1:19-20

AMBITION - AMBITIOUS
Evil **a**. causes. Pride. 3:6

ANGELS
Nature. Elect. 5:21
Purpose. To minister to Christ. 3:16

APOSTASY
Discussed. 4:1-5
Marks of - Characteristics of.
Asceticism. 4:3-5
Seared consciences. 4:1-2
Source of.
Doctrines of devils. 4:1-2
False prophets & teachers. 4:1-2
Seducing spirits. 4:1-2

APOSTLE
Meaning. 1:1; 2:3-7

ARGUE - ARGUMENTS
Discussed. 4:7; 6:20-21

BACKSLIDING - BACKSLIDERS
Described as. Shipwrecked faith. 1:19
Results. Can **b**. so far that one is turned over to Satan. 1:20

BEHAVE
Meaning. 3:14-15

BEHAVIOR, GOOD
Meaning. 3:2-3

BELIEVER
Duty. To be a man of God. Marks of. 6:11-16

BISHOP
Discussed. 3:1-7
Qualifications. 3:1-7

BLAMELESS
Meaning. 3:2-3

BODY
Duty.
To exercise. 4:8
To take care of **b**. 3:2-3

Outline & Subject Index

BRAWLER
Meaning. 3:2-3

BROTHER - BROTHERHOOD
Among various ages. 5:1-2

CALL - CALLED (See **MINISTER**)
Purpose of. To lay hold of eternal life. 6:12

CHARGE
Meaning. 6:17-19

CHILDBEARING
Promise to women in c. 2:15

CHURCH
Described.
  Church of the living God. 3:14-15
  Family of God. 3:14-15
  House of God. 3:14-15
  Pillar & ground of the truth. 3:14-15
Discussed. 3:14-16
  Behavior & relationships in the c. 3:14-6:21
  Duties, order, & organization of the c. 2:1-3:13
  Spirit & discipline of relationships. 5:1-2
  Women of the c. 2:9-15
Duty.
  First d. To pray. 2:1-8
Ministries of.
  To various age groups. 5:1-2
  To widows. 5:3-16
Names - Titles.
  Discussed.
  C. of the living God. 3:15
  House of God. 3:15
  Three pictures. 3:15
Nature.
  Described. 3:14-16
  Symbolized in the family. 3:4
Officers of. Bishop. Discussed. 3:1-7
Organization.
  Deacons. 3:8-13
  Elders or officials. 4:14
  Government, policy of. 3:1-7; 3:8-13

Ministers - Overseers - Bishops. 3:1-7
Presbytery. 4:14
Who the c is. 3:14-15
Worship. An early w. service. 4:13

CHURCH DISCIPLINE
How to *rebuke*. 5:1
Of a minister. 5:19-20

CITIZENSHIP
Duty.
  To leave judgment up to God. 5:24-25
  To pray for authorities. 2:2

CIVIL AUTHORITIES
Duty toward. To pray for all in authority. 2:2

CLOTHING (See **DRESS**)

CONSCIENCE
A Closer Look. Discussed. 1:19
Function - Purpose - Work. To approve behavior. 1:5; 1:19
How not to offend.
  By holding a pure, good c. 1:5; 1:19
  By not shipwrecking. 1:19
Kinds of.
  Good - clear. 1:5; 1:19
  Pure. 1:5
  Seared. 4:2
Reaction to. Hardening, searing. 4:2
Warning. Can be put away, neglected. 1:19-20

CONTENTMENT
Discussed. Secret to c. 6:6-10
Meaning. 6:6-8
Source of. Godliness, not wealth. 6:6-10

CONVERSION
Illustration. Paul's c. to show God's mercy for great sinners. 1:15-16

COVETOUS - COVETOUSNESS
Described as. Root of all evil. 6:10
Meaning. 3:2-3
  Love of money. 6:10
  Willing to be rich. 6:9

Results.
  Acute mental anguish. 6:10
  Disqualification of pastoral call. 3:3
  Enslavement. 6:9
  Many hurtful lusts. 6:9
  Many temptations. 6:9
  One to fall. 6:9
  Wandering. 6:9

DEACONS
A Closer Look. Discussed. 3:8-13
Qualifications. 3:8-13
Wife of. Discussed. 3:11-12

DISCIPLESHIP
Duty. To make disciples. 1:1-2

DISCIPLINE, CHURCH
Described. Delivered to Satan. 1:19-20

DOUBLETONGUED
Meaning. 3:8

DRESS
Duty.
  Not to dress to attract attention. 2:9-10
  To be modest. 2:9-10
Can cause problems.
  Attracting & being subjected to someone other than own spouse. 2:9-10
  Immodesty & insensitivity. 2:9-10
  Rebellion (unfaithfulness). 2:9-15
Discussed. 2:9-15
Proper d.
  Must be based upon faith & love. 2:15
  To be modest & sensitive. 2:9-10
  To d. as a godly person. 2:9-10
  To watch one's adorning - demeanor. 2:9-10
Results of proper dress. Discussed. 2:9-15
Saves one in childbearing. 2:15
Warning against. Being overly dressed - living extravagantly. 2:9

Outline & Subject Index

Drunkenness
Duty. To abstain. 3:2-3

Elder
Discussed. 3:1-7; 5:17-20
Qualifications. 3:1-7

Elderly
Ministry to. Discussed. 5:1-2

Employee
Discussed. 6:1-2
Duty. Toward a Christian. Supervisor. 6:1-2

Evangelism
Duty. To reach the world for Christ. 3:16

Eve
And Adam. Function of both in creation. 2:12-14
Fact. Was deceived, but not Adam. 2:14
Was deceived; Adam was not. 2:14

Evil Spirits
Work of. To seduce into false teaching. 4:1-2

Exhort - Exhortation
Meaning. 2:1

Fables
Meaning. 1:4

Faith
Meaning. 6:11
Warning. Can be shipwrecked. 1:19-20

Faithful - Faithfulness
Duty. To be **f.** in all things. 3:11-12
Meaning. 6:11

False Teachers (See **Teachers, False**)

Family
Duties. Function of husband & wife. 2:12-14
Leaders must rule **f.** well. 3:4-5; 3:11-12
Nature.
    Miniature of the church. 3:4-5, see Ep.5:22-33
    Woman more easily deceived. 2:14

Orderly arrangement necessary. 2:12-14
Parents. Aged **p.** to be cared for. 5:2-8

Favoritism
Duty. Of minister. Not to show **f.** 5:21

Filthy Lucre
Meaning. 3:2-3

Genealogies
Error. Discussed. 1:4

Gifts, Spiritual
Purpose. To predict & encourage Timothy in his call to the ministry. 1:18

Gnosticism
Discussed. 4:3

God
Deity. One God. 2:3-7
Names - Titles. God our Savior. 1:1; 2:3
Nature.
    Is perfect—no imperfection whatsoever. 2:3-7
    One God. 2:3-7

Godliness
Meaning. 6:11
Mystery of. 3:16
Results. Contentment. 6:6-8

Government (See **Civil Authorities**)
To be prayed for. 2:1-3

Grave
Meaning. 3:8

Hope
Comes through Christ. 1:1

Hospitality
Meaning. 3:2-3

Humanism
Fact. Preached by some ministers. 6:5

Hymenaeus
Discussed. 1:19-20

Immortality
Source. Jesus Christ. 6:14-16

Imperfection
Discussed. Man is imperfect, therefore unacceptable to a perfect God. 2:3-7

Incarnation
Discussed. Six facts. 3:16

Intercession
Meaning. 2:1

Jesus Christ
Ascension. To be crowned with glory. 3:16
Death.
    To give Himself a ransom. 2:3-7
    To save man. 2:3-7
Deity.
    Did the works of God. 3:16
    God incarnated in human flesh. 3:16
    Incarnation. 3:16
    Lived a sinless & perfect life. 3:16
    Proven by the resurrection. 3:16
    Proven by three things. 3:16
Exalted. To rule & reign. 3:16
Humanity. Begotten as man - sent by God. 2:5
Life. Ministered to by angels. 3:16
Mediator. Discussed. 2:3-7
Mission. To save man. 1:15-16
Names - Titles.
    Christ Jesus our hope. 1:1
    The one mediator. 2:5
Nature - Origin.
    Immortal, King of kings & Lord of lords. 6:13-16
    Sinless, perfect. The Ideal Man. 2:3-7
Work of - Mission of.
    Redemption. (See **Redeem - Redemption**) 2:5-7
    To save man to the uttermost. 1:15

Outline & Subject Index

JUDGMENT
Duty. To leave j. up to God. 5:24-25

LABOR - LABORERS
Duty. Toward employers. 6:1-2

LAW
Purpose. Discussed. 1:8-11

LEADERS - LEADERSHIP (See **DEACONS; MINISTERS; AND RELATED SUBJECTS**)
Of the church.
Deacons. 3:8-13
Ministers - Overseers.
Bishops. 3:1-7

LUCRE, FILTHY
Meaning. 3:2-3

MAN
Depravity.
Hunger for material things. 6:9-10
Imperfect; therefore, unacceptable to God. 2:3-7
Errors. Hunger for material things. 6:9-10
Nature.
Craves God & His Word. 6:4
Imperfect; therefore, unacceptable to God. 2:3-7

MATERIALISM
Discussed. 6:6-10
The passion for wealth. 6:6-10
The rich man. 6:17-19
What m. does. Causes many harmful desires. 6:9-10

MEEK - MEEKNESS
Meaning. 6:11

MEN, ELDERLY
How to treat in the church. 5:1

MERCY
A Closer Look. Meaning. 1:2
Purpose. To show God's great m. for sinners. 1:15-17

MINISTER
Call.
Credentials. 1:1
Enabled & counted worthy. 1:12-17
Entrusted with the gospel. 1:11
Must be called by God, not just choosing a profession. 1:18
Ordination by God. 2:7
To guard ordination. 5:22
Commission - Mission.
Enabled & counted worthy. 1:12-17
Described as.
Good. 4:6-16
Man of God. 6:11
True. 1:12-17
Discipline of. Discussed. 5:19-20
Discussed. 3:1-7
A good m. Twelve qualities. 4:6-16
Charge to the young m. To be a warrior. 1:18-20
Four charges. 5:21-25
Restoring a fallen m. 5:22
Testimony of a true m. 1:12-17
Duty.
Discussed. 6:11-16
Fourfold. 6:11-16
Must not fear the face of man. 5:21
Not to neglect the gift that is in him. 4:14
Not to ordain others too quickly. 5:22
Primary duty. To devote himself to public worship. 4:13
To be a good m. 6:6-16
To be an example to believers. In six areas. 4:13
To be a man of reason & purpose. 4:11
To be a trusted son. 6:20-21
To be a warrior. 1:18-20
To be honored. 5:17-18
To be impartial. 5:21-25
To exercise physically & spiritually. 4:7-8
To fight & lay hold of eternal life. 6:12
To guard himself & his teaching. 4:16
To guard ordination. 5:22
To instruct believers about false teachers. 4:6
To keep the commandments of God. 6:13-16
To labor strenuously. 4:10
To leave judging others up to God. 5:23
To meditate & to wholly give himself to the Scriptures. 4:15
To nourish himself in the faith. 4:6
To reject false teaching, that is, profane & old wives fables. 4:7
To take care of his body. 5:23
To various ages. 5:1-2
Toward m. 5:19-20
To widows. 5:3-16
Twelve duties. 4:6-16
Twofold duty. 6:20-21
False m. (See **TEACHERS, FALSE**)
Financial support. To be paid double. 5:17-20
Names - Titles. Elders. 5:17
Qualifications. 3:1-7

MINISTER, FALSE (See **TEACHERS, FALSE**)

MONEY
Discussed. Love of. Causes four things. 6:9-10

MYSTERY
Of godliness.
Discussed. 3:16
Six facts. 3:16
Of the faith. Discussed. 3:9-10

NOVICE
Meaning. 3:6

ORDAIN - ORDINATION
Duty.
Not to o. a fallen minister too quickly. 5:22
Not to o. too quickly. 5:22

OUTLINE & SUBJECT INDEX

Source. God is the One
who ordains. 2:7
To be guarded. 5:22

PARTIALITY
Duty. Of minister. Not to
show **p**. 5:21

PASTORAL EPISTLES
Purpose for writing. 3:14-15

PATIENT
Meaning. 3:2-3

PAUL
A Closer Look. Conversion
& call of. 1:12-17
To be a pattern of
God's mercy & long-
suffering. 1:15-16
Former life of. Discussed.
1:13-14

PEACE
A Closer Look. Meaning.
1:2

**PERSECUTION - PERSE-
CUTORS** (See **PAUL,
SUFFERINGS & TRIALS**)

**PRAY - PRAYER - PRAY-
ING**
Different kinds of p. 2:1
Discussed. 2:1-8
Duty.
First duty of the church:
to pray. 2:1-8
To pray for all men to
be saved. 2:3-7
To pray for all rulers.
2:2
How to pray.
Three essentials. 2:8
Who is to **p**. The
church: its first duty.
2:1-8

PREACHER
Meaning. 2:3-7

PREJUDICE
Duty. Of minister. Not to
show **p**. 5:21

PRIDE
Caused by. Being "lifted
up" - given responsibil-
ity too soon. 3:6
Of the false minister. What
he takes **p**. in. 6:4

Results. To be condemned
with the devil. 3:6

PROPHECY, GIFT OF
Work—exercise of. Pre-
dicted Timothy's call to
the ministry. 1:18

**RANSOM - REDEEM - RE-
DEMPTION**
Discussed. 2:3-7
Purpose. To redeem men.
2:3-7
Source. Christ. 2:3-7

REBUKE
Meaning. 5:1

RELATIONSHIPS
Discussed. Spirit & discipline of r. 5:1-2

REPENTANCE
Of a fallen minister. Discussed. 5:22

**RESTORATION, SPIRI-
TUAL**
Of a fallen minister. Dis-
cussed. 5:22

RICHES (See **MONEY**)
Dangers of. Three dangers.
6:17-19
Discussed.
Charges to the rich
man. 6:17-19
Secret to contentment.
6:9-10
Duty. Discussed. 6:17-19
Results. Four significant r.
6:9-10

RIGHTEOUSNESS
Meaning. 6:11

RULERS
Duty toward. To pray for
all **r**. 2:2

SALVATION - SAVED
Duty. To pray for **s**. of all
men. 2:1-8
Source - How one is **s**.
By Christ. 1:15-16
By Christ the Mediator.
2:3-7
By God our Savior.
1:1; 2:3-7

SATAN
Fell by pride. 3:6
Work - strategy of. Se-
duces men through evil
spirits. 4:1-2

SIN
List of. 1:9-10
Results - Penalty. Imper-
fection. Makes man un-
acceptable to God. 2:3-7

SLANDER - SLANDERER
Meaning. 3:11-12

SLAVES
A Closer Look. Discussed.
6:1-2
Duty. Toward a Christian
supervisor. 6:1-2

SOBER
Meaning. 3:2-3

SPECULATIONS (See
TEACHERS, FALSE)
Discussed. 4:7; 6:20-21

SPIRIT, MAN'S
More important than
physical. 4:8

**SPIRITUAL STRUGGLE &
WARFARE**
Discussed. To be a war-
rior. 1:18-20
Duty. To fight a good war-
fare. 1:18
Weapons. Faith & a good
conscience. 1:18

SPORTS
Exhortations to. Exercise
for godliness. 4:8

STEWARDSHIP
Duty. To support minister.
Double honor. 5:17-20

STRIKER
Meaning. 3:2-3

SUPPLICATION
Meaning. 2:1

TEACH
Duty. Must be appointed,
qualified to **t**. 2:3-7

TEACHER
Meaning. 2:3-7

OUTLINE & SUBJECT INDEX

TEACHERS, FALSE (See **APOSTASY; DECEIVE - DECEPTION; JUDAIZERS; LEGALISM; RELIGIONISTS**
Characteristics - Marks.
Does not preach the words of the Lord Jesus Christ. 6:3
Five **c.** 6:3-5
Pride. What he takes pride. in. 6:7
Description of false **t.** & their apostasy. 4:1-5; 6:20-21
Discussed. 4:1-5; 6:3-5; 6:20-21
Danger of. 1:3-11
Errors of.
Are seduced by evil spirit. 4:1-2
Consciences are seared. 4:1-2
Deception & seduction. 4:1-2
Protection against.
Knowing their danger. 1:3-11
Turning away from. 6:20-21
Teachings of.
Are profane & old wives fables. 4:7
Discussed. 1:3-11; 4:3-5
Vs. true teaching. 1:3-20; 6:3-5
What he teaches. Self-help; self-esteem; humanism. 6:5
Where are false teachers. Within the church. 1:3-20

TEACHING, FALSE
Teachings of.
Are false science & knowledge. 6:20-21
Are profane & empty words. 6:20-21

THANKSGIVING
Meaning. 2:1

TIMOTHY
A Closer Look. Discussed. 1:2
Call of. To ministry. 1:18

TRUST
Meaning. 6:20

VIGILANT
Meaning. 3:2-3

WEALTH (See **MONEY**)
Danger - problem of.
Passion for. 6:6-10
The root of all evil. 6:10

WIDOWS
Discussed. Treatment of. 5:3-16
Duty. To be cared for by children. 5:3-8; 5:16
Traits. Gossipers, idle, busybodies. 5:13

WINE
Duty. To abstain. 3:2-3

WITNESS - WITNESSING
Duty. To proclaim Christ. 3:16

WOMEN
Duties of **w.**
In childbearing. 2:15
In dress & clothing. 2:9-10
In the church. 2:11; 2:12-14
Not to teach or take authority over a man. 2:11; 2:12-14
To be submissive before men in church leadership. 2:11; 2:12-14
Elderly. How to treat within the church. 5:2
In the church. Discussed. 2:9-15
Leadership of.
Example after example. 2:12-14
Place in the church. 2:12-14

WORD OF GOD
Fact. Man's heart craves God & His Word. 6:4

WORKMEN (See **EMPLOYEE**)

WORLD
Reached by earlier church. 3:16

WORSHIP
Of early church. Services. Described. 4:13

YOKE
Meaning. 6:1

YOUTH
Men. How to treat within the church. 5:1
Women. How to treat within the church. 5:2

ILLUSTRATION INDEX

1 TIMOTHY

Illustration Index

Subject	Scripture Reference	Page Number
ASSURANCE		
• Only through Christ.	1 Ti. 1:3-11	Page 13
BIBLE (See **CHRISTIAN LIFE; WORD OF GOD**)		
BOLDNESS (See **WITNESS - WITNESSING**)		
BORN AGAIN (See **CONVERSION**)		
CALL, OF GOD		
• God chooses the minister.	1 Ti. 6:3-5	Page 136
CARE (See **SERVICE; WIDOWS**)		
CHRIST JESUS (See **SALVATION**)		
CHRISTIAN LIFE, THE (See **FOCUS**)		
• A reminder on how to behave in the church.	1 Ti. 3:14-16	Page 73
CHURCH		
• A description of the c.	1 Ti. 3:14-16	Page 75
• What if Paul visited your c.?	1 Ti. 3:14-16	Page 72
COMMITMENT (See **CHURCH**)		
COMMUNICATION		
• Learning how to listen.	1 Ti. 2:9-15	Page 49
CONSCIENCE		
• Convicts you of your sin.	1 Ti. 1:18-20	Page 29
• The embarrassment of not listening to your c.	1 Ti. 1:18-20	Page 34
CONVERSION		
• The critical need for biblical discipleship.	1 Ti. 3:1-7	Page 62
CORRUPTION		
• Of the mind.	1 Ti. 6:3-5	Page 134
DEACON—DEACONS		
• Qualifications of a d.	1 Ti. 3:8-13	Page 65
DECEPTION		
• The sinister schemes of fallen angels.	1 Ti. 4:1-5	Page 82

ILLUSTRATION INDEX

SUBJECT	SCRIPTURE REFERENCE	PAGE NUMBER
DISCERNMENT		
• Are you listening clearly?	1 Ti. 6:17-21	Page 158
DISCIPLE (See **CONVERSION**)		
DISCIPLINE		
• Of an elder in the church.	1 Ti. 5:17-20	Page 116
• Restoration—not reproach—is the goal.	1 Ti. 5:1-2	Page 100
DISTRACTIONS (See **FOCUS**)		
DOCTRINE		
• Beware of false **d**.	1 Ti. 4:1-5	Page 85
EXAMPLE		
• Kill the spiders of sin.	1 Ti. 3:8-13	Page 67
• Warning: don't allow your behavior to contradict your words.	1 Ti. 3:1-7	Page 58
EXERCISE (See **GODLINESS**)		
FAILURE (See **CONSCIENCE**)		
FALSE TEACHERS (See **DECEPTION**; **DISCERNMENT**; **DOCTRINE**)		
• How to detect a counterfeit.	1 Ti. 4:1-5	Page 81
FEAR (See **WITNESS - WITNESSING**)		
FOCUS (See **SALVATION**)		
• Are you concentrating on the finish line?	1 Ti. 6:11-16	Page 149
GODLINESS		
• Breaking free from the shackles of sin.	1 Ti. 4:6-16	Page 92
• Living the godly life.	1 Ti. 2:9-15	Page 53
GREED (See **MONEY**)		
HEAVEN (See **ASSURANCE**)		
HOLY - HOLINESS		
• Does your purity affect others around you?	1 Ti. 5:1-2	Page 103
HOLY SPIRIT (See **WITNESS - WITNESSING**)		
HOPE (See **ASSURANCE**)		
• The power of **h**. in Christ.	1 Ti. 1:1-2	Page 5

ILLUSTRATION INDEX

Subject	Scripture Reference	Page Number
INTEGRITY		
• Do you take *shortcuts* at your workplace?	1 Ti. 6:1-2	Page 130
JESUS CHRIST (See **SALVATION**)		
JUDGMENT - JUDGING		
• Does God *really* need your help in this area?	1 Ti. 5:21-25	Page 124
MATERIALISM		
• Exactly, how much is enough?	1 Ti. 6:6-10	Page 144
MERCY		
• Undeserved, but freely given.	1 Ti. 1:1-2	Page 7
MONEY (See **PASTOR; WORK**)		
• Does the love of **m**. drown you?	1 Ti. 6:6-10	Page 142
• Why God makes a man rich with **m**.	1 Ti. 6:17-21	Page 156
PARTIALITY		
• Believers are to serve without **p**.	1 Tim 5:21-25	Page 118
PASTOR		
• Is your church being financially fair to your **p**.?	1 Tim 5:17-20	Page 114
POWER (See **WITNESS - WITNESSING**)		
PRAISE		
• From the heart and soul.	1 Ti. 1:12-17	Page 24
PRAYER		
• A **p**. for government leaders.	1 Ti. 2:1-8	Page 39
• A recommitment to **p**.	1 Ti. 2:1-8	Page 38
• To reach beyond the church walls.	1 Ti. 2:1-8	Page 44
PRIDE		
• What goes up must come down.	1 Ti. 6:3-5	Page 133
RELATIONSHIPS		
• How to bridge the generation gap.	1 Ti. 5:1-2	Page 102
SALVATION (See **ASSURANCE**)		
• Run to the only One who can save.	1 Ti. 1:12-17	Page 22
SERVICE (See **DEACON - DEACONS; WIDOWS**)		
• For God or for self?	1 Ti. 4:6-16	Page 98

ILLUSTRATION INDEX

SUBJECT	SCRIPTURE REFERENCE	PAGE NUMBER

SIN (See **CONSCIENCE**; **DISCIPLINE**; **EXAMPLE**)
- What is s.? 1 Ti. 6:11-16 Page 151

STEWARDSHIP (See **MONEY**)

TEMPTATION (See **SIN**)

WIDOWS
- The blessings that come from caring for the w. 1 Ti. 5:3-16 Page 106
- Experiencing comfort in time of sorrow. 1 Ti.5:3-16 Page 106
- One example of how a family cared for a w. 1 Ti. 5:3-16 Page 111

WITNESS - WITNESSING (See **EXAMPLE**; **HOLINESS**; **INTEGRITY**; **LIFESTYLE**; **WORK**)
- Are you free from the fear of men? 1 Ti. 4:6-16 Page 93
- At what level do you share the gospel? 1 Ti. 5:21-25 Page 119
- Only by the power of the Holy Spirit. 1 Ti. 3:8-13 Page 70

WORD OF GOD
- Warning: Do not settle for an artificial substitute. 1 Ti. 4:6-16 Page 90

WORK (See **INTEGRITY**; **WITNESS - WITNESSING**)
- Is your employer grateful to have you at w.? 1 Ti. 6:1-2 Page 128

WORLDLINESS (See **MATERIALISM**)

OUTLINE BIBLE RESOURCES

This material, like similar works, has come from imperfect man and is thus susceptible to human error. We are nevertheless grateful to God for both calling us and empowering us through His Holy Spirit to undertake this task. Because of His goodness and grace, **The Preacher's Outline & Sermon Bible®** New Testament and Old Testament volumes are now complete.

The Minister's Personal Handbook, *The Believer's Personal Handbook,* and other helpful **Outline Bible Resources** are available in printed form as well as releasing electronically on various software programs.

God has given the strength and stamina to bring us this far. Our confidence is that as we keep our eyes on Him and grounded in the undeniable truths of the Word, we will continue to produce other helpful Outline Bible Resources for God's dear servants to use in their Bible Study and discipleship.

We offer this material, first, to Him in whose Name we labor and serve and for whose glory it has been produced and, second, to everyone everywhere who preaches and teaches the Word.

Our daily prayer is that each volume will lead thousands, millions, yes even billions, into a better understanding of the Holy Scriptures and a fuller knowledge of Jesus Christ the Incarnate Word, of whom the Scriptures so faithfully testify.

> You will be pleased to know that Leadership Ministries Worldwide partners with Christian organizations, printers, and mission groups around the world to make Outline Bible Resources available and affordable in many countries and foreign languages. It is our goal that *every* leader around the world, both clergy and lay, will be able to understand God's Holy Word and present God's message with more clarity, authority, and understanding—all beyond his or her own power.

LEADERSHIP MINISTRIES WORLDWIDE
PO Box 21310 • Chattanooga, TN 37424-0310
423) 855-2181 • FAX (423) 855-8616
info@lmw.org
www.lmw.org - FREE Download materials

LEADERSHIP MINISTRIES WORLDWIDE

Publishers of Outline Bible Resources

- **THE PREACHER'S OUTLINE & SERMON BIBLE® (POSB)**

NEW TESTAMENT

Matthew I (chapters 1-15)	1 & 2 Corinthians
Matthew II (chapters 16-28)	Galatians, Ephesians, Philippians, Colossians
Mark	1 & 2 Thess., 1 & 2 Timothy, Titus, Philemon
Luke	Hebrews, James
John	1 & 2 Peter, 1, 2, & 3 John, Jude
Acts	Revelation
Romans	Master Outline & Subject Index

OLD TESTAMENT

Genesis I (chapters 1-11)	2 Kings	Isaiah 1 (chapters 1-35)
Genesis II (chapters 12-50)	1 Chronicles	Isaiah 2 (chapters 36-66)
Exodus I (chapters 1-18)	2 Chronicles	Jeremiah 1 (chapters 1-29)
Exodus II (chapters 19-40)	Ezra, Nehemiah,	Jeremiah 2 (chapters 30-52),
Leviticus	Esther	Lamentations
Numbers	Job	Ezekiel
Deuteronomy	Psalms 1 (chapters 1-41)	Daniel/Hosea
Joshua	Psalms 2 (chapters 42-106)	Joel, Amos, Obadiah, Jonah,
Judges, Ruth	Psalms 3 (chapters 107-150)	Micah, Nahum
1 Samuel	Proverbs	Habakkuk, Zephaniah, Haggai,
2 Samuel	Ecclesiastes, Song of	Zechariah, Malachi
1 Kings	Solomon	

KJV Available in Deluxe 3-Ring Binders or Softbound Edition • NIV Available in Softbound Only

- **The Preacher's Outline & Sermon Bible New Testament — 3 Vol. Hardcover • KJV – NIV**
- *What the Bible Says to the Believer* **— The Believer's Personal Handbook**
  11 Chs. - 500 Subjects, 300 Promises, & 400 Verses Expounded - Italian Imitation Leather or Paperback
- *What the Bible Says to the Minister* **— The Minister's Personal Handbook**
  12 Chs. - 127 Subjects - 400 Verses Expounded - Italian Imitation Leather or Paperback
- **Practical Word Studies In the New Testament — 2 Vol. Hardcover Set**
- **The Teacher's Outline & Study Bible™ - New Testament Books**
  Complete 30 - 45 minute lessons – with illustrations and discussion questions
- **Practical Illustrations — Companion to the POSB**
  Arranged by topic and Scripture reference
- **What the Bible Says Series – Various Subjects**
- **OBR on various digital platforms**
  See current digital providers on our website at www.outlinebible.org
- **Non-English Translations of various books**
  See our website for more information or contact our office

— Contact LMW for quantity orders and information —
LEADERSHIP MINISTRIES WORLDWIDE or Your Local Christian Bookstore
PO Box 21310   • Chattanooga, TN 37424-0310
(423) 855-2181 (9am – 5pm Eastern) • FAX (423) 855-8616
E-mail - info@lmw.org • Order online at www.lmw.org

LEADERSHIP MINISTRIES WORLDWIDE

PURPOSE STATEMENT

LEADERSHIP MINISTRIES WORLDWIDE exists to equip ministers, teachers, and laymen in their understanding, preaching and teaching of God's Word by publishing and distributing worldwide *The Preacher's & Sermon Bible®* and related ***Outline Bible*** materials, to reach & disciple men, women, boys and girls for Jesus Christ.

MISSION STATEMENT

1. To make the Bible so understandable – its truth so clear and plain – that men and women everywhere, whether teacher or student, preacher or hearer, can grasp its message and receive Jesus Christ as Savior, and…

2. To place the Bible in the hands of all who will preach and teach God's Holy Word, verse by verse, precept by precept, regardless of the individual's ability to purchase it.

The ***Outline Bible*** materials have been given to LMW for printing and especially distribution worldwide at/below cost, by those who remain anonymous. One fact, however, is as true today as it was in the time of Christ:

THE GOSPEL IS FREE, BUT THE COST OF TAKING IT IS NOT

LMW depends on the generous gifts of believers with a heart for Him and a love for the lost. They help pay for the printing, translating, and distributing of ***Outline Bible*** materials into the hands of God's servants worldwide, who will present the Gospel message with clarity, authority, and understanding beyond their own.

LMW was incorporated in the state of Tennessee in July 1992 and received IRS 501 (c)(3) nonprofit status in March 1994. LMW is an international, nondenominational mission organization. All proceeds from USA sales, along with donations from donor partners, go directly to underwrite our translation and distribution projects of ***Outline Bible*** materials to preachers, church and lay leaders, and Bible students around the world.

www.ingramcontent.com/pod-product-compliance
Lightning Source LLC
Chambersburg PA
CBHW062215080426
42734CB00010B/1894